I'd Like To Thank
Manchester Air Rifles

Published by Grey Tiger Books

GTB, 10–16 Ashwin Street, Dalston, London, E8 3DL

10 9 8 7 6 5 4 3 2

A catalogue record for this book is available from the British Library

Edited by Fergal Stapleton and Tara Cranswick

Designed by Zoë Anspach

Printed and bound by CPI Group (UK) Ltd, Croydon, CR0 4YY

ISBN: 9780956441973

Cover photograph: © James Ernest Williams

I'd Like To Thank Manchester Air Rifles

~~Scarlet West~~

A Memoir

THE ARREST

November 5th, 2006

01:41 pm

Yesterday I woke up in a police cell. Savile Row police station was the location although I had no idea where I was. Well, I knew I'd been arrested and that was it.

I started to get flashbacks after a while. The handcuffs, the van, Soho Square. When they put me in the cell I tried to smash it up by hitting the walls. As you know, smashing up a police cell is impossible. After failing I tried to smash myself up by hitting my head as hard as I could against the tiled wall. I then curled myself up in a ball and cried myself to sleep.

They gave me some breakfast at 8:30am. I only knew it was 8:30 cos I asked. I wondered when I'd be able to leave but they wouldn't tell me. So I sat and began to recollect things.

The night had started off in a pleasant way. I purposefully went out quite late so I wouldn't get so drunk. I met Siobhan in The Coach and then I went off to Gerry's. I sat and drank wine. I texted Damon Gough and he came down around 2am. We talked and everything was fine. When Gerry's closed we decided to go to Trisha's. This is when things start to go black.

The next thing I know I'm being arrested. After thinking about things and waiting for what seems like ages, the police officer comes and tells me he's getting me some lunch and then I can go. The lunch was rather nice: steak stew, green beans, potatoes and rice. I even got an afters of apple crumble and custard. I started to think that my predicament wasn't a bad one; I had saved a whole day's food rations.

An hour after lunch they let me out. "Do you know what happened this morning?" the policeman asked.

"I was drunk," I replied.

"We found you curled up in a ball in Soho Square. We thought you were a rare panda." This was due to my fur coat.

"Anything could have happened to you." And so they gave me the lecture that I'm well aware of by now.

It was 3:30pm by the time I left the station. Anyone else would have gone straight home but I texted Siobhan and we met in The Blue Posts on Berwick Street. Malik joined us after a while and we started to laugh about it all. "It's not funny," I kept saying and then laughing all over again.

It really isn't though. I want it to be my last straw. I really want to stop drinking. How many more wake-up calls do I need? I wish I had enough money to go into a drying out clinic. As soon as I'm sober it starts all over again.

"PEOPLE AREN'T EQUIPPED FOR MY FILTH..."

November 11th, 2006

11:01 pm

I remember grabbing a carving knife as a six-year-old. Well, maybe I was five. All I can remember is threatening to kill myself with it. It was at the Sunday dinner table when I had a family. Someone must have pissed me off.

If anyone cared now, I'd be grabbing something and threatening something else.

I stayed off the alcohol for two days. For those days I lay in bed staring at my star-covered walls drifting in and out of consciousness, crying at forty-five minute intervals. Ridiculous really. So today I woke up and went into a crappy job in a call centre. After forty-five minutes of that hell I left proclaiming I was ill.

I was happy sitting in Liverpool Street station by 11:18am. I then went to Hamley's to get an application form for demonstration staff. What could be better than playing with toys all day? Speaking to children all day? I hate children. Absolutely can't stand them. Especially the ones that hang around in Hamley's. Can't stand their parents as well. Can't stand people as well. Perhaps it's not the right job. Perhaps nothing is.

So I went to The Coach to fill in the pathetic application form that asks you stupid questions like, "What superhero would you be?" E.T.

Luckily Keyhole Joe was in there really pissed. He inspired me a great deal and despite my proclamations after Wednesday of never drinking again, I bought myself a £3.60 pint of Becks with my rent money that I mistakenly left the house with. We hung around all afternoon and talked about the good old times that I was born quickly enough for. We popped into Dan Cook's and Joe tried on different suits. Keyhole Joe's becoming the face of Beefeater Gin so this is why, y'see…

I left him to have dinner with Leo Washington but he was too messed up from the previous night and so I went back to The Coach and Horses and then got my usual Thai buffet dinner thus spending the last of my rent which is due tomorrow.

I'm not happy. I'd love to just do myself in now. It always ends like this. I look at stuff like mydeathspace and see stuff like, "sadly missed…" You would never miss me. I may just kidnap one of you for the fun of it. Just to see what people write on your journal when you're away. All I used to think about was suicide, but all I can think about now is dragging an indie kid from the street by knife-point and getting my accomplice to drive them to my garage. If you're wearing a beret and a necktie beware. Be very aware.

SEATING ARRANGEMENTS

November 13th, 2006

06:36 pm

I'm ill. I've been given my diagnosis from my good friend Jupiter who rang me up this afternoon. I'm suffering from Sohoitis. Simple as, eh?

Not to worry then. Off to Soho again in a bit. I'm protesting about the Coach and Horses' new seating arrangements by hanging around The French House instead. I never thought I'd say that but I just don't like having my back to people. Especially in Soho. They're all out to get me.

"SLEEP WALKING WITH ACTIVITIES"

November 16th, 2006

08:02 pm

Drinking again. Yes, I know, that's all I seem to do. It just sort of happens though. On Monday I popped down to Soho to pick my wages up. The next thing I know it's 1pm Tuesday and I'm still downstairs on Dean Street drinking. I mean, I didn't even sleep. I can't remember getting home. The next thing I know I'm lying in bed and it's dark. I check the clock and it's 5:30pm and I've got to go back to Soho to rehearse with my new band.

Last night I was doing the rather sane activity of DJing at The Arts. Then my friend who quite often leads me astray came down. We went to Camera Repairs and then ended up in a hotel. This was 5am. It's nothing like what you're thinking. A hotel has bad connotations I know but it was just cheaper than getting a taxi. We weren't thinking straight as usual but at the time it seemed logical. And so I missed my job interview. Well, I wouldn't have but after that night I really couldn't make it.

Val rang me up today and got me a gig DJing next Thursday at The White House in Clapham Common. They want indie stuff. I told the man I'd do it and that I was a professional DJ and that I just played indie stuff. The truth be known I own about five indie songs. Don't worry though. I'll have a whole collection by next Thursday. I remember when I first started DJing and all I had was three CDs. It's all about manipulating people. Life is easy and you can be successful as long as you know how to do it properly.

I'm the most hated person in Soho at the moment. I can hear people groan as I walk into every bar. Their eyes avert to the floor and I'm left alone. I've done some bad things in these last few months just from being drunk. It doesn't matter though. I need to get out of that place and I need to get out of it alive. I cried on the tube again this morning. I can't stop sometimes. I can never stop. Tonight is an exception. I'm only in this internet cafe because my house is filled with rather large mice. They've taken up residency behind my wardrobe, in the cooker and behind the microwave. They need somewhere to live as well. We can coexist peacefully I guess. If you've got mice it means you don't have rats. Although I did see a rat in the back garden the other day. Going back to bed now.

EARLY MORNING, SHOREDITCH

November 17th, 2006

04:49 pm

YE OLDE AXE
69 HACKNEY ROAD, SHOREDITCH E2
1am-6am

I'll be on the door. Tonight and tomorrow night. I've got a guest list as long as my arm so feel free to pop down if you're in the area. It's a strip club. I wrote about my fascinating night there a while back. Tomorrow is rockabilly and tonight is I don't know what. If it's anything like last time there'll be lots of gay sex going on in toilet cubicles and gangsters and prostitutes hanging around. Then, bring your own gun and we can go to the Hackney snooker hall after. Sounds like fun eh?

"STRIPTEASE WITH A DIFFERENCE"

November 19th, 2006

10:58 am

I like strippers. You know what you're getting. Well, sometimes they may offer you extras but it's always more money than they say and you'll always feel bad about it if you bargain. If you just watch a stripper it's kinda nice. As long as you're not too pissed the memory can stay in your mind and you can re-play it in your head when you're in that kinda mood and have a wank.

I've been working on the door at Ye Olde Axe, 69 Hackney Rd if you wanna go. You should see their bodies. They're really great. They have these wonderful arses and their breasts are really fantastic. Not like girls you'd meet in indie clubs at all. Depends what you're into though I suppose. D'yu wanna grrlfrend? Huh huh. It'll all end in tears y'know.

I can't be doing with company. Company in the sense of the word that means someone asking how I am. I'd much rather be seen objectively and be able to pay my rent...

I can't pay my rent and it's due today. If anyone wants to give me £60 for something that they'd enjoy...

Robin Simon, V and me went to the Russian snooker club in Dalston after. Wow. How fantastic was that? Absolutely. I've still got a can of Stella in me handbag so I'm gonna have that in a bit. This snooker club is really fabulous. It's like being backstage at a 1980s Top of The Pops. You gotta go.

It was weird really, considering how the day started off. I went to Mass in Covent Garden and watched some Frank Sinatra soundalikes. Then I went to Sloane Square in an attempt to find an AA meeting. If I had been successful I wouldn't be writing this now. There's always today. As one of the benches was engraved with in Eaton Square: "Sieze the Day". Bet you'd not heard of that before?

I read the first few chapters of "The Curious Incident of the Dog in the Night-Time" yesterday. Kevin Evian and Alwynn Davies said it was just like reading my previous diary. I'M NOT AUTISTIC. I'M NOT AUTISTIC. I'M MAD NOW. REALLY MAD.

WEDNESDAY SOHO

November 21st, 2006

02:56 pm

I've got a residency at The Arts on Mondays and Wednesdays now. They said they'll let me promote it with my friends as long as my friends don't cause trouble. I know you people wouldn't cause trouble but my other friends, well they're a bit different, but they do spend a lot on drink. I get more money if more than £500 is taken behind the bar.

Woke up in my own bed this morning. My make-up had been taken off and by the look of the opened jar I'd applied moisturiser. Always a good sign. Still can't remember how I got home though. Angel, taxi, Coach and Horses, Arts, Airport, Gerry's. Night Bus perhaps? Wow. That's so new!

THERE'S A CLUB WHERE YOU'D LIKE TO GO TONIGHT

November 29th, 2006

02:31 pm

Alwynn Davies said this journal's a bit crap. He said it's not as good as my previous one. Well, it's not supposed to be. I don't want to give you the x-rated version of events when my real name is involved. Well, we all know that even this isn't my real name. My real name has connotations with debt and depressing things like my family. Not that they're bad or anything but bad things do tend to happen in Oldham.

My sister rang me up last night. She said my Dad's got a massive lump on his stomach and he won't go to the doctors. She said that when she saw him last he was eating tomatoes dipped in salt and was drinking whisky from the bottle. Death wish anyone?

She was saying loads of other bad things that are happening to each member of my family but I can't go into any of the rest cos it's all personal.

I was saying how everything in London is fantastic at the moment. I'm in employment. I don't know for how long but this new job I've got is fantastic. My office overlooks the Thames by Tower Bridge so I can see Canary Wharf and The City and everything. And I get free tea and coffee. Don't worry, I've not sold my soul. I'm only working 5pm-9pm and eventually I'll only have to go in three days a week cos I'll have enough money by then.

I was waiting for my Night Bus on Monday after DJing at The Arts when I got a phone call from the man that always leads me astray. He was on Oxford St as well. "Come to Chelsea, there's a place with a 24 hour licence where millionaires hang out." It's 4am and I don't need much tempting after an offer like that. So we get in a cab and

12

the next thing I know I'm eating smoked salmon and scrambled eggs and drinking fine wine. I couldn't see any millionaires. We were the only people there. We stayed until 8:30am. I couldn't speak. I had nothing to say. I couldn't really find much common ground. I have nothing in common with any of my friends. I'll never find anyone who I have something in common with.

"AS USUAL, I'M OUTNUMBERED"

December 8th, 2006

02:47 pm

I've lost three days again. It wasn't my fault though. It was The Arts Club's fault cos they double-booked me. I've started to only drink on the nights I'm DJing and everything has been quite calm for about a month. I was a bit down about being double-booked as it's obvious to everyone that I'm the best DJ in the world. But, of course, this tracksuited man is bringing down fifty people so I'm out of the door, up some stairs and down another set on Dean Street where wine is given to me.

The conversation was one of murder. Female murderers. Ruth Ellis, Myra Hindley. I started it and I stood up for both of them. As usual, I'm outnumbered.

I wake up on a bench in the same place. It's midday and a glass of wine is still by my side. I drink its contents and head to The Coach and Horses or Norman's as I'm now going to insist on calling it to be awkward. I drink several glasses of wine over the course of two hours bought by several different alcoholics. Kevin Evian turns up fresh from his holiday. He says I should leave and go somewhere with him. "I can't leave. I'm not leaving Soho today!" So he leaves and Angus McAndrew finds me. He takes me to the French House where we eat the nicest fish and chips ever.

Samuel talks to me. Tells me that I'm wasting my life away. Tells me I'm being sucked into Soho like so many people have been before me. He knows; he's seen them all and their deaths. He tells me the wisest things but then I leave him. I can't face any more truth into what I'm becoming.

I find solace in Norman's. I manage to get a few more glasses of wine from various men. Then it's 8pm and the landlady is refusing to serve me. It's strange how men always serve me when I'm there but not women. Well, they're women. She tells me to go home. Home? My Mum'd kill me. So I go back downstairs where Michael immediately says, "A glass of red perhaps, darling?" That's the nicest thing I've heard all day and so I sit there and it's nice and I'm warm and I'm sinking slowly into that quilt called oblivion. Then Keyhole Joe shouts, "Go home! Just go home!" Michael has left so there's no one to stand up for me anymore. It's 10:30pm. Arts Club, I think to myself. And so I go and Woody, the homosexual barman is watching Kill Bill. The violence crashes into my vision and makes me nervous.

There's no DJ that night so I tell them I'll DJ. I have my records still. I've been carrying them around for twenty-four hours. So that's what I do. It was a busy night. I made it busier by playing what people want. I kept collapsing in the DJ booth every half hour and I was having trouble breathing but then Woody mixed me a vodka, cranberry and orange juice and then he gave me some wine and then some more wine and all of a sudden I'm feeling back to my old self and I start dancing. Then there's a fight. It's a pretty violent fight but I'm just laughing my head off and then I stop the music so it makes everything more dramatic and then when the bouncer eventually shoves him out I play Jailhouse Rock really loud and everyone starts jiving and laughing their heads off.

At the end of the night I play Hallelujah by Jeff Buckley and everyone's slow dancing and it's all really beautiful. Snooker anyone? I find a couple and take them to the snooker hall where they've started to serve drink again. We drink pints of lager. We leave around 9am.

I go HOME. Yes. No memories but I wake up at 3pm surrounded by noodles and toast. I have to work from 5pm-9pm and then DJ 11pm-3am again. I do it. I don't drink. Physically can't. I'm taking short laboured breaths and my heart is palpitating. Did I do drugs? I have no idea. A black man starts swinging his rather large penis around to Babies by Pulp. I try not to look. Another black man proclaims he's in love with me and wants one of my bracelets. I know exactly what that's for. Black Magic.

It's 3:13am and I can't smile anymore. I play Jump in the Line as the last record and disappear into the Soho pouring rain.

Tonight the party begins. I'm DJing for an hour and half only at The Soho Arts Club. 10:30-12. Weekends are horrible there. I'll be in The Coach and Horses 9:30-10:23pm preparing myself.

ONE NIGHT ONLY THIS WEEK

December 11th, 2006

04:26 pm

And that's tonight.

I've lost my job again. The snooker club want me to go to Brazil with them to do some drug smuggling. Is that an offer I can't refuse? Can you make me a better offer? This will probably be the last Christmas I see. That's why you should come down to my night. None of you have been yet, apart from Jamie Manners.

MONDAY AND WEDNESDAY DON'T GO TO SOHO
As I'm DJing...

December 18th, 2006

02:49 pm

I've been spending far too much time in the snooker club lately. They have this special cordoned off VIP area that only I'm allowed in. I even have two security guards at each end so no one can break their way through to see me. I sit there on my own most mornings while drinking an endless supply of Newcastle Brown Ale and I'm always thinking, wow! I've really made it now. I've arrived.
I can't write that much here anymore as I'm out of it too much. I don't get back until 10am and then I go straight to bed and I tend not to leave the house until late in the evening when I start drinking again.

A woman has moved into my house. She lives in a room with her boyfriend. I don't think they're married. It's just not right that. You wouldn't find me living with a man unless I was married to him. She's just a free prostitute, that's how I see it.
Anyway, I could smell bleach yesterday evening as I was clambering down the stairs to get some chocolate cake. It turns out she was cleaning the kitchen. The kitchen is filthy I know, but it's not me who's made the mess. Then she tells me that there must be a couple of mice living in the kitchen. I didn't want to tell her the truth. The kitchen is infested with mice. There's a nest of them that live inside the cooker and in the toaster.
That's why I'm never ill. My immune system is so good from living in filth that I don't get ill anymore. And the alcohol helps. I'm like human Dettol. I was hoping they wouldn't move a woman in. I knew this would happen. She'll start some kind of cleaning rota next and try and get friendly with me. She'll think I'm a prostitute from the strange hours I keep. Men don't care and that's why I like them. My time has gone.

"I KNOW A PLACE WHERE WE CAN GO TO SCORE CRACK"

December 20th, 2006

02:22 pm

I'm going home tomorrow. I'll use my time in Oldham to detox. I hate that word. It's nice in Oldham, I can't wait to go back. Well, I can kind of as I'm DJing tonight. I hope my Mum makes some soup.

I'll have to pretend to everyone that I'm a really successful DJ and that my band is really big. I can't stand going back to my home town as a failure. Sometimes I think about the stuff that I imagine in my daydreams and it seems so real. I start to believe stuff myself and once I tell other people about it, it becomes even more real.
Anyway, all is not bad.

If you're in the unfortunate position of being in Soho on New Year's Eve, I hear the brothel on Greek Street is the best one but the one opposite Somerfield on Berwick Street isn't too bad either. You can go there after you've been to my night. Mind you, it's so easy to get laid in The Soho Arts Club. Hence the reason I've renamed it The Soho Tarts Club.

The man who owns the karaoke bar on Frith Street came down on Monday night. When the night finished I went along with the suited regulars to the karaoke bar and we went in a room at the back and sang stuff. I didn't bother singing too much as I can't sing. Well, not karaoke. My voice has a different key to everyone else's, that's what I like to say.

I, as usual, was the last to leave and he chucked me out at seven. The party never ends until I'm unconscious so I went to the snooker club. There was no security on the VIP area at that hour so I had to sit at the bar with the manager. There was only me, him and his cousin in there. My friend told me the snooker hall is a place where people go if they want to score heroin. Apparently, it's always been that way. I wondered why people keep asking me for heroin and crack down there. Funny really.

When I go home I'm just going to hang around and do nothing. I'm going to The Smiths night on Friday. If anyone wants to meet up with me then Friday's probably the best day. Merry Christmas and a prosperous New Year. Let's hope it's my last.

BILLY DIAMOND

December 27th, 2006

02:56 pm

I'm sitting here in Oldham wearing a red wig, three jumpers, two pairs of socks and gold sequined shoes. I'm freezing.

I arrived on Thursday and I've just seen my Dad for the first time since my birthday. I had given up hope of seeing him this time. He bought me "The People's Prayer Book" and "An Advent Journey of Prayer for Marriage and Family Life". Of course, I'd have only bought those books anyway if he gave me book tokens.

I've spent a lot of time hanging around pubs in the Werneth area. That's my area you see. The Cambridge pub was full of under-sixteens drinking Magners. People stare at me a lot round here. I don't mind though. They stare at me a lot round Soho but here the stares are of a more threatening nature.

I've got a habit of telling people exactly what I think of them when I've had a bit to drink. Last night was one of these times. I told my sister's fancy man that he had wasted his life. I just went on and on saying he was pointless etc, etc, etc. I think it might have done him some good. Maybe he'll be a better person now.

My Mum's just opened the present my Dad left for her. Bread mix. How predictable.
"What do I want with bloody bread mix?"
"You could make some bread," I offer.

Anne and me went to a convict's house last night. They were doing drugs. "I'm right pilled up," they kept saying. I gave them all a lecture about the badness of drugs. Needless to say, I didn't partake.

My old drinking pal is locked up this Christmas. He's been done for paedophilia. He locked some girls in his house and made them watch porn and then assaulted them. Bad eh?

Then the man from the chippy told me that the woman that used to own the newsagent's was killed in a car crash on Snake Pass. It's all rather depressing. I spent three years doing my paper round for her. Well, for the money to buy alcohol and cigarettes actually, but it's still bad.

It's rather depressing here. A fine mist cloaks the derelict streets while the only people that roam them are drug dealers and child alcoholics.

Now, I'm off to have a turkey sandwich and a pork pie. Lovely.

"BUT IT SAYS YOU'RE OPEN ALL NIGHT"

January 4th, 2007

01:54 pm

Another packed night down at Tarts last night. Wuh-huh. I attacked the homosexual barman again cos he started attacking me. I drank NBA and then tried to get some more of the stuff down the snooker hall but they wouldn't let me in. Brave decision methinks. And so I ended up in Subway eating a Subway melt. I resisted the Yazoo this time because money is short.

I had a nice New Year's, thanks for asking. Coach and Horses from 4:30 to 10am. They should do that more often. On New Year's Day I went on that big erection thing in Leicester Square. It didn't go for long or fast enough for me. Lovely view though and the rain added a nice effect.

Just been to Iceland to buy a bag of sugar. Why do people pay their bills in Iceland? I was under the impression that it was a frozen food supermarket. I suppose it's a bit like going to Tottenham Court Road station at 5am to get a drink. Or a bit like when you go to Ireland and there's a bar in the post office.

I'm lucky to be back in London and up to my old tricks. My Mum wanted to send me to a drying out clinic cos I got pissed on my last night in Oldham. She prays for me every night. I'm not going back there for a very very long time.

Tonight I'm taking Phill Gatenby on a tour of Soho. Well, just to The Coach and Horses, The French and Gerry's. He's the man that wrote a book on Morrissey in case you didn't know. I'm not taking him to the snooker hall though. Early night for me. I've got things to do before midday tomorrow. Do you wanna know what they are?

HELP KEEP SCARLET WEST IN EMPLOYMENT

January 8th, 2007

05:52 pm

Make your plans. If no one starts coming down to my DJing at The Arts, the homosexual barman is making me turn it into a hi-energy pop night.

I went to the lesbian and gay AA yesterday. It was all rather depressing. Everyone was saying how they were mad. I would never admit to being mad because I'm not mad. A man next to me gave me Opal Fruits throughout the meeting. I felt a bit bad about the unwrapping and chewing noise while people were saying how awful their childhood was and how they used to feel bad about being gay. But still, I like Opal Fruits. I didn't look too anonymous. I was wearing my bright red jumper and I'd just cut my hair into a weird style.

After we'd all held hands and said the serenity prayer I made a sharp exit and didn't make an offer to help with tidying up. There wasn't much of a mess anyway. Just Opal Fruit wrappers and coffee cups.

I got on the tube at Holborn making a big detour so I wouldn't have to enter the slow suicide that is Soho. I went to the Spiritualist church in Notting Hill which I sometimes frequent. A man was sat behind me and as I sat down he said it was the second time he'd seen me that day. "Where was the first?" I questioned. "Covent Garden," came the reply. By the looks of him I reckon it was AA but some people are just too polite.

The service was nice and the medium put me in mind of Norman Balon.

I went straight home after. It was nice to be alone. It's always nice to be alone when you're not lonely. I talked to the E.Ts. for a bit then went to sleep where my dreams were filled with terrorists and Channel 4 News.

This morning I had to go to work. I was excited about it as I wanted to be part of society again and this was the first time the people in Tower Bridge had offered me such a thing. I got up at 6:50am. It felt weird. I'm usually in the snooker hall, ordering my second to last drink at that hour. Catching the tube was strange. I was wondering if the commuters would recognise me from being really pissed every morning and complaining about their choice of newspaper. But I was well disguised: spectacles, no make-up, parka. I rarely recognise myself on days like those.

Anyway, I've just got back from work. It was a bit crap. I didn't get any surveys while everyone else got about six. I started to fall asleep around eleven. At one, I ate a chip butty on a bench in a housing estate. I fell asleep again from three onwards. By the end of the day they told me that no more work was to be had by me. That means I don't have to go back. I made an effort as well. I didn't part company without telling them all to come down to my club nights, that I played the stuff they were into like R'n'B. Yeah, like yeah…

So now I'm free. Please join me.

PHOTOS OF PIES

January 9th, 2007

08:19 pm

I've just bought a tin-opener from 99p Stores. It's a rather nice tin-opener. I smashed the kitchen up the other day cos someone had stolen my old tin-opener. Well, it wasn't really mine. It came with the house. I was desperate for meatballs though. Really desperate. I ended up just eating a potato and feeling bitter.

I drank red wine last night. I've heard there are some incriminating pictures of me and a certain news anchor floating around The Coach and Horses. They say they're going up on the wall. It will be nice to be alongside Jeffrey but he looks so demure and thoughtful.

I went out for two days again the other day without going home. I slept downstairs. That's the last time I do that. There are entities down there. I was alone and something kept grabbing me. I was chased around the place by it. There was more than one of them as well. I turned all the lights on and put the music on but the lights kept flickering and the music kept skipping and then the phone starts to ring. I answered it but it went dead. I actually did a 1471 but it was dead. Soon's I put the phone down it rings again. Same thing. Any other person would have just got out but I poured myself another drink. I was after all waiting for The Coach and Horses to open but it was only 5am. Something kept stroking my hair. I looked at him from the corner of my eye and guess who it was? Yes, it was Jeffrey Bernard. So Jeff's tryna seduce me from beyond the grave. How cool is that?

I spent the next day in The Coach. Norman Balon bought me a drink in return for me giving him the number of the stage manager of the opera house. I have most people's number in Soho. Well, just men's numbers. I've never used them for anything cos they've never used me for anything.

I've just woke up. My landlord's chasing me for the rent. I'm in trouble. I'd like to justify the tin-opener though. It was a justified buy.

The snooker club has well and truly lost their patience with me. I went down there last night with a Trash reject and they asked me to pay. Then they wouldn't let me sit in the VIP area. I drank three bottles of NBA then went home. Today I woke up surrounded by two tomatoes, a bag of mushrooms, four packets of Koka noodles and an onion. What was I thinking? No porn though. I think I've overcome my porn addiction.

and from my hospital bed

January 15th, 2007

12:35 pm

they give me these fantastic pills that are green and yellow. i feellike im flying. and cnn andpies and everything. like it here. nice... ucl ward t7 bed 26 b4 8 pleaseonly 2day

A CLEAN BREAK FROM SOHO

January 17th, 2007

08:48 pm

I've broken my leg in two places. Just in case the last entry caused you any confusion.

I made a decision last Thursday morning at 3:30am to go to Camera Repairs after I'd finished DJing. After my first bottle of lager I popped to the toilet and then slipped on the constantly flooded floor on the way out, thus twisting my leg. I took my cowboy boot off to have a look at the damage. My foot was facing a strange direction. I tried to twist it back and then my strange acquaintances tried to put my boot back on which they did successfully. I couldn't stand on it but I was still hoping for the best. I was carried up the stairs by a Virgin record company executive and taken to UCH in one of those dodgy taxis.

There I waited and waited. Eventually they did an x-ray and confirmed the worst. Then they cut my jeans and underwear off. I was kept occupied with a supply of gas and morphine while they stretched it back into place; this involved four people of my own age pulling the leg in different directions. I didn't waste time in explaining that I was once in the prestigious squadron of 317 Air Training Corps and that I knew how to not feel pain. Maybe it was the morphine or maybe I was just ignoring the pain. I told them to all come down to my club night once they'd made me better. I can't remember them agreeing.

So then I'm on a ward with three elderly ladies. I was glad of getting rid of the young people. I lay there with my morphine drip having a thoroughly good time. Talking to the ladies about different stuff. Jamie Manners was my first visitor. So shout out to Jamie.

After a while they made me sign a form and sent me down to the basement for an operation. Everyone seemed to be fascinated about my occupation as a DJ. I made out like I was a really good DJ and told everyone they could come down on Mondays and Wednesdays in a few months when I'd be better. And then that was it. A bit like my alcohol induced blackouts apart from I was still and lying in an operating theatre instead of a gutter.

When I came round I was back on the nice ward with the nice old women. I lay there again clutching my morphine drip and pressing it every five minutes. I ate something after a bit even though my appetite was dead. I then proceeded to puke it up. By this time Kevin arrived. Thanks Kevin.

For the next twenty-four hours I veered in and out of consciousness and my face veered in and out of the grey cardboard sick bowl. It wasn't bad though. The sleep was pleasant and complete. Even the bedpan wasn't as bad as some folk make out.

Over the next few days they gave me pills and weaned me off the morphine. Then they gave me a Zimmer frame and a nice pink nightdress. I was happy. Me and the ladies talked about past holidays and jobs, the people next door and the past in general. At last I'd met some people who I could relate to.

Every day a black man would come round with a menu for the next day's meals. I'd spend twenty minutes colouring in the boxes and working out what accompaniments would go with the mains, and asking the ladies what chicken or pear surprise would actually consist of. Every day I was surprised at how nice the menu read but how different the reality of the dish was. Every day the food trolley smelt the same. But who was I to complain? I can't cook and even so I was still having a bloody good time.

At around 8pm every evening I would look out at the BT tower and watch it change colour. Everything seemed so nice. The colours of London were so clear. Then I'd go back to my ward and watch people rushing in and out of Euston Square station. Everything seemed perfect. Sometimes I'd watch TV after I'd taken my pills and they'd turned the lights out. I'd watch nature programmes about fish or late editions of Coronation Street. Then I'd drift off, taking comfort in the sound of the machines and the nurses' footsteps.

On Sunday I asked the nun if I could receive the sacrament. She was very pleased to oblige. I prayed about everything and told God how sorry I was about the inconvenience I'd caused the nice people.

So after six days I had to leave. They needed the bed and all that. As I was waiting for my Mum I said to my new-found friends, "Well, I don't know about you but I've had a really good time!" They weren't as enthusiastic about it all but I had the idea that they enjoyed my company.

I was glad to see my Mum. I had to give her a daylight sober version of the events leading up to my accident. My Mum only let me go back to London on the condition that I attend AA and didn't drink. I promised. I fucked up as usual.

My Mum had taken the trouble to book a buggy to take us to the platform at Euston and another buggy to take us to the taxi rank at Piccadilly. So now I'm here. Safe and sound. I've never felt better. I look really good as well. Really rested and translucent.
Expect to hear more from me. I'll be here for a while…

I MISS SOHO

January 18th, 2007

02:19 pm

I'm not missing drinking. I'm missing Soho. I'm missing The Coach and Horses. I'm missing the patrons.

While the wind howls around my old house I think back to the good times. I suppose there's been more bad than good times, but still. I think back to the beginning of my nights. Mainly because I can never remember how they end. The conversations. Everything's just so alive. It's been nine days since someone has verbally challenged me. I'm so bored.

This is how life ends. Maybe it's just temporary but as I sit here in this darkened room, smelling bad in my dressing gown I can imagine this being the end. I know it's only a broken leg and I'm only twenty-five but I feel like I've lived enough life to be able to say Amen, that's it.

I feel like I've never lived without Soho. I spent twenty-one years without it but I really can't remember those times. When I talk about Soho I'm talking about only these places: The Coach and Horses, Gerry's, The French, The Colony, Blacks, Trisha's (even though some serious trouble got me barred). Erm, that's it really. At least that's what Soho means to me. Now I realise it has become my life. Maybe I would never have known that if it hadn't been for this break.

It was the only place where I have ever been accepted. A place where people have just talked to me. I started out in London going to places like Stay Beautiful, Trash, White Heat, The Ship, Hoxton, 333 and the list goes on. I always felt so alone. I'd meet the same shallow people night after night. Night upon night people would tell me the same things no matter who they were. Stuff like, "Where did you get your shoes from?" I can't believe anyone would be bothered about a pair of fucking shoes. If someone asked me that now I'd tell them to fuck off.

Walking into The Coach for the first time that September back in 2003 I felt like I'd come home. Home for the first time. The first person I spoke to was Antonio, the stage manager of The Opera House. The next person was Richard Haydn, now my longest surviving friend. Quality people, that's all I've got to say. Quality.

Along the way there have been rumours about me. I like the rumours. People don't buy me drink anymore because they know they'll never get one back and my looks are fading fast. But I don't mind. I just like sitting in Jeffrey's seat and watching everyone. I belong there now.

I can't quite bring myself to say goodbye to Soho. This is the true extent of how empty my life has been. Soho fills it up. It's a labyrinth of colour and adventure. It's also a black hole that I've been sucked into.

"I've seen many a man ruined by Soho."

Now I can understand why.

IN WHICH DIRECTION IS THE SEA?

January 23rd, 2007

09:13 pm

The consultant told me it would take a year. My leg. To heal. Oh dear. I still can't walk on it. They like to say, "It's still not weight-bearing". They've given me another appointment at The Royal Oldham Hospital for a month's time.

I called the benefits helpline yesterday, but they just reduced me to tears. I have to get a letter from my landlord but he's not supposed to be renting out rooms. It's a casual arrangement. I can't go back to London and move all my stuff out of that room as I do eventually want to go back but I don't know how I'm going to pay my rent until then. And then I've got all those credit card bills. Shit. I owe loads. Thousands of pounds. And with no income from anywhere. Oh God, everything's gone wrong. And I've no one but myself to blame.

I've nothing more to say. It's been rather an abrupt end to the life that once was. I'd rather be dead than in this state. At least I chronicled it all on here. When I came back from the hospital I slept for the rest of the afternoon. It tired me out greatly. I'm glad I've lived my life the way I did. I'm not happy about spending the amount of money I spent. I still can't work out how that happened as it's not as if I ever bought a drink. I'd like to thank all those people that have bought me drinks over the years. I'd also like to thank the people that entertained me verbally. We all know there was no other entertaining going on.

I've sent two postcards from here. One to The Coach and the other to Gerry's. They should get them tomorrow.

My final request is to have a Requiem Mass. Thank you.

THE FACTS ABOUT THE MENOPAUSE

January 26th, 2007

10:22 am

So I died here and went to Blogspot for a bit. But the next day it wouldn't let me back in. Maybe I was a bit controversial or something. Anyway, just like The French and Trisha's they've barred me.

So I'm back here. This internet thing is keeping me really entertained. I've never really used the internet before. I know I've written all my journals in internet cafes but that's all I've used the internet for. Sometimes I check my hotmail thing. I use that MySpace thing more though. I've been adding people for my band Iraq. Yesterday I spent six hours browsing through people that I thought might appreciate them. Like Muslims. I've got a few Muslims but they mainly come from the Queens district in New York. Cool eh? Then I found this comedy Rat Pack style band and they're called Iraq Pack. They play in Leytonstone and have a man called Osama Bing Crosby in their band. They dress up as famous people like Hitler and Saddam. Well, when my band next do a gig I'm gonna wear a hijab and I'm gonna make the boys wear backpacks just like the 7/7 bombers. My Mum said I'd get into trouble and that I'd be arrested. It's only a joke though innit?

My Dad came round last night. The most comforting thing in the whole world for me is to hear my Mum and Dad talk, just their voices when they're not arguing. It's a nice sound. They're gonna take me out in the wheelchair on Sunday. Our destination will be The Bridgewater pub on Manchester Road and I'm gonna have a roast dinner there. I'm looking forward to it. Next Thursday I think my Dad's taking me to the free 'n' easy afternoon at one of the pubs. My Mum said I can't have anything alcoholic though.

My broken leg feels really heavy. It feels double the weight of the other leg. It doesn't look much different, it's just that metal rod in it.

I wonder if I'll ever be able to swim again. I haven't been swimming for seven years so I don't know why I'm wondering that now. I was once a champion swimmer. I was in all the school competitions as well as Air Training Corps ones. I used to win as well. Then I used to win all the cross country competitions. And sprinting competitions. Then I did weight training once a week. I was good at any sport where there was no teamwork involved. Mind you, I was on the football team and I was quite good at that. If you look closely you can still see my muscles. They're perfect.

WHAT IS THE ORIGIN OF THE OTTOMAN EMPIRE?

January 30th, 2007

11:57 am

I've stopped going downstairs now. I don't get dressed either. There's not much point. Can't afford my rent in London either. Everything's gone.

Perhaps this is depressing for you. I wouldn't bother reading anymore. As I said, I hate depressed people. I could be dying in Sudan. I always say that. But instead I'm in Oldham. It doesn't matter where I am. I still haven't left the house. I still can't walk.

My optimism has gone. My leg has black marks all over it. It's difficult to lift as it's so heavy. I've got nothing good to say so I shouldn't say anything at all. I've also stopped speaking.

The only person that's visited me is Paul Thompson. Thanks Paul.

When I do eventually return to Soho I'm going to start out where I left off. I've found out exactly what I want. I want the life I was living before the accident. I loved all that drinking and everything else that went with it. Even being arrested wasn't that bad. And all those dangerous characters I was hanging out with. I loved them all.

The thing I miss most of all though is the walk from The Coach and Horses to The Arts on Mondays and Wednesdays. I loved that. Then I'd get there and drink and play records and smoke and I was happy.

I enjoyed those three-day drinking sessions. I miss the people that served me. The people behind the bars were the only stable things I had. Here are my favourites:
Edward Joyce (Gerry's)
Minty (Gerry's)

Michael (Coach)
Cherry (Coach)
That girl that looks a bit like KD Lang but better (French)

I miss my favourite drinks. Here are my favourite drinks:
Löwenbräu
Rosé wine
Red wine
Grolsch
NBA
White wine
Champagne

I've got nothing else to think about apart from the day I will return. Until then I have no control over anything that happens. My Mum's not allowing me to drink. I hate being controlled. It's in my best interests though I suppose. If I had a visitor I'd feel better.

I'D LIKE TO THANK THE COACH
AND HORSES...

January 31st, 2007

11:09 am

For ringing me up last night and sending their love. I got to speak to most of my cronies who were all terribly concerned. And they rang me up on The Coach landline as well.

I'm quite happy now. Sitting here with my porcelain cat and my flask of coffee. Life is really great. I'm glad I broke my leg. It's been really fun. I like sitting around. And I've been reading more than usual. I now know the answers to the following questions. Why not test your knowledge?
1. Who was the first king in the world?

2. In what battle was a British army commanded by a Frenchman defeated by a French army commanded by an Englishman?

3. Who were the Mohocks?

Now that's enough to be going on with. I'll return later to see how you've done.

WHISKY AND TOLERANCE

February 2nd, 2007

10:22 am

Gerry's called me yesterday afternoon. Well, Edward Joyce actually but he is Gerry's. He said he didn't know about my accident until he got my postcard. Then he said he would have come to visit me in UCH. "But I was out of it on morphine," I said.
"We could have shared it, darling," he replied.

So that's just great now. I was only bothered about those two places not realising I had disappeared but now they both have and that's all that matters. My bar-stools are awaiting my return.

I'm desperate to see that film "Venus". For obvious reasons. I've hitched a plan to get in touch with my old acquaintances from school cos they have cars and they could take me somewhere.

I deserve all this. I've been bad and spoke bad about near enough everyone I've ever known. I don't have a bad word to say about very few people. I can list the people I have nothing bad to say about. I'm into my lists at the moment and I was about to list the people I don't have a bad word for. But that would do me no good. Most people are nice to me. Most people tolerate me. People do eventually stop tolerating my behaviour but they tend not to tell me that they're going to stop tolerating it and just never bother to call or stay in touch.

I'm still not bothered about not drinking alcohol. Although yesterday afternoon my Dad came round with a bottle of whisky for him and a computer table for me. His glass evaporated while he was assembling the table. Then I fell asleep. The whisky gave me a warm sinking feeling. It didn't do much more than that.

Whenever I look at the clock I envisage the clock above the bar in

The Coach. Like now, I'll imagine it getting ready to open. Then in twelve hours from now I'll imagine last orders.

I'm spending a lot of time on my band's MySpace. We've written more songs than the one featured. And they're still rehearsing without me. Half of my band are from Paris. How cool is that? I've got a good feeling about them as usual. I love Iraq.

HALF A PINT OF RED WINE
WITH ICE PLEASE...

February 5th, 2007

08:59 pm

I got dressed today. It made me feel normal for a few minutes but didn't really do much more than that. Then my dad came wandering down at 4pm. He was a bit pissed and asked my Mum if she wanted a blow-up santa. My Mum declined the offer.

They decided to take me out to the pub in the wheelchair. My Dad pushed and I was a bit nervous as cars kept swerving to avoid my Dad's drunken driving of the chair. He insisted on pushing the chair in the middle of the road and assured me that we had "right of way". We successfully made it to The Royal Oak. I had a glass of red and smoked cigarettes. A haggard looking woman talked loudly to us from the other side of the bar about her battle with breast and cervical cancer. It was all very predictable. Not like The Coach at all really.

However, the cancer survivor did buy me a drink. I'd never heard of it but she ordered me a double red wine and then asked me if I wanted ice in it. The wine came in a half pint glass. I was quite happy after that. Just sitting there with my half pint of red and smoking some rather vile cigarettes I'd found.

My Dad always drinks half pints of bitter followed by straight double whiskies. He started getting loud so my Mum said it was time to go. I wasn't too bothered. Nothing exciting ever happens in Oldham. I should know. I spent twenty-one years here and nothing much happened. Well, the riots were kind of exciting in 2001 but that doesn't seem to be going on much anymore. I don't mind it being boring. It's just the people. They all say the same things. Everyone has the same "outlook". They'll say crass things like, "You're not here for long, you've got to enjoy it while you can," or, "you're only here once," and all the time, to me especially, "cheer up". Every sentence they string together is second-hand. The art of independent thought just never happened for them. It's nothing to do with education. I shunned it all and I'm still thinking.

I'm glad I can watch The Sky at Night on BBC Four. I've always enjoyed Patrick Moore. Sometimes I imagine getting married to him. I know he was married a while ago but I haven't really done my research properly so perhaps it's not love.

I went round to my sister's house on Saturday. She rang me up at 11am and said she was having a party and hadn't been to bed. I got there at midday. The room was thick with smoke and terrible looking people were lying around the place. I felt awful, not being able to walk away. I had to just sit there for nine hours with the smoke stinging my eyes while they talked non-stop about crap. My Mum was out so even she couldn't rescue me. I worry about my sister. She's vulnerable. I'm gonna set her up with a nice man from Liverpool soon. He's the network manager at John Moores University. I think he might be able to help her.

My tally chart of visitors still has only one stick on it and I've been here three weeks. You're bastards, that's what you are.

DON'T BOTHER READING.
SAME OLD STORY.

February 9th, 2007

11:46 am

It's still awful here. I hate The North. It's oppressive. Once you're here it's difficult to get out, especially if you're born here. Maybe the middle classes are different. They're willing to send their children to university and they have enough money to do so. But for me it was different. I was told to get a job at Setons, the body bag factory, that it was a good career and then I could just shut up. Everyone's so proud to be honest and hard-working, but what for? I've never aspired for people to say that I'm a good person or that I'd do anything for anyone. Well, maybe I would depending on the price. But anyway.

The only thing my Mum aspired me to do was to work in an office. My Dad says different things depending who he is that day. When I was eighteen he said he'd be proud to see me on page 3 of The Sun. When I was seventeen he told me to get a job in a factory. He still thinks I'm working as a pole dancer in London and needless to say, so do all the pubs in Oldham.

I don't wish I'd done anything differently. I've had my moments. I do wish I hadn't spent seven years in a band that didn't get anywhere. That's my only regret, but how was I to know? You believe in people and then they let you down. The usual story I suppose. It's nothing new. It's like any marriage or any friendship. Everything ends and it's always someone else's fault. I always feel so free without friends.

"LONDON, BECAUSE OF ITS VAST SIZE, CAN OFFER MORE THAN THE SMALLER PROVINCIAL TOWNS."

February 17th, 2007

10:31 pm

For the first time in my life I've found myself interested in what other people are doing. Well, I'm not interested, it's rather more due to the fact that I have fuck all else to do. I'm listening to other people's bands on MySpace for heaven's sake. How bored must I be?

I've never held an interest in anyone but myself. Even if you've known me for a bit, you probably notice that my eyes wander or I make an excuse and leave. So anyway, I've read all your MySpace pages and your blogs and yes, it's true, I was right all along; I needn't have bothered because you're all the same. It's not very original for me to be saying this as everyone says that everyone's the same so I'm just wasting my time and sounding exactly the same by doing so.

Blogspot is shit. I opened up another account with them the other day so I could comment on my eight-year-old niece's holiday experience. Unfortunately I forgot she was still eight and now need to delete my comments and I can't get back in. My sister's gonna go mad.

My fourteen-year-old cousin has found me and Iraq on MySpace. It's great how that brings families together. I mean, they would never have known I was as talented and wonderful as those spaces make me out to be.

Meanwhile my mother thinks I'm running a terrorist network cell from the spare room. She keeps telling me to change my band name or I'll be taken to Paddington for questioning. Not bothered. Anything to get out of Oldham.

I'm kind of wishing I'd called my band Iran now. There's more of a youth culture out there and they're crying out for a band like mine. As soon as I can get past the censors I'll be adored out there. I've found a few Iraqis that are into Iraq but the rest of the people with MySpaces there are American. So maybe a name change is in order. Perhaps I can run two MySpaces. One called Iraq and one called Iran. Maybe one called Afghanistan or Israel for good measure. Finger in all war zones, that's the way to go.

STAGNATION. SUICIDE. SALVATION.

February 18th, 2007

10:28 pm

I was lying in my bed just now, listening to Jeff Buckley. I was crying loads. About everything but mostly about being born. That sounds a bit teenagerish but yes, that's what I was crying about.

If I was able to walk I'd be out of here. You know that by now. Even my mother knows that by now, but instead I'm in my bed staring at my glow-in-the-dark stars through the blur of my tears. Don't give me sympathy, my predicament is my own and you have your own worries.

I think about my brother and how lucky he was to just die like that. He was twenty-three. I mean, that's a nice age to die although I think twenty-five would be better. I can't leave my Mum now, she's been through enough. If she hadn't I'd be out of this life so fast. It's not that I can't cope with it, I mean, it's fine. In London. Life is wonderful in London. I was attempting to explain to my Mum how wonderful life was in London earlier on in the evening but she took it all personally, as to mean that life was terrible here with her.

My father, as usual, hasn't been in touch. I'm not going to call him Dad anymore. I've given up all hope in him. Everyone says he's a bastard and they've been right all along. It's a bit like when you're going out with someone and you really like them but your friends don't. Remember, your friends are usually right.

I haven't been out since last Sunday. Father is drunk all the time. People have said he's normally out of it by midday. Last Sunday he came into the pub where my sister and I were at 2pm and he couldn't even stand. Sometimes I wonder when he will actually die. He gets beaten up a lot so I don't think it will be long until he does.

I don't wish he was dead though.

My sister's ex-boyfriend who I was going on about at Christmas is in a critical condition in hospital. If you're an avid reader of this, you may remember a fight I had with him in the Christmas special. Well, he's now in hospital with brain damage. I'd like to add that it's nothing to do with me. He was found outside his house. The blood's coming out through his eyes and he's got bleeding on the brain. My sister seems to have fallen back in love with him and spends her time at the hospital even though he doesn't care for her.

My sister's like that though, she's just a victim. I think it's due to the "Oldham condition" AKA "They'll do anything for anybody".

Soon's I get back to London I'm going to be the worst person you've ever met. I'm going to rob, lie and murder. As long as I don't get caught I'm gonna find a way to survive so I never have to come back to this fucking hell hole.

"GROWING UP, I'D HATED THE WHITES."

February 21st, 2007

10:41 pm

A vague acquaintance of my Father's has been wheeling me to the pub recently. Just cos my Father can't be bothered.

I've been sitting in pubs watching horse racing. I'm now an expert on horse racing. I remember how I used to hang around The Coach during the day and the old men used to talk about bets they'd placed. And I'd drink and drink. I still drink and drink but know there's only so much I can take before I get into the dangerous territory of being unsteady. I can't be unsteady anymore and that pisses me off.

So this man, he'd press the doorbell at 3pm and wheel me up the road. I didn't like him or anything, he was one of these honest types: "I say what I think and if they don't like it then they can fuck off". That was his motto. But he bought me drink so the situation was kind of alright. He started getting pissed off with me though, the fact that I never spoke and rarely smiled. They take that as an insult round here. I still didn't bother. That old phrase made its well-trodden path back to me after two pints of Guinness. Not that he was bothered. Men only like me cos I've got blonde hair and blue eyes. I'm their "ideal woman" in a Nazi kind of way.

I edged the conversation towards politics the other night. "We don't talk about that round here," came the laughing reply.
"Go on, go on, go on. I'll keep saying that until you tell me your political persuasion," I said. He gave in and so did the whole table.
"B.N.P."
"Why? Protest vote then?"
"You just don't understand, you don't have to live here."
Erm, yeah I'm glad I don't have to live here. A registrar told me I had another month to go yesterday. This IS hell.

And you get down to the root of the problem and everything's obvious and I never wanted to come back here to work out what had gone wrong. I just wanted to go away and remove myself from it. And forget what a slum I'd come from.

Growing up, I'd hated the whites. It's weird but I still do. In Oldham, things are different. Growing up, the English hated me and they still do. Now they think I'm Polish.

I'VE GOT A BAND. IT'S CALLED IRAQ.

February 25th, 2007

11:27 am

I've lost all desire to leave the house. Now I just stay in and look for new MySpace layouts.

At night I get frightened. I'm pre-occupied with things beyond this realm and I can't stop thinking about death. I keep getting visions of butchered bodies in the bathroom. It's like a horror movie. I feel like someone's constantly watching me. Thing is, I don't know whether I'm the victim or the murderer. My Mum says it's because I've been watching too many films. But I've only watched two since I've been here.

Last time I went to a psychiatrist they tried to take me away. But the next week I said I was alright and that it wasn't happening anymore and they let me be. I had to say that. I didn't want to end up anywhere, and I know I'd end up at Broadmoor if I told them about the inner workings of my mind.

Thing is, I'm fine in London. I don't have problems like this. My house there is fine too. And the clubs and everything like that, that keeps me busy and I lead a normal life.

I should be at church now but I couldn't face it this morning. I was up all night with the light on, too scared to sleep. I feel like the priest in The Omen.

THE DEATH OF THE PARTY

February 27th, 2007

03:38 pm

I've been Googling myself again. There's absolutely nothing on me. Nothing of interest anyway. I found out that I organise Meetup groups about David Bowie, The Smiths, Marilyn Monroe. Thing is, I don't. I just registered with meetup.com thinking I'd go to some of these things and it would be an excuse to sit around the pub with people and get pissed. I organised one on Marilyn Monroe cos I thought it would be a good way to meet girls. No one turned up.

Last night I went to a comedy night in Chorlton with my old pal Bob Bolton. I was quite involved in the comedy circuit at one time. 1999-2002 actually. In fact so involved that I lost my virginity in 2000 to a comedian. That's a bleak story that you probably already know. A taxi I was in ran the poor man over in Barlow Moor Road so it all stemmed from that. After that I had three dates with him, each time meeting in The Briton's Protection. On the third date I made him do it, if you can make anyone do it that is. He didn't want to and I didn't particularly want to but I was worried about getting raped in Oldham so I thought that in a bed in a loft in Chorlton would be a much more viable option. After I got it over and done with I didn't bother with him again. He didn't bother with me again so it was all alright.

I didn't bother with sex again for a good few years after that. I still haven't come round to the idea of sex and every time it comes on the telly I have to turn away.

My Mum's just brought me up a letter that says I'm not entitled to Incapacity Benefit as I've not paid enough National Insurance contributions. Fuckinghell. Income Support don't want to know either. My Mum hasn't got enough money to pay my rent or keep me for much longer. I've missed all payments on my credit cards so I can't even take out new ones now. I feel pointless and helpless. It's as if I'd be better off not existing. I can't even turn to prostitution cos I can't fucking walk. I wish the suicide attempt had worked all those years ago. I wish they hadn't revived me at birth. Is this an overreaction?

I will return to Soho, there's no way I'm dying in Oldham. When I do return I shall drink day in, day out until I turn yellow and die, and I'm gonna start taking drugs as well, whatever I can get my hands on. Anything. Anything not to smell this awful stench of failure. I don't care whether you smell it, I'm leaving.

February 28th, 2007

FAVOURITES

THE CENTRE POINT SNOOKER HALL
02:46 pm

The Centre Point snooker hall, best used at 3:30am. Ladies free. Men £5 or however much the big black man thinks you're worth. Pints of Kronenbourg 1664 and bottles of NBA. Cigarettes behind the bar.

THE BLUE POSTS BERWICK STREET
02:53 pm

I don't hang around here that often. I did after my arrest though as they were fitting a new carpet in The Coach. I usually get Kronenbourg 1664 in here. I'm not keen on the telly in the corner or that crackly radio station that you can hardly hear. It interferes with my mind. I like going in here at dusk.

THE COACH AND HORSES
02:58 pm

The Coach and Horses is my favourite. I don't mind what time I'm in here. In fact my favourite time to be in here is when I don't know what time it is which is most of the time. People still talk about Jeffrey Bernard as if I admire him in some way. In fact I only found out who he was in December. I'm not keen on the prices in here. It's £3.80 for a pint of Löwenbräu but this is what I drink. Sometimes I'll have wine as that's more cost-effective. That's £3.20 a glass. I'd still like to thank all those men that have bought me drinks over the years. They never got one back and I feel bad about that. If I ever had any money though I would buy people drinks. I wouldn't give them anything else but I'd be sure to buy them drinks.

I usually use the side entrance and walk to the other end of the bar if it's not too busy. Just so you know where to find me on my return.

D. HUGHES DEMOLITION 620 6498

March 2nd, 2007

02:39 pm

The most exciting thing happened this afternoon. A big bulldozer came and demolished the flats opposite where I live. They were built in 1979 from a nice red brick as sheltered housing for old people. When we moved here in 1990 the old people would sit outside by their nicely tended gardens and drink tea. It was all so nice until they died.

Then the council decided to use the flats to house drug addicts and people with "problems". They used the flats as drug dens. It's all getting a bit Daily Mail eh? One by one they went to prison or OD'd so the council left the flats empty and now today has been the day.

There was one man that lived in the flat directly opposite our house. He was a bit odd but not a drug addict. He used to stand at the side of the window on the landing and look into my bedroom while having a wank. He was a vile character but I was still rather flattered. He didn't think I could see him so I started doing my S Club 7 and Steps dance routines in front of my bedroom window. (I was working as a dancer at this time for the prestigious nightclub chain, Jumpin' Jaks). Anyway, this went on until I moved away. He lives in Shaw now. I wonder if he has new wank material.

As I was eating my cheese and pickle sandwich and watching this demolition, I was hoping for bodies. I looked carefully but couldn't see any. It all got a bit boring in the end and I went back to MySpace.

Last night I hung out at The Castle, Oldham's premier music venue. I watched a Beatles tribute band called Semolina and Pilchards which my friend sings in. I don't like The Beatles. I've tried but I still don't like them. They're just so obvious. All that love and everything. They appeal to the masses because the masses all feel the same. Basically, John Lennon and Paul McCartney were no different from you, and that was the genius of it. Maybe I just like to champion the outsider and that's my downfall. I remember Anthony saying that we wouldn't get anywhere because my lyrics wouldn't appeal to many people. I don't know about that. I mean I'm sure everyone thinks about killing people and setting off bombs. I would like people to buy my records and store them under their beds like Escort magazine. I always appeal to myself in every single way. I also appeal to my new band members and they don't complain about my lyrics. However, English is not their first language so I'm not too sure how much they understand me.

I'm freezing cold. I'm always freezing cold.

KEEP THE HOME FIRES BURNING

March 3rd, 2007

02:54 pm

Last night fires were lit on the rubble of the old flats. It wasn't long before the whole site was ablaze. I couldn't decide whether the view of this looked more like the blitz or Beirut. The fire engines took their time and eventually put out the fire but it wasn't long before someone else started a new one and they returned. They were outside my window for most of the night and tonight will be the same.

Looking out at what remains is a sight that you can imagine. Just think of any news picture of a bombed out town. I feel like I'm being pushed back here. I never wanted to return. Anywhere else would have been fine. I'm sure I'd have had my usual problems, but Oldham? Why was I born here? Why did they never better themselves through free education and get out? Why was a family so important? Why are they just happy to struggle along and complain constantly?

My mother's not got enough money to pay my rent and I'm still receiving nothing from the government and my debts are increasing. And I still can't walk. I know that my whole family want to see me back here. They never wanted me to leave and they certainly never want to hear about my life in London. No one round here does so I've learned to remain silent.

I want to drink enough to forget where I am but I have no money to do so. I want to go back to my room and be left alone. She's looked after me like the best mother in the world but to see what she has to go through to pay my rent makes me feel like the worst person in the world. She's a cleaner. But why? Why did my father turn into an alcoholic? Why did he have to drink everything and leave her with nothing?

I'll carry on and I'll do what I have to do on my return to London. I've been looking into selling my eggs but that's illegal in the UK. Maybe I'll have to go back to medical experiments. I now know that I will do anything to have to not come back to Oldham. Anything.

I'M GOING TO DO SOMETHING BAD

March 12th, 2007

03:48pm

This has been the worst three months of my life. I can't even speak about it.

My sister and niece are over from Australia. I haven't seen them for three or four years and now I won't be able to hang around with them because I've got no money. I'm desperate. Really desperate. I was crying while on the phone to the income support people this morning. They say they're not going to backdate my claim so all I'll get is £57.45. I can't even use my credit cards now cos they've all been stopped and I've got no idea about how I can pay my rent that doesn't involve anything illegal.

And my Mum's got no more money. It's got to the point where the church are paying my rent. I feel really sick about everything. But we have to carry on. I'll do something bad and pay my Mum back and then she'll be happy. I've wrecked everything, that's official so things can't get any worse. Now I know how desperate I've become. But less of all that, I'll find a way. If I'm willing to do anything then that means there are more opportunities.

I'M BACK!!

March 14th, 2007

03:20pm

I'm sitting in my favourite internet cafe in Leytonstone. I'm well happy now. Many thanks to Kevin Evian who picked me up from the Megabus stop and carried my bag to Leytonstone.

Last night I just stayed in, I was so happy. And my room was just how I left it, no rats or mice, just a thin layer of dust everywhere and a few dead flies.

I'm going back to work on Monday, to my little job in Tower Bridge. I love that job. Just 5-9pm and weekends like but I'm happy there. Then I rang up all the credit card companies and explained my situation and they're fine with me. Then I rang NatWest and they said that my overdraft was a "hefty" sum. But I don't think £1,250 is a "hefty" sum. Maybe I don't understand the value of money. I'm glad I don't, that's well boring. I'm typing too loud as I'm overexcited.

The bodybuilder and my landlord remarked about how fat I was. They said, "You've put on weight". I don't think I look much different but it's good to be a bit fat cos now I won't have to waste my money on food. I'm not bothered about my weight, I've never been concerned about it, it's not something I really think about. There's people in Sudan starving. Really starving y'know.

CIGARS AND TWO BREAKFASTS

March 16th, 2007

04:15pm

I've had the most wonderful two days. I've just been hanging around and DJing. I DJ'd at the usual place on Wednesday, that was alright. I found this massive cigar and I was well happy when I was smoking it. I love cigars.

They let me stay for a drink at the end and so I didn't get out of there till 7am and then I went to McDonald's and ate my usual two breakfasts.

Last night I DJ'd at Slappers Club at the venue on Soho Street formerly known as Pop, now renamed Punk. The bar staff in there have T-shirts that say "Sex Worker" on the back. Bet people go up to them all the time and ask them for a handjob or anal. It's a bad idea, it really is.

The Coach and Horses is alright still. I'm going there tonight if you wanna join me and buy me a drink. I've not spent any money whatsoever since I've been back. I haven't got any money to spend as you probably know too well. I don't even take my purse out with me anymore. I'm relying on the kindness of strangers. Maybe I can blag more drinks cos I'm on crutches. It's all a bit bad though and I feel really bad about everything.

Last night I found a wallet in a doorway on Soho Square belonging to a Mr Warren Scott. I have two of his credit cards, a debit card and another bank card. He seems to live in Maidstone, is a member of the National Trust, The Horticultural Society and he also gets his hair cut at a posh salon. Does anyone know him? No phone number otherwise I'd be ringing up and sorting out a deal. Guess he's cancelled his cards by now so it's all become a bit pointless. I'll have to hand it in now. He seems like a nice person.

My room's become a magpie's nest of all these things that I've got. I'm selling a Pentax MZ-32 camera. Is anyone interested? I found it under a tree and handed it into Chingford Police Station but no one claimed it. It's worth around £200. It has a variety of different lenses to go with it.

I also have a wooden carved statue of Madonna and Child, I mean The Blessed Virgin Mary, not the pop icon. I'm selling that for £500 as it's by Henry Moore and worth about £10,000. I'm not familiar with the underground art black market. You can come round and have a look if you like. Get me some tins in though. I'm not good at carrying tins yet.

LONDON'S ONLY FIVE-STAR SAUNA. VIEW PHOTOS OF GIRLS

March 21st, 2007

01:32pm

It all started again, that drinking thing. Yesterday I spent all day in The Coach and Horses. I'd slept downstairs again. I dunno, it's not good is it? I wish I wouldn't.

I came back with a few useful things that people gave me: three coat hangers, two apples, a bunch of grapes, one banana, one orange and two pieces of artwork.

I could go on and on about how I've got no money. Well, I haven't. I'm scared, really scared.

On Sunday I went for healing at The Methodist Church in Leytonstone. They said I have to change my life around and then I can be healed. I said alright. I really need to see a doctor though. They still haven't given me an appointment at UCH. It's really painful. I wish someone could get me some food in. I can't carry anything but I've got no money. I'm gonna have to start going to soup kitchens again.

Byron Williams won't help me anymore. He said he was hurt cos I didn't give him a mention in this journal after he'd picked up my clothes from my flat when I was in hospital. There is a reason though. When I was in hospital he made me cry and his girlfriend said, "Where's your boyfriend?" And that's why I got upset, cos I realised I don't have anyone and maybe back then someone would have been useful. I don't usually want anyone, just someone to get stuff for me like some tins or something.

Henry Moore sculpture – £5000

06:43pm

Last night my longest-standing friend Richard Haydn gave me 40 euros. I promptly went to the bureau de change and received a sum of £25. Cool eh? Then we went to The Groucho with Lisa Stansfield. I spoke to a lady about my Henry Moore sculpture and she said it would be worth around £30,000. Now that's a lot of money. I forgot to take her email though. She said she's not au fait with the art black market. I don't know how I'm gonna get rid of it.

I handed in Mr Warren Scott's wallet to HSBC. I left a note with my address on it. Perhaps he'll give me some money eh? I'm not feeling well. I'm constantly bleeding and feel faint all the time. This is bad.

A man in The Coach and Horses said there's a man in Covent Garden that would pay me £70 to watch me have sex. He offered me that to have sex with him. Urgh, I wouldn't want to be doing any of that business. He asked me not to tell anyone. Doesn't know about this diary though.

I went to the hospital yesterday. After waiting three hours the doctor said I was alright. He said it's healed very well for two months. Must have been the healers though. I liked them. I want to go back there.

I'm staying in a hostel from tomorrow until Friday. It's in Russell Square and called The Generator. It's a 24 hour party place and there's a bar where it's only £1 a pint. Wow! My sister wants to use my room for her and my niece. I'll tell you all about it soon enough. You'll be well excited about that won't you? I'm gonna be staying in a female-only dormitory. It'll be just like Some Like it Hot. Won't it?

I WILL PISS FOR £20 A TIME

March 26th, 2007

12:10pm

I've just had my Coco Pops and made my sandwiches for the day out of the bread I'm supposed to toast. Free breakfast here y'see. I'm on the bottom of a bunk bed in a dormitory where about fourteen other girls are staying. They're all around eighteen to twenty-four. They're not very friendly though. And my sister said I'd make loads of friends. Well, I've got until Friday.

The girls talk about hairdryers a lot and other people a lot. There was a nightclub tour last night but it cost £9 to go on so I didn't bother. Not my kind of clubs really. I'm thinking of setting up my own pub tour but they're not really the kind of people to appreciate the English pub experience. I'm not keen on foreigners. They're always into sport and stuff. Especially white foreigners.

So tonight there's a quiz. Wow. Sounds like real fun. I hate quizzes. Maybe it's because I don't know anything. Quizzes are for people that know loads of boring stuff that you don't need to know anyway. The only chance they get to feel that their boring minds are justified is by doing a quiz. Same with exams and degrees.

PHOTOS OF NAKED TEEN GIRLS

March 27th, 2007

06:53am

Another hour and breakfast will be served. It doesn't seem much like a 24 hour party place to me. I met some Americans tonight. I'm taking them on a tour of Soho tomorrow. Bet that will be something they won't forget too soon. They'll get me drinks and stuff. Huh huh…

There's these people here with bleached hair, just at the tips though. I keep saying, "Bet you're Australian aye?" They keep getting offended and so they should. I like the Americans though. I keep talking about the war and Pearl Harbour. It's always interested me that, but they don't seem so.

I DJ'd tonight at The Arts. Wish they'd give me warning, then I'd be able to let you know, not that you'd come like, but I like to let you know.

Forgot to mention that the girls in my dormitory walk round in their underwear.

LOSE WEIGHT: KILL YOURSELF

March 28th, 2007

02:39pm

I had ideas, I had things that I wanted to tell you about, but now it's all gone. I can't remember a thing.

I'm doing my club tonight but first I shall be rehearsing with my band Iraq. It all sounds quite optimistic doesn't it? It's not though. I have a bad bad feeling deep down and I'm scared about everything. And I'm so lonely.

I went to the bar in this building last night. £1.50 a pint. It was so disgusting and they had Sky Sports on a big screen and everyone seemed fascinated by the cricket. Wow! Cricket! Fucking bores. Everyone bores me. I can't stand people.

Last night I took an American to White Heat. He hated it as much as me. I'd not been to a club since I played that gig back in April. I've got no need to go to clubs anymore. They're all fucking boring. If there's one thing I hate more than anything else it's indie kids. They should all be lined up against a wall and shot. They repulse me. So White Heat wasn't a good idea. It was really packed and quite difficult for me to manoeuvre myself on the crutches and those indie kids won't move. I got a bit of room when they all went to dance to that shit band called The Gossip. I can't stand that woman's voice and why doesn't she lose some weight? I've looked after myself only cos I'm in a band. I like to be easy on the eye. Some kind of feminist protest then? I hate feminists. If I was married then I'd look after my man and stay at home and cook and look after the babies. I'd stop drinking as well.

I can't concentrate. I'm writing this by a pool table where Australians are talking really loud about last night's P. Diddy afterparty in Chinawhite. God, I couldn't think of anything worse. And they all walk round in here in flip-flops and shorts. I can't stand Australians.

I know my sister's Australian but even she says she's embarrassed about the rest of them. They're too laid back. They want the simple things in life but they are simple. To want the simple things in life then you must be.

SAVE UP TO £150 ON SELECTED PEOPLE

April 1st, 2007

08:37 pm

"We pray for the young people that think the easy way out is to stick a needle in their arm or to down six pints of lager."
That's what he said during the prayers an hour ago. Six pints though?

I drink six pints and a bottle of wine. That's what I do. And anything else I can get my hands on until I'm completely unconscious. It is an easy way out though, he's right. And if heroin is as good as that morphine drip I had in my arm in January then I can understand why folk go in for that.

So I went back to Leytonstone Methodist Church. I like it in there. We split up into groups during the service and I talked to them about how my broken leg had strengthened my faith and changed me and made me more committed to God. Sometimes I just like the sound of my own voice. From the way I've been behaving, my broken leg has made not one shard of difference to who I am. I went on to say how God was in control of me now and my life is in his hands. Well it is. There's no one else around.

There were sausage rolls, sausages, weird potato things and crisps and cakes after. And diet coke and tea and chocolate biscuits. I ate everything but no one was bothered. They don't mind me in there. And I can use my real name and wear no make-up. That always makes me happier. I like it when I don't have to be that person or this person but even the person that I just was doesn't exist. Not really. Y'know I have four different names now. I'm not gonna say what they are. Sure you could make a few up.

I made my sister cry the last time I saw her. She asked to see my credit card bills and so I showed them to her and she said how she was upset that when I went to meet her I asked her for food as I hadn't eaten in two days. Well, it was true. I was very hungry but my church has a meal once a week. So I'll be alright then. The money that people donated got swallowed up by my bank fees. I don't want to talk about this anymore.

Last night I worked in the cloakroom of the strip club and made £52. But when I'd finished, the tube still wasn't open so I had to spend £4 getting back on two buses. I was exhausted when I got back and couldn't even take my clothes off. I just slept, surrounded by all my E.T.s.

When I woke up I was so hungry, I ate a raw capsicum that my sister had left. It was pretty vile but helped a bit.

I might DJ tomorrow night. The Arts Club never tell me when I'm DJing so I just turn up there every weekday night just in case. Wednesdays are definite though so come down Wednesday. Tomorrow might be happening if they're not having one of those crap raves.

BONE COLLECTION

April 6th, 2007

07:41 pm

There is a framed picture of me on the wall at Gerry's. I believe you can purchase it for £75. It's a lovely picture, as I said, taken for the book Gerry-go-Round. I stood in a packed Gerry's on Wednesday night from 1:30-3am staring at it and telling anyone that would listen that "that's me". I meant something else perhaps, something more terrible. I mean, I'm not here anymore, that's me, in the frame, trapped in that Friday night, not here, not now.

I have a problem. My broken leg is longer than the non-broken one. I'll be like that for the rest of my life now. Everywhere I walk I look like I'm stepping down a step. It's horrible. I am a cripple. I watch other people walking and all I feel is envy. I want the past to come back. I want to be right again but it will never happen. I'll never walk properly again and I feel sick constantly at this thought. Boys don't see how I look anymore, they just see me limping. I would never go out with anyone that couldn't walk properly. So that's it.

I'm not that struck on boys fancying me anyway. It'd just be handy sometimes. Money and presents and stuff.

I think I've killed something. I've got a collection of bones in my bag. I feel like torturing things. Then killing things now. I was getting over my murderous streak but this accident has changed me. I'm angry at everything, especially things that breathe and live a normal life. Most of my so-called friends abandoned me after I came back to London. I suppose I never had any real friends anyway and I don't believe I've ever had any real friends. People say that's because I'm a terrible person. Well, my mother says I'm not right, that I don't care about anyone except myself. I don't think she's that right. I mean, I'll always speak to the tramps and the mentally ill at church. But that doesn't count does it?

I only write this cos I've got no one to talk to. Have I depressed you enough now? Be thankful for your own life while it lasts. I'll soon be hiding in your kitchen cupboard with an axe.

TERRORIST MEETUP GROUP EVERY WEDNESDAY

April 9th, 2007

02:51 pm

I worked in the strip club on Saturday. I made £35. I got talking to the owner. He took a shine to me and kept calling me Ruth Ellis. People always do that. I don't even know what Ruth Ellis looks like. So anyway, he's put me in touch with a good lawyer and I'm suing the Duke of Westminster for being responsible for my broken leg. Cool eh? He reckons I should get £30,000.

Robin Simon took us all for breakfast after and then we all drank lager in Hoxton Square all morning and talked to the pikeys. That's what Robin calls them. I said as it's Easter Sunday we should all go to church, so we all went into the Catholic church and lit candles. Robin lit three for the three girls that blew him out. Clever. I lit one for myself. Robin said that was wrong.

After that we went back to Hoxton Square where I carried on drinking lager while Robin and Bud fell asleep. I had some blue nail varnish in my bag so I painted Robin's nails while he slept. When he woke up he didn't seem to notice. I don't know how he failed to notice. We then went to Anti Social and Robin bought us all pints of lager. Everyone was really tired so it got a bit boring. I wasn't tired though and I'd been up since 7am Saturday.

Bud and Robin decided to go home and advised me to do the same. Home? Never. So I caught a bus and went to meet my new boyfriend in The Angel on St Giles High St. You should meet my boyfriend sometime. It's not often I get one. He's very good to me. He buys me chicken and lager. Don't tell him about this though. He won't want to go out with me then.

So we went drinking. Coach and Horses, French House, Glasshouse Stores and then French House. I think. I can't really remember much. I think he bought me more chicken after that and then we caught the bus and woke up in Hainault. I woke up on my bed with my coat still on. He left me a note. It was nice of him not to take advantage.

Come down to my club on Wednesday. It's always a good night. And famous people are always there. Miranda Richardson and Rosamund Pike go. And Sean Bean. I think I'm DJing tonight as well so give it a try if you're around. Yeah, it all goes on at Tarts.

GET THE TRUTH. THEN GO.

April 12th, 2007

02:32 pm

After DJing at Tarts last night I decided I hadn't quite had my fill. Where can I get my fill? I wondered. The Spanish Mafia bar. So it was decided I would make a return trip.

It was all going on down there. The floor was soaking as usual and people were sliding around. I stayed seated. My friend Jeremy who's partial to cocaine introduced me to one of his friends.
"My name's Jude."
"Yuh what?"
"Jude."
"Yuh what?"
"Jude."
And then I bothered to look at him. Oh yeah, it was Jude Law. So I rolled up my cut-off tights and showed him my scar.
"Yuh wanna be careful down ere. Dangerous. Wet floor."
But he really wants to be more careful about hanging around with my cocaine friends. That's an even more slippery path.

My Asian friend bought me a meatball footlong Subway sandwich after. I was well happy. And he let me have Yazoo as well. I love that stuff. The food is the best part of going out I reckon. I like Asian people the best. They're my favourite. Apart from the man that lives downstairs cos he's a drug dealer and beats up his girlfriend. That's bad.

There was a hen party last night at Tarts. It was pretty packed. Everyone kept thinking I was part of it cos I was wearing a tutu and tiara but that's my usual garb. Yeah. You've seen me around haven't you?

There's a man that's awake but snoring in this internet cafe. I'm gonna have to leave. I wanna go to bed now. It's not often but it needs to be done. Perhaps you can text me jokes and stuff. Don't bother sending me picture messages of penises though cos I've got a 3210 Nokia.

I AM GOING TO ASSASSINATE G*****
*R*** in 16 days and 26 minutes

April 13th, 2007

04:36 pm

Alwynn Davies told me he'd met up with my sister in my house when she was staying here while I was in the hostel. They met up to discuss me and the problem of me. I said well, it's fine to discuss me but when will anyone actually help? They discuss me like I'm some kind of mobile soap opera. They discuss me to entertain themselves. No one actually cares. And then Alwynn Davies sends me a text message while I was in the Jobcentre this afternoon which reads, "Self pity is only acceptable when matched by concern for others". Who's talking in cliches now eh? And who else needs my concern? There is no one that wants or needs my concern. He just wanted me to help him with his DIY, that's all he wanted. Then he told my sister that once he was contemplating asking me to marry him. And be condemned to a life of DIY. That's all ahead for his new girlfriend now. It's a wonderful life.

I haven't paid my rent for two weeks. Cos I can't. You don't want to hear this do you? I found a Tesco clubcard £2 voucher under my bed last night. I was so happy. It was like I'd found a key to a magical kingdom. I promptly took a walk out to the Leytonstone Tesco and bought mushrooms, a tin of beans, some ham, an apple, an orange and some milk.

I've been in the Jobcentre all afternoon trying to ring the income support people to sort out my back pay. I can't get through though. It's engaged all the time and the man said I can't see anyone in person. He said it usually takes around four hours to get through. Four hours? They're bastards. They're all bastards and I'd kill em. I would fucking kill em. It's the Department of Work and Pensions that have driven me to the edge. I mean, I'm working now but I don't get paid till the 25th.

I was walking past a car. They had left their window open. It was in a car park with a ticket on the window. So I lurked around. Then I thought no. I just couldn't do it. I can't drive can I? Fucking hell. Some fathers at least pay for driving lessons for their seventeen-year-olds. What the fuck did mine ever give me? I need an accomplice but even he can't drive and he already has a girlfriend. But he buys me lager and chicken and the other week he gave me £40 so it's not too bad. But I need someone who can drive and they could teach me to drive and then I could go round stealing cars.

BEA SAHARA'S BARBECUE

April 16th, 2007

12:14 pm

I haven't been home since Saturday. I did my crazy twenty-four hour drinking thing again to see what adventures I could have. It was all rather good. I worked in the cloakroom of the strip club on Saturday and made £45. My friend Bud always hangs round when I'm working there. He pisses me off a bit cos it ends up ruining my chances with other men cos people reckon he's my boyfriend. I hate all that. Anyway, in walks the most attractive man I've ever seen. I was mad for him and just staring at him all night. Then I tell my friend Bea Sahara so she goes and chats him up for me. Then he comes over to me and we make a date. Cool eh? Nicely done I say. I'm not that keen on all that stuff. But the most attractive man I've ever seen! Yeah, I'll make an exception. So Thursday it is. At Bethnal Green WMC.

At 6:30am when the strip club closed I went to my friend Pedro's flat. He lives opposite. We drank Corona and listened to psychedelia and talked about stuff. At 8am we went to visit his friend who lives in Herbal, that nightclub near the bridge. He was foreign also and he was talking about some kind of genocide where he grew up. I love them foreign people. They've always had such a hard time. It makes me feel slightly better about my OIdham ghetto roots. Anyway, he was called Nanoo and his flat was well nice. He fixed up some really strong vodka Red Bull while I DJ'd using his iPod. It's getting very of its time this diary thing. They'll be using this as a historical document in a few years, mark my words.

I got a bit bored at around 10:30am so went to meet the man that I'm the other woman of. We hung around and went to pubs then made our way to my friend Bea Sahara's barbecue in Bethnal Green. There's these people on Bethnal Green Road that sell all the shit that they don't want. I bought a brown jumper for 50p and some Arrested Development tapes. They gave me the Arrested Development tapes. How kind.

The barbecue was good. I just sat outside with my lover with my plastic rain mac on. People took pictures of me cos I was wearing my rain mac with my sunglasses. It was a kind of Hoxton thing to do.

We left at nightfall. We passed some bags of jumble outside a church. I couldn't resist nicking the stuff that I liked. I've got a pair of swimming goggles, a Monsoon top, a blue jumper and a pink jumper which reads, "Let's Fight". We then went to a quiet little pub in Bow. He keeps saying, "I'm crazy about you". I advise him to stay with his girlfriend but to give me £10 for each meeting. Or else. Cool eh? I've got it sussed now. I might up it to £20 tomorrow. We don't have sex. We don't even kiss so I've got it made haven't I? I might get pictures. For evidence.

Night night. I'm going to bed now.

TERRORIST MEETUP CELL GROUP TONIGHT

April 18th, 2007

03:01 pm

I just wrote an entry but I lost it. Gone forever. It was quite good as well.

I didn't mean to write anything. Just wanted to do my advert. Three minutes left.

OUR DEAR CUSTOMERS ARE REQUESTED TO PAY BEFORE USING THE COMPUTER

April 26th, 2007

07:28 pm

That's what it says in this internet cafe. It's a new one. They all sit in here with headphones on speaking in foreign languages really loud. And they look at porn. It's not as bad as that one in Leyton where that man started wanking. Ha ha. I couldn't stop laughing.

My disco went really well last night. I always get presents from my groupies. Last night I got a bottle of wine. It's better than asparagus. That's what I got before I broke my leg.

I can't write this anymore. I really can't. I'm sick of wasting my time on it. I could have written a book by now. And I'm sick of putting my life into words. I don't know why I even began doing this. I always used to laugh at people that kept their diaries online. I used to think it was a bit immature. It is. It's completely ridiculous. I did it cos I didn't have a telly. Or friends. There was no one I needed to impress. I was upset about how the world had left me as some kind of outsider. I felt like James Dean.

But now I don't feel too bad. I'm happy. I have everything. My band are starting to gig again and I'm a successful DJ and people love me now. I've nothing more to say. Goodbye.

LAST EVER WEDNESDAY TARTS CLUB!!!

May 8th, 2007

06:32 pm

Celebrate the life and works of Scarlet West with special guest Scarlet West as DJ.

Aaah! Someone's attacking me! He keeps punching me. And he's calling the other man a nigger!!!! This was one of my favourite places. This internet cafe I mean. The one on High Road Leytonstone. It's brightened up my day a bit actually. I'm not into racism but I find retards hilarious. He's one of those ones that can't speak properly. Well funny.

I'm doing Mondays at Tarts instead now. Wednesdays are Bloomsbury Bowling Lanes and I'm starting at The Roxy as well. How cool am I? I still don't know how to use headphones though. It's amazing what can happen when you're as stylish and fantastic as me.

Hope you all miss me. ha ha ha ha ha ha ha ha ha huh huh huh.........
....I'm gone

IRAQI PROUD DISCO TONIGHT AND TOMORROW

May 14th, 2007

05:59 pm

Do you miss me? Strange how I have everything now. I shouldn't say stuff like that. I've begun work on my novel. I'm writing full time now.

Coach and Horses from 10ish.

Oh yeah, I lost everyone's number when my phone fell down the toilet the other night. Luckily I was with the only person whose number I really need so I wasn't too bothered. However, it would be useful to have your numbers so I can annoy you with gig invites and other Scarlet West Enterprise stuff.

SEE ME IN THE NEW RUBBISHMEN VIDEO!!!

May 17th, 2007

04:44 pm

I was on one of my twenty-four hour drinking sessions. I was quite pissed by the time I met them at 11am.

I'm right at the end. Don't think they could use the rest of me. I was wrecked although I do feel I was looking rather alright still. They wouldn't serve me in The Coach though.

Was DJing at Bloomsbury Bowling Lanes last night. I am also DJing there tonight for a corporate event. How cool am I? The owners are alright. Not like Tarts.

Tarts is crawling with cockroaches. I'm not enticing you to come down am I? I keep pointing at them when they're crawling across the dance floor and the owner keeps telling me off. And they're all round the DJ booth as well. When I get back to Michael's he has to check me for cockroaches. Yeah, how bad is that?

Still come though. It's just like a zoo now.

IRAQI PRIDE TONIGHT!!!

June 26th, 2007

01:16 pm

Nine minutes left so I'll give you an update of the life you're all fascinated by. I was in the Mama Shamone video on Saturday. They got me pizza and so I ate and ate. It was a bit boring waiting around and all that. Anyway, the next day I got food poisoning. I was puking outside Kentish Town tube. It was well bad. I mean, I couldn't even drink alcohol. Michael took good care of me though. I'd probably be on a Megabus home back to Oldham today if it wasn't for him.

My Dad's in hospital cos he fell out of bed after drinking too much and he's broken his right arm in three places. My Mum's been hanging out with him in hospital. He's quite an endearing creature really. I do feel rather sorry for him and can't help but like him even after everything he's put my mother and sisters through. I know what being an alcoholic feels like. I should visit him before he dies.

THE RETURN OF THE SUICIDE NOTE IN WEEKLY INSTALMENTS

July 5th, 2007

12:26 pm

I can't keep my mouth shut for long. Well, I can actually but I have trouble not writing. I just like going on about myself. Everyone else is just incredibly dull.

A medium mentioned me the other day. Bea Sahara told me. I have no idea what this medium has been saying about me. I reckon it's bad. I've had a real bad feeling in the pit of my stomach for about a month. It's like I'm about to die or sommat. Like sommat real bad's about to happen. Do you ever get that?

I went to Tesco's this morning. I bought some pies and cordial. I always like that 14p cordial they do. The water in London's well vile.

That Coach and Horses is well crap without me. I'm gonna change the name of this journal to "I'd Like to Blame The Coach and Horses". I don't like them anymore. And I know that Anja doesn't like me. And them foreign bar staff well piss me off. They're deadly dull. I don't mind that goth one though. Do they know I've settled down? I popped in sober the other day to check if anyone was eligible to come to Iraqi Pride. It was then I realised. I thought, these people are all pissed. I can't stand pissed people. I just hate it. I think alcohol should be made illegal. I mean they've banned cigarettes so they might as well ban alcohol. I wouldn't be bothered if I could never drink alcohol again. It's what people with no confidence use to prop themselves up. I don't need it. I'm constant. I only ever drank because people bored me. Michael's the only person that doesn't bore me.

You know I've got no friends. You know that though yeah? I've not had a phone for two months and no one's attempted to come down to any of my nights or make any kind of contact with me. I could be dead. I could be cut up in bin bags behind Soho Books like I always used to say. But this is London and no one's supposed to care.

I'm gonna have a read of my People's Friend then I'm going back to bed.

DJING FOR IDIOTS

July 24th, 2007

03:24 pm

I went to the Jobcentre today. I'm always the only white person there. Why is that? I'm not bothered like. Cos once I went to Oldham Jobcentre and that was well crap. I couldn't even sign on cos I was too young.

I was talking to Theo Saxon last night about getting my manuscript published. Does anyone know how you go about these things? I'm sure you've all written novels and stuff eh? I wouldn't be arsed about getting it published cos it's just a laugh but I'm well skint since that bitch Victoria Maybury sacked me from Bloomsbury just cos I'm better looking than everyone else.

I got a letter today that informed me that I didn't have cancer. Well, at least that's some good news eh? I've got cirrhosis of the liver. Well, I will have soon.

I made a mushroom omelette this morning to celebrate my smashing health.

I'm in the library. I was reading a book called The Idiot's Guide to DJing. I've picked up lots of useful tips. It just says you should play what you want even if it clears the dance floor. Didn't need to read that bit did I? Every time someone reads this they always say it's getting worse and that it's not as good as previous entries. More good news then.

SCARLET WEST – A THREAT TO NATIONAL SECURITY

July 27th, 2007

05:05 pm

My house got raided the other night. The police kicked the door in and raided all the rooms. They'd had a tip off. As usual I was out so they kicked down my door and turned my room upside down. I mean literally. I got back and everything was on the opposite side of the room to where it was before. My make-up was smashed. They'd even been through my underwear drawer and laundry basket.

Well, I predicted this would happen. I asked the landlord what they were looking for to which he replied, "Guns". So um, yeah. But I'm thinking oh shit this is all my fault for threatening to kill prime ministers and going on about Iraq all the time. They reckon I'm a terrorist threat. I only did it cos I wondered how far I could push it. I mean talking about that in the way I do is real anarchy. People always said I shouldn't have called my band Iraq. I'm not gonna stop now though. My friend said it's due to my pattern of self destructive behaviour.

Mind you, I just think things like being raided are dead exciting. I mean, it's like a film or sommat. Like The Bill a bit. So I don't mind. I tidied it all up before I left for my gig and I changed the sheets on my bed and did the washing so I don't feel too bad about it now. The landlord said he'd fix the door. He seemed a bit worried about it all. I said, "Do you reckon it's cos you're Asian?" He just put his head in his hands and said, "I don't know, I just don't know".
"Don't worry, I'll still keep the room on. I like it here."
Even more now. But if we've been raided once then that means we won't be raided again. Surely. Anyway, raid anytime, I just wanna make sure I'm in next time.

I wasn't feeling too well yesterday. It's all cos I stopped drinking. Well, I haven't had a drink since Saturday. It's been a bit dull really; I mean when I'm DJing at The Arts. That's the only real time I drink. It just makes the night go faster. It's been really empty so I just sit there and read my People's Friend or think about Michael. I don't want to be a DJ anymore. I'm bored of it. And when there are people there I can't stand them.

So I digress. The day before the gig I feel a fever coming on and then I lose my voice. But y'know, the show must go on and all that. We played in a candlelit room to a mostly seated audience. I told them all about my terror raid. They seemed a bit bemused by it all. Very normal looking people just out for a nice evening of bands before they have to go to their dull jobs. It's not the kind of place I'm used to. Far too clean. And I don't think they even served pints. Anyway, Michael got me some alcoholic medication for my throat and I went on and struggled through the set. It all ended in chaos when I went into the audience and the audience went onto the stage and started dancing. Michael was throwing cigarettes at me. Some kind of smoking ban protest. I turned back to see a man on the shoulders of my guitarist, just like grinding against him or something. Feedback. Then I take my bow and I'm out.

So The Babalou in Brixton (St Matthew's Church) liked us so much that they want us to come back and play again on 9th August. That's cos Iraq are the best band ever. So get to that.

IRAQ PLAY BRIXTON TOMORROW.

August 8th, 2007

01:23 pm

Oldham was nice. Michael and I sat in my backyard on deckchairs for the majority of the time while my Mum made us cups of tea and fed us E.T. cake. It was very pleasant indeed. My family were very impressed by my choice of life partner.

I received a letter this morning. I receive the debt collecting letters most days but this one was handwritten. You can tell a lot about people by their handwriting and I could tell that this man was a psychopath. I nervously opened it expecting the worst. Here's what it read:

Dear Scarlet,
Hope you are well – according to the barmaid in the C & H, you haven't been seen for "a few weeks".
I saw this in the paper the other day and thought it might be a good opportunity to enhance your "media profile".
Best wishes,
Mick

And so attached with brown gaffer tape was a newspaper advert. The following was circled: "or maybe you know someone who's already had the dress, the cake and the party without The Man?"

It is true, I did do that. I had a page boy, bridesmaid, maid of honour and best man as well. Those that know me well may remember the 28th October 2002. Don't think I'll bother with the documentary though. They'll only make me look cheap.

The Jobcentre was alright today. My old manager Keith was in there organising a scheme for jobseekers. He said I should go on it. It's bricklaying and carpentry. I'll be alright at that. It's just drinking tea innit?

We had to close The Arts Club at 2:30 this morning due to lack of interest. The night before that it was just me and Johnny Vegas. Well really it was just Johnny Vegas as I was playing records. He was telling me all about his venture into the priesthood. I don't blame him for hanging around on his own a lot. He seems very down at the moment, but the kind of people he attracts he hates. I think he's looking for a woman so if any of you want to cheer him up then you should come down. He's there about three times a week. Mainly Mondays, Tuesdays and Wednesdays.

Who's coming to my free gig tomorrow? We're on at 10:30 at The Babalou in Brixton next door to Mass. I haven't learnt my lyrics proper yet. It's very difficult cos I don't have a tape recorder. Anyway, that's not your problem is it? DJing at Arts tonight. I'm not gonna be doing that for much longer so get down while it lasts.

IRAQI PRIDE!!!!!!!!!!!!

August 14th, 2007

03:28 pm

I was DJing last night in my club. Them old boys that come down to play cribbage are hilarious. You've got to come just to check them out. They arrived relatively early last night; 1:30am to be precise. I was playing "I Know it's Over" when they walked in. There was only me there as usual and I was drinking Jack Daniels and coke and trying to learn the Hail Holy Queen. The alcohol had no affect cos I'd been drinking heavily on Saturday night. I never intend to drink the way I do and I'm not going into it for the eighty thousandth time as it's boring everyone.

But when I wake up and my legs are covered in bruises I do tend to think Shit, I never intended this. I just intended to have a moderate drink. Sometimes I do have a moderate drink but it has no affect so what's the point? I don't enjoy it. I mean the only reason I drink is because I get this feeling in the back of my throat like a weird feeling and then once I get the drink the feeling doesn't leave, it just gets a bigger and bigger feeling like I need more and more. And it's not to do with my mental state cos I'm alright now. It's a chemical state.

So that's that then. I'm never going to talk about my alcohol abuse again.

WHERE IS GOD IN THE CHAOS?

August 22nd, 2007

01:08 pm

I didn't DJ last night. I just put on 2 Many DJs, that CD that doesn't have any gaps and it's all like electro stuff, then I went to sleep on the bench. That Soho Arts has got so bad. I mean the only movement I saw all night was a cockroach crossing the dance floor. I reckon it's cursed. They could sell it for quite a bit so they might as well do that. It's definitely haunted as well. A lot of the time when I'm behind the DJ booth and there's no one there I sense someone just standing in front of the booth and watching me. And last night was weird cos I could see shadows every now and again out of the corner of my eye.

So nevermind eh? I try and do stuff that's good but it's everyone else that's crap and that's got nothing to do with me. I'm gonna do some flyering for Matthew Black to top up me funds.

One of the old men turned up at 2:00am. He said the last time he saw me I was "bladdered". I don't like that word. I mean, I wasn't having any trouble urinating. I was DJing there on Saturday y'see. Just filling in for Bud. They like him cos he plays Motown but if there's one genre I hate it's Motown. Northern Soul, yeah but Motown. Fuckinghell. You might as well be into Luther fucking Vandross.

Anyway, the old man said as I was out of the door last night, "It's a shame there's no one here. She's the best DJ we've ever had down here and the crowd love her as well". Aaah, isn't that nice? I always linger at doors to see what people say about me when I'm gone. At one point I was hatching a plan to fake my own death just to find out what people actually think of me. Well, not actually think but they always say good things about people that are dead don't they?

I'm DJing there again tonight if you wanna go. I've heard that people are coming down on Thursday, Friday and Saturday nights saying they're Scarlet's friend. Can you not read? Then when Trevor tells them I'm not there they say they're meeting me down there. He doesn't have any of it though cos everyone knows I seldom venture into town at that end of the week. "Definitely don't let them in." That's what I say. I mean you expect me to DJ to an empty room for three days of the week and then you're gonna quote my name when I'm long gone. That's like someone dying and you pretending you're a friend of theirs just cos people are saying nice things about them for the first time.

Right, I'm off to get some sustenance. (I stole that word from Michael.)

MY SPECIAL DISCO FOR SPECIAL PEOPLE IS TOMORROW

August 31st, 2007

02:21 pm

My band played another gig last Friday at The Half Moon in Brixton. I didn't bother telling anyone cos Michael brings his friends now and my "friends" have all abandoned me anyway. But fear not says Our Lord! Where should I find all my old Gerry's crew but on that fascinating website called "Facebook".

They all keep adding me and saying, "We were both members of Gerry's" when it comes to the "How do you know this person" bit. You know I got barred yeah? I'm not arsed cos Michael's much more exciting. But those folks were the only people who would speak to me for three years so it's nice that they're still out there and drinking about me.

I wanted to leave London but Michael said that if I do then I would succumb to my own vanity and return within two and a half months. London needs me apparently. I don't need London though. I've been very depressed about London. It's got a lot to do with that stupid DJing job I've got. Three nights a week at least and then I'm exhausted cos of the free drinks.

I'm flyering outside Ladytron at ULU for Stay Beautiful tonight. Give me a £1 if you see me. You won't be able to miss me.

PORNOGRAPHY AND DRUG DEALERS

September 4th, 2007

12:07 pm

LANDLORD: Let me know when you've got some new porno DVDs.
ITALIAN TENANT: Sky, satellite?
LANDLORD: No, y'know?
ITALIAN TENANT: Aaaah, yes. Porno DVD.
LANDLORD: That last one you lent me. Good.

This is the conversation I woke up to this morning. Relayed at full volume I hasten to add. When we were raided, the Italian tenant, Gonzales, needed a translator. And ten years he's been in the country. He's alright though.

The landlord's brother went to prison. It was nothing to do with me after all. It's just that when I told people about the raid, everyone's initial reaction was that it was my fault. Even mine was. But no, it was the drug dealer downstairs. It's a lot quieter there now. I never mentioned on here that there was a drug dealer downstairs. Didn't want to get him caught really. Could I have made any money on turning him in I wonder? I didn't think of that.

I was purchasing mushrooms and a tin of macaroni this morning when the Asian man mentioned that he hadn't seen the landlord's brother for ages. Me, whisper, "You mean you don't know? Got raided didn't he? Five years. His dogs have been put into care. Drugs". I do like a good gossip but don't know whether it's a good idea to gossip with the Muslim shopkeeper about his supposedly good friend. I mean come on. I'm naive and I knew what was going on. Can I get into trouble for saying that after the event?

My disco was rubbish again last night. I can't be bothered with it anymore so I'm not gonna talk about it. I just put on a Smiths CD for Malik and Sahib Mahadeo and sat down.

I'm gonna get a proper job soon. My Mum's coming to London next week to give me a good telling off. She reckons my life and my financial situation are out of control. But you know what you can do don't you?

WHEN YOU CAN TELL A GOOD STORY, THE WORLD IS A MAGICAL PLACE.

September 5th, 2007

02:18 pm

Them wankers from Gerry's came down to my disco last night. I didn't hate everyone in Gerry's but there was a group of coke addicts that did my head in.

They're all in their late twenties and make pointless short films that never get anywhere but they all reckon they're gonna be so bloody successful when it's obvious that one strand of my peroxide hair has got more strength and talent than they will ever have.

Anyway, they left cos there was no girls. There are never any girls at my disco. They don't like it cos the music's too good. All girls wanna hear are rubbish songs like Groove is in the Heart. Like how fucking shit is that song? And the Dirty Dancing soundtrack. Fuckinghell, if one more person asks for that, I'm gonna smash my Newcastle Brown Ale bottle in their face and grind the pieces of glass in at asymmetrical angles.

My landlord was cleaning the drug dealer's room out this morning. Does anyone fancy living in my house? Think it's about £60 a week inclusive, if you're interested. Don't worry, you won't have to deal with me cos I'm not there that much. I just don't want any of those stinking Eastern European perverts there. Don't mind Eastern European girls though.

Anyway, the only person who I've got a good word to say about that's come down to my club is Johnny Vegas. He's always so depressed and thinks of himself as a failure. I was thinking, if you're that kind of person, I mean, a person with addictions who's "made it" then you're gonna be more depressed about it all than when you first started out.

I can't be arsed explaining it all cos I've got a tin of macaroni waiting for me at home.

Oh yeah, Michael's been to my club. He's the best person. Yeah. That's all I really think about now.

WE'RE BORN, WE LOOK AROUND, WE DIE.

September 13th, 2007

02:39 pm

Let's just pretend that nothing bad's happened. With me? Why do they place a 24 hour internet cafe opposite my Night Bus stop? I've questioned this before. It's just a conspiracy against me. That's all it is. They get me pissed and upset and then they get me to write cos they reckon it's funny when I'm pissed and I'm writing about killing myself.

I had to ring my friend, Father O'Reilly and ask him to delete it. Some people do worry about me y'see. I don't just exist for your petty entertainment. Sometimes my feelings are real.

And surely I can change my mind about things? Aaaaah. What are all these colours that surround me? Is this really life?

Does anyone want to take over my disco on a Monday or Tuesday? You can have the bloody thing. It's just a noose around my neck, that disco. All that drinking. Fuckinghell. I'm sick of it.

I keep finding these handwritten notes all around Leytonstone. They say stuff like:
"Pray this: God made them marchettes or swords for your warriors".
"God made them to inanimate things."
"Sir, study The Holy Quran. Play the tape, CD, DVD. It can be revealed to you. Please."
Then it says something about Gordon Brown.

Should I hand it in at the police station or just leave it in my flat and wait for the next raid? If I'm caught in a bomb, I bet the notes will survive and be found on me and I'll be done for it. Fancy discarding something like terrorist literature? They're not very careful are they? I wanna see the tape and the DVD though. I'll play it down The Arts when I find the DVD. Just Wednesdays now. Think I can cope with that.

At 2:30am this morning they shut the doors and let everyone smoke. Now that's a reason to be getting down there. I could get them fined now couldn't I? Would they know it was me that told? Don't tell anyone, readership of 1000 people.

NO PLAN SURVIVES FIRST CONTACT WITH THE ENEMY

September 19th, 2007

01:24 pm

If you content yourself with standing still you will go backwards. Bloodyhell, that Charles Verrall must have a good book of quotes. I'm going back to his acting class tomorrow. And that film that I starred in ages ago is being wheeled out again and screened at Filthy McNasty's next Thursday. All welcome. Especially if you have a sick desire to see me in a nurse's uniform faking an orgasm. How vile is that? Absolutely the most disgusting thing but it's one of the most unsexual things you will ever see. I'm the best thing in that film. And my hair is bright yellow.

I decided to grow up a bit and get back my old job in Tower Bridge where all the drinks are free and the view is of the River Thames and Tower Bridge and that beautiful city skyline. I feel all the better for it. It's a bit like being at a disco but everyone's sober and you can hear what everyone's saying. I sometimes have a genuine interest in people when I'm sober.

This morning I got up at 9am and watched Homes Under The Hammer. Now that's a show with a good concept. You get involved with people's purchases and then after fifteen minutes they go back to them, but three months have passed and the house they were so enthusiastic about has been stripped bare, is now riddled with damp and the only thing left to do is demolish it and sell the land. Also, by this time they've had a nervous breakdown, their wife/husband has left them and they're about to declare themselves bankrupt. Property developing eh? What's the point? I have no intention or desire to own anything. Just E.Ts. Loads of them. That's all I want. I dream about them a lot, like finding them in car boot sales and knocking down the ransom money and rescuing them.

That meteorite that hit America yesterday and made people ill. That's a laugh, that. It'd be funny if they all died or weird things started happening to them. Ernie Talbot said it was his neighbouring planet. It's the bacteria in the meteorite that caused everyone to be ill. The bacteria came from the aliens' bodies. They all died but they saved their DNA into little slides of rock that formed the meteorite. It's all because it got overdeveloped out there and no one would re-cycle. Now it's harming E.T.'s planet cos it's in close proximity. Michael. Are you listening? Recycling is important.

DISCO FOR BET LYNCH TONIGHT!

September 26th, 2007

02:18 pm

I hope that doesn't sound like she's dead. I can change the name of my disco every week if I want cos no one bothers with it anyway. Say you're Scarlet's friend but don't say you're Scarlet's friend any other night.

I'm gonna be DJing on one of those party boats that go up and down The Thames soon. Cos I am…

I've been offered three gigs this week but I can't do any of them cos my drummer's on tour with his heavy metal band. Does anyone want to be a replacement drummer in my band?

My film is being shown tomorrow at Filthy McNasty's on Amwell Street in Islington. It starts at 7:30pm and Ricky Gervais said it was "the strangest thing I have ever seen". Or perhaps you wanna make a crap short film of your own and you wanna do some networking. That's what the director seems to do a lot, so if you wanna talk bollocks with him come along.

DISCO FOR IRAQ. EVERY WEDNESDAY.

October 16th, 2007

12:54 pm

I'm gonna be having two birthday parties this year. One of them in Chicken Fantastic next to London Bridge Station and the other one in Glasshouse Stores either this Wednesday or next. You can come to both if you like but I know some of you have worked your way up the food chain to eat lettuce so won't be into the former. As usual, I'm not expecting many people so even if you've never met me you can turn up. I'm not bothered. Serial killers, rapists, paedophiles. All welcome.

COME TO MY BIRTHDAY PARTY THIS WEDNESDAY!

October 22nd, 2007

12:52 pm

It's at Glasshouse Stores on Brewer Street from 9pm. It's a Samuel Smiths pub so only £2 a pint. Inevitably I'll be doing my disco after, but I'd rather you come to the pub than go to that. I'll be wearing my gold suit. Cos I'm special.

I didn't mean to stop writing this diary y'know. It just sort of happened. Cos I used to write about personal stuff but I've got to be careful nowadays. There's no point writing about the twee stuff like charity shops and hanging around shopping centres. I lost my job again. I was a bit rubbish at it anyway. I'm still ticket touting so if you want any tickets to the England game let me know. Starting price is £300.

I'm off down the Walworth Road now to check out the charity shops. Let us know if you find a job for me. Text preferably but before 9pm or Michael will hurt you.

I MARRIED THE WRONG UNCLE

November 9th, 2007

02:58 pm

I haven't forgotten about you y'know. Before Facebook people used to pass the time away by reading this, but things change. Even I've got really into Facebook and now I waste my life looking for Robbie Rotten groups and attempting to find people from my old squadron. I don't think Facebook is right. I find myself looking at my old school and reminiscing about it too much. The memories seem to have faded into a nice sort of memory though. But I'm not remembering rightly. I know I'm not. Them were bad days and I'm living a glamorous life now, so why am I looking back?

My party went down a storm. Some people got the wrong pub as there are two pubs on Brewer Street with the word "glass" in the name. It all went well though. At my disco after, Nigel Piss-lover was throwing some interesting shapes on the dance floor and no doubt in the urinals as well.

At 1:30am my friends from the pop group Valerie turned up and then the rest of the night descended into chaos cos Elvis kept tryna DJ but I kept chucking her out of the booth. I should have just let her but the music she was playing was kinda electro punk stuff but by that hour all I wanted to hear was Gene Pitney.

On my actual birthday I got pissed out of my head in The Coach and Horses. I didn't intend to but I can't really recall how it got to that point. Siobhan and Malik put me in a taxi to Michael's, so many thanks to them. I banged my head at some point in the night and I've been having dizzy spells ever since. It's like I'm going down in a lift. That's what it feels like. I'm not going to the doctor but I'm presuming it's bleeding or bruising on the brain.

When I woke up the next morning Michael was really mad at

me so I went to Southend for the day. I'm not overly keen on Southend but I'd never been there before and thought it would be a bit like Blackpool. I didn't like the beach and there wasn't enough amusement arcades. I wanted to find a gypsy but I couldn't find one anywhere. I'm desperate to find out what's gonna happen to me y'see. Like where I'm gonna end up. On the streets with a bottle of gin I'm guessing. I keep thinking something bad's gonna happen to me. But I know that's just alcoholic paranoia. And all the bad's already happened.

The charity shops were ok in Southend. I bought David Bowie's Black Tie White Noise Album and a book called 23 Steps to Improve Your Life. It advises that Michael should be the one to get the coal in from the coalshed and I should cook him nice food for when he gets home from work. We're going in the right direction then. Apart from the food thing.

My sister sent me a cannabis leaf through the post for my birthday. She's so sweet.

I'm looking for a new drummer for my band. Let me know if you're interested.

YOU'RE GONNA GET YOUR FUCKIN HEAD KICKED IN

November 21st, 2007

12:35 pm

I've not got long. I'm in Leytonstone library as usual. I am a member here but am still using their CDs which I got out in October 2006 to DJ with so I'm not allowed to take anything else out.

I'm rubbish at borrowing stuff. Like money as well. If you lend anything to me you won't get it back. Even buying me a drink. Even if I won the pools I wouldn't bother buying you one back.

I've been enjoying Channel 5's Cannibal Season. That Japanese one was impressive. I've never really fancied eating another person but if it tastes like posh pork I might be tempted.

I sold my England ticket to Michael. He's a hooligan so I'm gonna watch it on telly to see what trouble he causes.

My favourite lyric at the moment is this:
"I came to watch a soccer match, not fairies dancin.
Think I'll just liven things up and give someone's head a good stampin".
It's from First Offence who are my favourite band from the early 90s. The chorus line is:
"You're gonna get your fuckin ed kicked in." Repeated and repeated.

There's no decent internet cafe in Kennington. That's probably the main reason that I'm not updating as often. Well, there is one but it's £1 an hour and no matter how much money I have I don't like the thought of being ripped off and £1 an hour is ridiculous.

ONE DWARF, ONE GIANT AND A FUNERAL

November 29th, 2007

12:52 pm

I just walked past a funeral party. Funeral parties fascinate me. I haven't seen one for ages. Maybe it's because I'm not up early enough and most funerals happen in the morning. Anyway, I was truly fascinated and then I bumped into the Co-operative funerals building on Kennington Park Road. I was staring so much. They had big flower arrangement things on top of the coffin and one of them spelt out "MUM". Doesn't that just make things more depressing than they are though? I remember my Nan was quite fond of chrysanths and they were out of season when she died or in season so her coffin was absolutely covered in them but that was alright cos it was quite badly done and I think it only cost £10 or something.

I'm fond of reading the Deaths column in The Oldham Chronicle. I mean, they don't even soften it by calling it "Obituaries". I like that. So, in Oldham, people write the death up in simple terms and there's always a note at the end that says, "No flowers but all donations to Doctor Kershaw's Hospice". That's better I reckon. Cos when I used to hang around Duckinfield cemetery after I quit college I would always watch the burials from the viewing point at the top of the cemetery. That cemetery's on a slope y'see and straight after, the gravediggers would come and put all the flowers in the big metal netted bin. I'd sometimes take out the roses when people had gone and give them to my Mum. Well, they were only going to waste and I am my Father's daughter.

My Dad took along a camera to my brother's funeral. Dunno why but he made everyone gather round and took a few snaps. I recall I'm smiling but at thirteen you don't know what else to do in front of a camera.

I went back to that place I sometimes work yesterday after a fortnight's break. As I was having a fag outside I saw a dwarf coming towards the building. "Hello, it's my first day," he said. I nearly started laughing cos there's something funny about dwarfs even though I'm all for equal opportunities and stuff. Then I went in and there was this other guy that had just started and he was seven foot tall. I'm not taking the piss or lying. I swear on Michael's life it's true. They must have been on the same training course for the job. How hilarious would that be? I suppose everyone's gotten over their amusement about it but between the hours of 5pm and 9pm I kept sneaking a look at them both and turning back to my screen and laughing. I wanted to just say to someone, "Ha ha! Look at them! Just look at them!" But you can't do that nowadays can you?

December 10th, 2007

03:08 pm

I just had my hair done. I noticed that they were selling condoms at the counter. I go to a barber's y'see. Well, it's unisex but it's mainly men. Mainly men in postmen's uniforms. There's a sorting office at the bottom of the road y'see.

So the cloakroom at Rock'n'Roll Wrecked was alright on Saturday. I made £80 in six hours and most of that time was spent reading and jumping. They have a small trampoline in there y'see. I think it's for the strippers to keep toned but it does a good job at keeping me warm.

I got some photos back today that were taken last year. I'm looking well good. Like really good-looking. I never think of myself as good-looking but the photos are really good. It's really great being good-looking. Michael reckons so as well. But sometimes I think that it takes away from other things. I mean everyone just thinks I'm good-looking and dumb cos my hair's peroxide and I hardly ever say anything unless I'm slagging off people for no reason.

I met John Cooper Clark the other day. He liked me. Some people just talk too much though and it gets boring and I take more sips of alcohol and then pass out.

I need to get two pieces of chicken, fries and a Pepsi now. Mayonnaise as well.

MY BOYFRIEND THE BLOOD TOURIST

December 18th, 2007

11:23 am

Some Triads came down to my disco the other night and tried to beat up my good friend with a sawn off snooker cue. Michael stopped it all apparently but I can't remember any of this. I was well pissed. I didn't know what Triads were anyway. Chinese Mafia. Fuckinghell, I bet there's a Pakistani Mafia as well eh? Or is that the one-man show that is Michael?

So yeah, but it was Michael's fault that the Triads were there in the first place cos he'd been to that awful Black Gardenia on Dean Street beforehand and brought them down with him. I didn't mean to get pissed but I was so bored of DJing. Just putting on record after record of songs I'd heard loadsa times before. Even if I put on a few different songs that I'd not heard then the crowd wouldn't like them. I hate music at a high volume. I'd be quite happy to put on Ernest Broadbent's Wurlitzer classics on a low volume and sit and sip my drinks at a reasonable speed, but I can't do that cos all them boring people wanna listen to Northern Soul, Madonna and a bit of punk.

I'll be in Oldham/Manchester from Friday till 27th so if any of you Mancunians are around, drinks at The Palace Hotel?

CHRISTMAS WITHOUT MADDIE

December 26th, 2007

01:01 pm

Me and Michael are having a well good time in Oldham. It's all been kicking off with our Asian brethren but nothing too violent. Michael threw a cigarette at them so that was nice cos they were taking the piss out of Jesus and that's just no good.

My Mum bought me a special phone that gets me in touch with E.T. and E.T. talks to me through this special phone. And it's not in my head cos everyone else can hear it too. My sister cooked Christmas dinner yesterday and that was well nice cos she hardly cooked the vegetables and I like vegetables that are kind of raw. Not potatoes though, they were alright.

Michael got me a Union Jack diamond encrusted skull necklace locket and when you open it up there's a baby skull inside. I got Michael a diamond encrusted skull ring. It was just a coincidence we both got each other skulls. Cool eh?

We hung out for a bit with my Dad yesterday in a pub called The Smut. We drank red wine and talked to this ancient rockabilly who must have been well old in the 50s anyway but he still had his comb on him and started doing his quiff up.

The other day we went to another pub called The Royal Oak. They had a blow-up snowman in a blow-up four foot plastic bubble with polystyrene balls that blow about in it. Well, I was fascinated and couldn't take my eyes off it. I'm in a rush as I need to eat again. My Auntie and Uncle are bringing Tony Blair to dinner here tonight. Well, my uncle's Sedgefield y'see. It was a shame not to get a Christmas card from the prime minister this year like I used to. I know you all hate everything like that and read The Guardian and will vote for something crap like The Liberal Democrats but it made me feel important when I got the Christmas card. Anyway, I'm in a rush cos I can smell a special dinner of some sort that my Mum's cooking and it's making me hungry.

JEWISHAM IS THE NEW ISRAEL

January 24th, 2008

05:36 pm

"Honey bun you are my world. I love you more than words can express. Love you. Jxxx"

"Honeybun. You are my poopie whom I love very much. Jxxx"

"I need my money Daniel. I am getting married next yr and I need u 2 start paying it BK NOW"

"Just a little message to say I love YOU HONEYBUN. I hope your day gets better my squishy love bunny. Jxxx"

"Honeybun you are my one true constant in my life without you it's all shit. Keep me going. Keep me smiling. Love you forever. Jxxx"

It's a nice thing kindness. A boy in the place where I work gave me his old phone yesterday. He didn't give me his SIM card but the text messages get saved to the phone in this day and age so I was delighted when I read these gems. J is his fiancee but I find it quite strange how she initials every text message. Not to mention that her name in his phone is just under "Girlfriend J". There were some other ones that got more and more vicious about the money. That person doesn't have a name because her number wasn't in his phone. I've always found it a bad idea to lend money to anyone. Especially me.

I was well laughing about the honeybun squishy stuff. I mean where do people learn that? Has it been on a TV programme? Princess Diana? I dunno. I call Michael Michael. Why would I call him anything else? I think it's just laziness. I mean, you can go from one relationship to another calling each lover by the same stupid pet name and how are they to know that you haven't called your last three girlfriends the same thing? I think it's vile. You should just use people's names. It's much more dangerous.

It's nice being financially secure. All those years I was skint, and now I'm loaded the rest of the world is skint. Well, that's fine by me. I've been splashing out in my favourite two High Street shops: Atlantic Clothing and Risky. They have some wonderful things in those places. I bought a gold sequined waistcoat to go with my gold pinstriped suit. That was from Risky. I mainly love the crap stuff they sell. They're the kind of things that the girls in Escort and Adult Spy magazine are taking off at the start of the picture story. The kind of stuff that even The Cheeky Girls would think twice about wearing. I also bought a Fall LP for 50p but that was from the St Trinians Hospice Shop on Walworth Road.

Anyway, must go. Got to go to the WMC in a bit. Bands and stuff.

APPLICATION FOR JOB

February 6th, 2008

01:13 pm

Who's coming to my disco tonight then? Use it or lose it. My disco must be the longest running failure of a "club night". I'm not bothered though. I get to drink free liquor and I still get paid.

13/2 I deleted this paragraph as got into real trouble for writing it. Ooooh bad.

Something bad happened yesterday. I was in that London Paper's "Lovestruck" section. It said, "To the blonde girl in Camberwell Charity Shop on 23 January buying The Fall album, This Nation's Saving Grace. I'm the guy who wanted it too. Fancy a drink? Anon". I admit it was me. I'm not a Fall fan. I was buying it for Michael. I was dressed in my parka, wearing no make-up and making eye contact with no one. I'd just like to explain myself. I'm not tarting around charity shops. What do you think I am? I do remember someone picking it up and then putting it back and then I picked it up and bought it cos it was only 50p so I wasn't bothered. I didn't tell Michael that I was featured yesterday, I thought perhaps it's best he reads it on here as I have trouble with words and speaking and he might presume things. Anyway, anyone that calls himself a "guy" sounds a right wanker to me. You shouldn't put adverts in the paper like that. I'm happily married. I know there's a load of desperate girls that read this. Perhaps you ought to write a message in saying that you like The Fall too. Get a shag or sommat. Might make you feel better.

So disco tonight. Pints of Grolsch, long songs, smoking outside then playing weird songs between 2 and 3. I got Madonna and Gene Vincent videos to play in the background. Cos I'm so fucking cool.

MY LIFE AS A JEW IN HENDON

February 18th, 2008

12:12 pm

I had to wait twenty minutes in the doctor's surgery this morning. It beats two and a half months ago when I had to wait two and a half hours, but still.

My doctor's an Indian fella, bit of a strange man. He had what I thought was a urine sample on his desk when I walked in. On further inspection I realised it was a paper weight the colour of crystallised piss. I'm so bloody bored today.

I'm going to Wetherspoon's in a bit for steak and chips. Then I'm meeting my friend, Steve Burns (who's a homosexual) for a drink at Molly Moggs.

Michael and I went drinking on Friday night. We went to The Coach and Horses then The Black Gardenia. Jake was singing. He was singing about shooting his girlfriend cos she was having sex with another man. A bit like Hey Joe but with better lyrics. "Her head fell off like a melon," was one of the more memorable ones. It was alright but Jake doesn't like me cos he overheard me once going on about how much I hated The Black Gardenia and I looked at him weird once when he was staring at my arse. I do that a lot. I turn round quick to check if they're looking and then I look at them weird. I can't stand people looking at me in that kind of way. I hate them bastards. Like I'm a piece of meat. Like that's not been said before but I really hate it. And I never wear anything tight or anything low cut but they still do it. Anyway, it gets on me nerves. One day I'll be old and no one will see me in the way they see me today and I'll be glad. I'll be so glad when my looks fade and I can just sit down and not be bothered by anyone again.

Michael can bother me though.

I worked at Rock'n'Roll Wrecked on Saturday night. It's in a big old building that usually functions as a strip club. One club-goer was having one of those waking nightmares. Perhaps you've seen it happen to other girls. Y'know when they drink too much and someone steals their bag cos they're pissed. Anyway, this girl starts getting really upset and panicked so she comes to the big empty cinema/cloakroom and her friend says, "Has anyone handed in a wallet?" I'm sitting there with my parka hood up crouched next to this heater and I say, "No". And then the drunk girl starts shouting, "Why are you alone up here? Why's no one here? Where is this place?" And I just stare at her and smile. And she keeps saying, "Why don't you answer me? Why don't you answer me?" Her friend dragged her away so it was alright and I was happy to be left in the peace and dark of the cinema warming my hands on the heater once again.

Sorry it's not that interesting this week but Samuel Tate was saying to me that it's always good to keep writing no matter how bad it is. Not that my life is bad. My life is good and that's why this has suffered. It's either me or this.

THE LENT GUIDE TO MARRIAGE
AND FAMILY LIFE

March 3rd, 2008

01:10 pm

I was gonna have a day out today. I got up incredibly early (10am) and made my way to Liverpool Street but then couldn't decide where to go so I didn't bother. Writing this is rather pointless as I have nothing to report on but it does make me feel a little better, like I've done something or something.

I was sitting reading my Family Guide to Advent prayer book in the cloakroom on Sunday morning while 50s hardcore porn was playing on the cinema screen (Robin Simon's brand new idea to get people hanging around in there). Well this girl starts going on saying religion numbs the brain etc. God makes a fool out of those who do not believe and sure enough an hour later her bag had mysteriously disappeared. She had some good stuff in it though, nice Chanel lipsticks and a Givenchy perfume. £20. Not bad.

I've been listening to U2 today. They're like my favourite band. I'm not keen on all that stopping the bomb stuff. It's a bit 70s. I remember I got into them cos I went to this wedding in Liverpool and the couple had their first dance to "All I Want is You". It makes me cry sometimes.

Me and Michael went to an acoustic night by mistake last night. We decided to go upstairs at The Dog House to check out the decor but then this woman takes to her guitar in a kind of apologetic way and starts singing. Her voice was very nice, very gentle. And me and Michael had to be very quiet because there were only four other people there. I find things like that excruciatingly embarrassing. Then she goes, "This song is all about loneliness," and Michael whispered to me, "E.T.'s on the floor. You've got to pick him up". That's all I needed to just start laughing. I was laughing so much

I started making weird noises and just shaking with my head on my knees. It was bad I tell you. Michael explained that I was just overcome with emotion, what with me being a songwriter myself.

Anyway I asked her for her MySpace so my band could have another fan and I told her to get down to my disco (which is on Tuesday for this week only if you're interested). Then Michael bought a veggieburger and some chips from which he got food poisoning this morning. I don't know what he was doing buying a veggieburger in the first place. Michael likes his meat.

I've got to go now cos there's a mad man in this library who's shouting. He's got bleach blonde hair and he's wearing a pair of devil horns. A £3 roast dinner awaits me.

ANOTHER CHRISTIAN CELEBRATION WITHOUT MADDIE

March 28th, 2008

01:17 pm

I don't usually leave the house when it's raining but as I hadn't left for two days I thought I'd try and get out. I wish I hadn't. I'm not one to complain about the weather but the rain was one of the reasons I left Oldham.

I passed the funeral parlour. The floral displays look so nice and peaceful. I'm not a Goth but I wish I could just go in and lie in a coffin for a bit. And there'd be a nice lamp on the side and a display of chrysanthemums or something. And I'd just lie there and go to sleep. I quite liked that about being in hospital. It was a bit like being dead.

I do get these nice highs sometimes but everyone says I can't be manic depressive or bi-polar cos I'm not a genius. I'm not bothered though. Things should stop being about me all the time. I've volunteered for Age Concern to befriend old people. I had my interview the other day in a 1970s office block in Brixton. I didn't say much but they've still got to do the CRB check and I reckon they might find out about my crimes. But that's discrimination if they don't employ me, surely.

On Good Friday I went for a walk with my Catholic youth group to eight churches. We said benediction in all of them and finished off at Westminster Cathedral for the Mass. Michael was outside and on seeing him I didn't feel like going in as he made me feel like a drink. The wind blew me over outside Westminster Abbey. My balance is terrible since the accident and I've been struggling a lot recently although whenever anyone asks me how my leg is I always tell them it's alright. I read that if you go around being negative about everything then no one wants to be around you. No one wants to be around me when I'm high about everything either. I've never won anything.

My friend got stabbed through the heart the other day. He's in intensive care but I think he'll be alright.

I'm in a Spanish internet cafe on Kennington Park Road. The music's doing my head in. I'm going back to bed.

ADOLF HITLER – WAS THE FÜHRER A BLACK MAGICIAN?

April 4th, 2008

11:32 am

The doctor gave me an urgent referral for suspected cancer this morning. Well, that's what it said on the form he faxed over to the unit. I'm not lying. Who would lie about having cancer? I'm not after your money anymore so there's no point. I'm not too worried though. I know I said I'd like to lie down in a coffin for a bit but only for a bit. I'd miss Michael if I really did die. Anyway, I haven't been diagnosed with cancer yet. It's a common thing to die from though, but I think I preferred the old days when people just died and you didn't know what it was from. In the end it's usually pneumonia but now they just call everything cancer. So I'll let you know how it goes and what the people in the waiting room look like and what the magazines are and all the other banalities of this banal and boring disease.

I had suspected cancer in 1999 as well. My Mum came with me to the hospital at the last minute as I didn't tell her until I was ready to go. The waiting room is pretty bad cos you see people that really have got proper cancer and it's bad and depressing. I've been hanging around in churches a lot lately so God's not gonna mind me if I hang around him sooner rather than later.

I went to a jumble sale at St John's in Leytonstone after my predicament. I wasn't really depressed but I just thought to myself, "You buy anything you want," and so I did:
The Giant Book of Bizarre and Mysterious People (brand new) – 50p
Electric blue nail varnish (only a bit used) – 30p
A birthday card for someone who's twelve – 25p
VHS Casablanca – 50p
Brit Awards album 2004 – 30p
Gwen Stefani, Love Angel Music Baby – 30p

Blondie, Denis – 30p
Will Young, Friday's Child – 30p
Cup of tea – 35p
Slice of cake – 30p

My new music selection is not really gonna tempt you to get down to my disco is it? You should have smelt the stench on Wednesday. Apparently there was a dead rat underneath the floorboards behind the DJ booth. And the cockroaches came back and were crawling everywhere and the place was completely empty. Robin Simon came down with the rockabillies for a bit but then left cos they were after girls.

My band has a drummer now so I hope you'll come and see us play. We should be gigging again in about a month and a half provided I don't get put in hospital. I'd do a gig there though. At least people would show up.

I was out on Sunday night recording people's conversations with my new tape recorder. Michael and I went to The Constitution in Camden. The music was really good and the conversations were even better. Having a tape recorder on you means you can get completely pissed out of your mind but not lose the night so you don't feel too bad about not remembering.

I might get my hair cut now.

A PLACE WHERE SADISTIC
PEOPLE CAN MEET

April 9th, 2008

01:18 pm

I went for my breakfast in Wetherspoon's this morning and what a fantastic breakfast it was. £2.49. It's set me up for the day and now I feel alright.

My Mum seems to have got the whole of the diocese praying for me, and my sister in Australia keeps ringing me up. It's as if I'm on my deathbed already but I don't think there's much wrong with me. It's when you lose your appetite you need to get worried, cos then you die soon afterwards. And I haven't lost my appetite or my thirst for large amounts of alcohol so I reckon I'm alright.

Yesterday Jupiter John and I went on a historical pub crawl. It was a lovely sunny day for it and we stopped off at the oldest Catholic church in London to say benediction then resumed with our refreshments.

When I got back to Leytonstone (I'm not here much nowadays due to my change in marital status) the drug dealer and his dog greeted me at the door. Yes, he's back. His bail was paid. £2000 apparently. He told me his friend had set him up. Oh dear, friends are dangerous things. He told me he was looking at five years. I thought he was in there for five years but anyway, he's alright and I told him how glad I was to see him and his giant dog back in the house, as well as the ten cars that he owns in the back garden. And he said that I must come in for a meal. Well I won't be up to that, having meals with other men when, you know...

My disco is tonight. My Michael will be there. He's the only reason to go. I've got some josticks to cover up the smell of decaying rats and blocked drains so you don't need to worry too much. I can't guarantee about any people being there or the quality of the people that do turn up but Michael will have his metal comb with him and he'll be slicing people with it on the way out if he doesn't like them. Good Michael.

I'm gonna have to buy some more wine glasses now cos we've smashed them all again. Then I'll get my hair cut. That's important that is but I don't like looking at myself in the mirror.

DEATH: THE HIDDEN KILLER

April 22nd, 2008

02:01 pm

It seems like ages ago now but I went to visit the cancer specialist last week and he reckoned I didn't have cancer, but I was supposed to go for a scan but forgot and walked out. I'm gonna leave it now though. I think I'll be alright.

Thing is I'd forgotten what the reality of death was like until the other day I heard a friend of mine was unconscious and was going to die. I eventually found out that she'd had breathing difficulties and it had just got worse and then I realised how bad it is and I can't stop thinking about her and the fact that she will be gone soon. I've realised that death is a serious thing. The last time I saw her she gave me a big hug, and usually I don't let people touch me in that way but I didn't mind her cos I liked her. Me, her and Steve went drinking in Molly Moggs, Glasshouse Stores and then The Soho Arts Club and it was strange cos it was quite an optimistic night and everything felt bright and nice.

So I think now I'd like to live until I'm seventy-five and I hope I'm lucky enough to grow old.

KILLING TIME = SUICIDE

May 8th, 2008

03:55 am

Sometimes I look at the people that surround me and I think: no one actually does anything, and people go to work and stuff and come home and survive in that sense but some people just never do anything. I realised last week that I'm the only person with any talent and creativity in London and probably the rest of England as well. I bet you may differ from this view and I don't give a shit if you do, but I'm doing stuff and you're probably not and I'm not talking about drugs.

I keep handing out these handwritten flyers for my band Iraq on Sunday 1st June at 8pm at 12 Bar. Just so you know. And I have this big feeling within my mind that, yeah, I'm doing something with this time that I've been given, as in the life, that equals time doesn't it? And if I sit in and stare at the walls I feel bad about it, like slow suicide or something, like I'm disrespecting God. So I have to do as much as possible even if I do end up sitting for three days staring at the TV but mostly, if I do that, I'm praying.

I've just given my flyer to a prostitute and a weirdo but earlier I gave my flyer to a dwarf. My friend, John Davenport said I might as well hire a circus. I always promote the things that I do with the so-called aliens in society, the people that everyone will stare at. Ugh. I'm not gonna go on like a fucking wanker. This whole thing has been fucking crap and I'll delete it tomorrow if I see fit.

9th May

I can't be bothered deleting this but I wish I would avoid going to internet cafes at 4am. It's all rather embarrassing and it's not that I'm pissed, it's just that I was overtired and when I'm overtired I have to be doing stuff.

I had a nice rest yesterday and didn't bother going to work. I've just had a cheese and onion pasty from Percy Ingle and all is right with the world.

I'M THE BEST THING THAT EVER HAPPENED EVER

May 26th, 2008

03:39 pm

I'm suffering from advanced paranoia. That's what they said about Princess Diana. Whenever I'm around other people I feel like they hate me. Like when I walk into the room it lets out a groan. "Oh no, not her again." I mainly feel like this around Michael's friends. I don't think they understand me. I think they've missed the point. I can count on one hand the people who get me. Even Michael doesn't really understand why I exist. Like today he saw that I had a plastic bag in my parka pocket and he was so upset about it he just walked away. The plastic bags seem to upset him immensely. I've always carried plastic bags on me. They come in handy for several things. Vomit and shopping mainly.

I'm back in my favourite internet cafe in Leytonstone. This is the internet cafe I wrote most of this stuff on before I broke my leg. I'm back here because Kennington is trying to kill me. There's this massive phone mast on top of the BT building opposite the tube station and it lets out these rays that blast my mind and make me feel suicidal. But as soon as I'm back in Leytonstone I begin to feel happy again and I want to be out and about and doing things. Anyway, Michael can't help where he lives and so I'm stuck and there's nothing I can do about it.

That's the main reason I don't write this journal anymore. When I'm there I can't get out of the flat. I just feel lethargic and depressed. Anyway, just so you know, I haven't given up.

My band are doing well. We're recording stuff with a producer at the moment and we also got a manager who's taking us to play in Turkey. We've also got a big gig to play at The Saatchi Gallery and we're being paid a bit of money for that so perhaps soon I'll be able to buy a big Edwardian house in Leytonstone and then I'll be able to blackmail Michael into living with me here.

My band Iraq have got a gig next Sunday 1st June at The 12 Bar on Denmark Street. We're on at 8pm and it's £3. It would be nice to have some of my supporters there cos it's Michael's birthday and he's invited all his friends that hate me and that won't understand my ad-libs. Michael's gonna kill me for this journal today but everything I say is true and he pissed me off last night so he deserves this.

My DJing is going incredibly well. When I last wrote I was going on about it being unpopular and cockroaches being the only things that are on the dance floor. Well, it's good that it's got really popular. With no promotion from me, it's happened just through word of mouth. They come up to me and say, "You're the best DJ ever. We only come when you're DJing". Then Trevor puts a sign that says DJ Scarlet outside cos he said that people only come if they know I'm DJing. It's cos I play decent stuff. Not Rolling Stones and Ska and not credible stuff. I've been doing Fridays as well. On Friday you couldn't move in there.

Last night me and Michael went to The Boston Arms for that rockabilly thing. I'm telling you, them people really don't like me. They won't even speak to me, they hate me so much. They don't think I'm cool enough but I think about them and I think, what the fuck have they done? I'm getting somewhere and all they do is hang around on the same scene with the same people and wear the same clothes and talk about the same shit things. I'm meeting different kinds of people every day when I manage to leave the house.

I'm the best thing that ever happened.

ON HOW I'M WASTING MY WHOLE LIFE ON DRINK

May 29th, 2008

04:11 am

I've been DJing. Funkinghell, I never work out why I bother. Well, there's all those terrible people who I hate that go down.

Michael told me last night that I'm an embarrassment to his friends.

I was in the cancer waiting room today for most of the day. It was quite boring but I decided to make it more exciting by exploring the hospital. I've had to turn up at Whipps Cross four times in the last two months. I like that hospital and pray that I might die there one day. I'm sick, I'm ill. Michael says that I'm ill for saying everyone, every girl that he has ever known, should die under the knife, from me. I feel bad, I feel terrible for saying that. But that's how I feel.

Anyway, this life and writing this in an internet cafe at 4:34am in Trafalgar Square, surrounded by prostitutes and lowlifes is where I am. Michael says I'm on my way to self-destruction. He's pissed off with how drunk I get and how I keep getting that way and punching myself and clawing myself and trying my bestest to jump out of windows. Someone always stops me then. Usually Michael.

Anyway, he says he's gonna leave me, how I'm giving him a heart attack, how he can't put up with my drinking anymore, how he's sick of my lies, how I've wasted everything, all the talent and writing and how now, it all means nothing, how when I get to forty I'm gonna regret never doing anything with my life when I probably could have become something. Huh. Well. I dunno about all what he's said. He said that everyone's said the same thing about me, how they said I'm wasting my whole life on drink. And that's it. I'm destined to become nothing.

PRESCRIPTIONS AND PISS

June 5th, 2008

03:15 pm

I bumped into that woman who told me I was a psychopath yesterday, when she read my fortune that time and she said I'd never be able to hold down a relationship because in the end they'd find out I was a psychopath. Anyway, it was something like that. I don't know why I'm bringing it all up. I've been having a lot of psychopathic thoughts of late. It's Michael who's the other psychopath though. He throws glass wine bottles off his balcony onto the ten-year-olds that are annoying. I don't bother stopping him though. I believe that he can do what he likes. I hate those women that are like, "don't do that," and then they'll give a reason. I just go into the toilet when he's smashing up the street.

Anyway, I guess you're all dying to know how my gig went seeing as not one of you turned up to my concert. You're all bastards and I've always said that but I don't like each and every one of you and I wouldn't be bothered if I saw any of you killed on my way to have a drink. I'd step over you and that would be that.

My band were the only band that got paid as usual and I stole the money just as the other band members were leaving and then me and Michael went on the piss in Camden for the rest of the night. It was Michael's birthday as well so we had a great time. And when I came offstage I got this massive bouquet of flowers and it was like I was Greta Garbo or sommat. Fuckinghell, it was well good. And the atmosphere was amazing and I was cracking everyone up with my jokes and my voice and the sound were to die for.

And even my acting coach turned up. He left his meal in a posh Chinese restaurant on Gerrard Street. That's what he did cos he was desperate to see me do my amazing performance.

Our manager is in awe of us. He can't believe he's found a band that's as good as ours. It's like we've got everything.

So this week I decided to take off. Yesterday I went to have my hair done at Toni and Guy and then I went for lunch at Wetherspoon's in Bank and then I went to The Nostradamus church in Leicester Square and lit a candle for Michael and then I went to The Prince Charles Cinema and saw The Diving Bell and The Butterfly. It had subtitles. I'm not keen on films with subtitles cos I can't read that well. Erm, joke. Cos I can't be bothered. Anyway, it was nice and the cinema was full of old ladies on their own carrying loads of bags and smelling of their prescriptions and piss and I felt quite at home.

Now I'm gonna check my fan mail.

LONDON IS A FOREIGN SHORE

June 16th, 2008

04:31 pm

I'm back in my beloved town of Oldham. I have been here for two and a half hours so it is still my beloved.

Mogwai died. I was sad about that when it happened and the house is not the same without her eccentric behaviour. E.T. has taken to wearing a tootle scarf. He tells me he was inspired by someone I've never heard of. He's happy enough and tells me to stop kissing him.

Our Pakistani brethren have written "gay" on my Dad's front door. Could have been worse. Could have been "paedophile".

Anyway, happy times are to be upon us soon as me and me Mum and Dad are going to Blackpool tomorrow and we're gonna have a good time and get some fish and chips. Blackpool is the only place I ever want to be. Apart from here in Oldham. London's dead. I find it really dull now. I don't reckon I'm bored of life though. There's some things I still enjoy. I'm stuck there now though, I'll be there until my band leave and until Michael leaves me. Then I'll go somewhere nice. Perhaps Michael will leave with me.

My Mum's making me pork chop, mash, broccoli and gravy in a bit. Avid readers will remember that this was what I was eating when I found out John Peel had died. It's my favourite meal and I'd have it if I was about to get executed, but only if my Mum cooked it. But if my Mum wasn't available to cook my last meal then I'd have pudding, chips and gravy from Wing Wah on Oxford Street, Werneth, Oldham.

I had a strange evening yesterday. I was so bloody bored as Michael was away doing some top secret business so I thought I'd pop into Soho but not get pissed or anything. Then Lisa Stansfield starts singing while someone played the piano in The Coach and Horses. It was all rather wonderful and you know you tend to leave your house for moments like that when an atmosphere in a room is so where it's meant to be. She sang "My Funny Valentine".

I went home after that and watched Nuts TV with the wonderfully talented Michelle Marsh who is also from Oldham. She was interviewing people in Jumpin' Jax, where I used to work as a dancer. I was watching these people and I thought, aaah, if only I could be them and life would be so simple and I'd work on the cold meat counter in Tommyfield Market and I'd just go out on a Friday night and get rat-arsed and things would be lovely.

A DAYTRIP TO BLACKPOOL

June 18th, 2008

12:18 pm

Yesterday me and me Mum and Dad went to Blackpool. We didn't think Dad would go cos whenever he's got to do something he always turns up late and misses the bus, but after much deliberation over what bus stop we were supposed to go to, we got on the bus and we were on our way.

If you ever wanna go to Blackpool from Manchester then you wanna catch the Stagecoach bus from Shudehill bus station. You pay on the bus and it's £5.70 for a day ticket so that'll take you there and back. However, if you happen to be as lucky as to be over sixty then it's free. Last bus at six.

In Blackpool we walked down to the promenade and sat there for a bit. My Dad drank coffee out of a flask and I had a cup too. I've never known him not to put whisky in his coffee so was sorely disappointed when I tasted it. I whispered, "Where's the whisky?"
"I ran out," he replied. I think he'd drunk a few glasses to get him out of bed but he was alright and wasn't too pissed. It was a bit cold so we set off to the Winter Gardens. Every time we passed a lap dancing club or a sex shop my Dad would shout out, "Ooooh! Look at that". My Mum got a bit upset about it. "Peter you're a dirty old man," she said.

The Winter Gardens looked lonely. "Where is everyone?" Mum kept saying. She said it was like we'd stepped into a strange time and everyone was gone, like the place was out of season. This used to be busy at this time of year, she said. Thing is, I liked it like that. I've always liked Blackpool like that. Like a musical star that ends up dribbling in a nursing home. Kind of gone but still there.

Charity shops are rife in Blackpool, so me and my Mum bored my Dad by going into every one we passed. There was nothing I wanted though. I kind of wanted a drink more than anything. My Dad suggested The British Legion and off we went, up a big hill. My Dad had his club card with him so entry was easy. He signed our names in and we went on through to the concert room. At last, I thought, this is it; I've come home and this is the place I was searching for. Old people were singing songs from the last era, the very old songs that I'd never heard on the radio. And a man was playing an organ. It was a bit like karaoke but each old person does three songs and they know the words. Free 'n' easy it's called. Their voices were amazing. No one sings the way they sing anymore. I leaned back in my chair and admired the singers and all the Union Jacks. I drank Fosters. It was nice but my Dad looked like he had left the gas on. I told him so but he didn't pass any further comment about it. He looked so sad, like everything had been taken away.

After a couple of hours we went back outside and looked at more charity shops. We eventually left my Dad in Whittles, a popular chain in Lancashire. Mum said he'd done very well to come round the shops he did with us before needing more drink. Mum and me then went into the Sacred Heart Catholic Church to say some prayers. We sat down in a pew and I started thinking, this is probably the last time I'll ever be in Blackpool with Mum and Dad again. Cos when I'm sad I always think of the time when the sun was setting and I was walking down the promenade holding Mum and Dad's hand and I must have been around 6. And it's weird cos whenever I cry that vision always comes into my head and makes me cry even more. I didn't cry though. After five minutes Mum gave me a hug and told me she'd prayed for me. Then we left and went to collect Dad but he was already coming out of O'Neill's. He said how he'd tried some new type of Guinness.

We then caught the bus back and I looked out of the window, planning to buy a house with a dome like the ones that were passing the window.

11 CHARING CROSS ROAD, WC2H 0EP

July 2nd, 2008

04:19 am

I was gonna go back to Oldham yesterday. I had an argument with Michael about my drinking, I think. It all got out of hand, or I did. And then I tried to strangle myself, which is a very difficult thing to do. I've got some marks round my neck so I can't have gone too far wrong.

Tonight I DJ'd at The Soho Arts Club. ITV were having a big party there and the only person missing was Trevor McDonald. I played loads of white music anyway so he wasn't missing much. They were all into my Joy Division, Smiths, Associates and Abba though.

I'm in that fucking internet cafe again. It stinks of puke. I fucking hate this place. Michael should get a computer but I always stick to my reasons: "I don't wanna bring the outside world in".

I never spend longer than an hour on these machines. What good would any more do me?

These late night places are for homosexual men that don't have computers at home. It brings back memories of all the nights I spent in easyEverything internet cafe in Manchester 2000.

What to do with my life I can never decide. Is it ever up to me though? I feel suicidal and lost for twenty-five percent of the time, determined and focused for sixty-five percent and looking around for the rest. Or does that count as lost? I wish I was somewhere else.

I have to go. Some homosexual's tryna get a shag. George Michael's relatives have bought The Soho Arts Club and they want to keep me on but they're changing the whole venue so none of you can get in free anymore. Well, you never bothered to come to my night anyway so I'm not gonna put any of you on my shiny new guest list and no one can get in by saying they're Scarlet's friend anymore. They're making the ceilings higher as well as my wages.

Tomorrow I shall hang around Elephant and Castle Shopping Centre.

MY WIFE'S MOTHER WALKED IN ON ME MASTURBATING

July 7th, 2008

05:19 pm

I've been in this library for almost three hours. I've lost my job. I didn't go into it much anyway, just a couple of times a week, so now I've got all this free time. I do stuff that I need to do for thirteen hours a week and the rest is blank. I've put an advertisement about my DJ skills on the internet.

"60s, 70s and 80s party DJ available. No equipment. £15 per hour." Now, that's reasonable. I've put up loads of adverts like that in the past but no one's ever got back to me through it.

Sometimes in life you have to be professional and being professional for me would be no fun so I'm not gonna bother. I'd rather have no money than be professional. It's boring but I'm bored doing nothing all day. And I feel bad as usual cos I feel like I should be doing something, at least. But my lethargy in these matters grows each day.

I forgot what I wrote in my last entry cos I was pissed in that stupid homosexual internet cafe again. George Michael's relatives bought T'Arts. And they're doing cocktails and having booths. I'm not allowed to say anything else cos I've signed a big contract with them.

I was at my new doctor's surgery this morning. Forty minute walk from my house cos the government closed him down for being a single-handed GP. He does have two though and he took my blood pressure and said it was low again. I reckon my heart will stop beating in my sleep and I'll just die like that. How nice would that be?

I remembered what I need to do on this internet and it's not do a "Scarlet West" search for the hundredth time on Google. I need to look up how I can donate my body to medical science. I'm worried about my family having to pay for my funeral so I thought that if I leave my body then everyone wins.

My disco is on Wednesday. So far ten people are not attending and forty-two people have ignored my invitation. I don't know why I bother with that stupid Facebook thing. No one ever comes from there but it's always packed. That website makes me look unpopular. And what's so wrong with being unpopular anyway? I feel like I'm being bullied by them all. It's strangers who are kindest to me. And Michael. Yeah, never forgetting Michael with his silver teeth and his leopardskin waistcoat. And his hair, oooh, his lovely hair.

SOON YOU'LL ALL BE ON MY SIDE

July 17th, 2008

01:24 pm

Is anyone coming to my gig tonight? Guess you're not but anyway, thought I'd write on here as I've booked an hour in this cafe on Walworth Road and I've done everything already.

Michael's bought me some lovely Vivienne Westwood earrings cos we had a bad argument the other day. It was cos I went on a drinking session. I was so bored and y'know when you've got nothing to do but you fancy just having a drink. I don't do that too often now but on Tuesday I just had that feeling. I always have to have an excuse for it so my excuse was that I wanted to become a member of those two big casinos round Leicester Square. Anyway, I'm a member of those now. I think it was cos they barred me from Gerry's. I have to be a member of somewhere cos I don't want to drink with the people. Casinos are always empty during the day apart from gamblers. They like casinos but they're on the machines. So the bars are empty and y'know me, there's nothing more that I like than an empty bar in the afternoon.

I went to The Colony after my time watching pop videos in the casino. Michael, the Colony man, was passed out on a bench. The place was empty but I needed a drink. I tried to wake him but he wouldn't wake up and then I thought, I'm in this room with loads of Francis Bacon and Damien Hirst originals, what if? Y'know… Well, I didn't steal anything cos I was in no fit state but I would have and I wish I had. But I thought what if he dies, what if Michael, the Colony man, chokes on his own vomit or he's OD'd on something else that I don't know about and then a Francis Bacon goes missing and they have me done for murder as well as theft. So I left.

Back in Kennington my Michael was mad that I was pissed. I walked out of the flat and lay down in the middle of the road, but then a car came and a crowd gathered and I realised I was blocking up the road so I went back to Leytonstone where I drank five cans of Kronenbourg that I tend to keep there in case of emergencies like that.

Anyway, I woke up the next day so that was a good sign. Then my friend Antonio who's the stage manager at The Royal Opera House texted me to say he had two tickets for La bohème so I told my Mum to get to London fast and come with me. Antonio gave us a backstage tour before the opera started and we even went onto the stage and onto the roof. Looking around the opera house I was thinking, this exists and this is all that matters. Why should I live my life in terrible poverty the way I have when this exists and I exist and everything can be exciting and shiny and good? It's only people around me who bring me down.

My Mum and I also went to see The Mousetrap. We'd been planning on seeing The Mousetrap for five years now. It's alright but don't sit in the gods.

The barman at The Soho Arts Club was found dead last night. Suspected overdose they reckon. I liked him. He was quiet but it always is those quiet ones that die. Last week my friend who was in the coma died as well. I'm used to all this death so it doesn't bother me too much. I feel almost autistic nowadays in the way I cope with my emotions. I just don't feel and everything seems to have a price. As long as I have enough money to dine out in The Connaught and drink in Claridge's then I'm happy.

Come to my gig tonight. Come to my gig tomorrow. Soon you'll all be on my side.

WIN A NIGHT OUT IN SOHO
WITH SCARLET WEST

July 21st, 2008

12:36 pm

I did that just now cos I'm a bit bored. It had a headline as well. KICKING FOR KILLING AND STABBING FOR FUN – ONE NIGHT IN SOHO WITH SCARLET WEST. But my headline was too long and I couldn't work out how to do it.

I've not seen Michael since I walked out on Saturday evening. It's all gone wrong. And he didn't turn up to my gig on Friday and that's the worst thing cos I played the best gig of my life and everyone else was there. Well, no one that reads this but the proper fans of the band were there and dancing, and the lesbians and scantily clad female fans were also enjoying it.
But no Michael. And he said he was too tired and ill and that he fell asleep.
Anyway, I don't know whether I can forgive anymore. I've always found forgiveness difficult and people don't change. Michael said that we both need to change but I don't know how it would be possible for me to change cos I know that I like a drink but there's nothing else I wanna change about myself.

Last night I went to Sunset Strip on Dean Street for the screening of a film by Lance Wrigley, the director whose film I was in a few years back. The film was called Soho Sunset and was set in Sunset Strip. Anyway I was standing at the bar and one of the actors starts doing my accent really badly so the regular man at the bar thinks he's taking the piss out of him and thus a big fight breaks out and as usual, I disappear. I don't know the outcome of it. Sometimes trouble follows me around. I went back to Leytonstone then and bought some chicken and chips from USA Chicken and Pizza.

HOW TO FEEL GOOD-LOOKING?
GO SHOPPING IN ASDA

August 1st, 2008

11:24 am

Yesterday I spent five hours waiting at the hospital. I'd taken a book called "Daily Bread" that my Mum had given me. It's full of bible verses and anecdotes for when you're going through bad times. I don't know what I'd have done if I didn't have that. I think I would have just left. Then I spent an hour left in a room on a trolley. All I could hear was distant voices and footsteps and I felt so alone that I started to cry. Then I went to sleep and then eventually the doctor came back.

Anyway, it's all suspected cancer isn't it? I suppose that's what most people die of as I've said but I reckon I might just be able to get away with cheating death. They gave me some tablets which I was supposed to eat this morning but they made me puke. Vile things they are. I'm no good at swallowing.

It's actually been nice not having to lose two days a week to that subterranean cockroach-infested club. I've been walking around, exploring things. It's been alright.

I went to the most wonderful Asda in a place called Crossharbour near Canary Wharf the other day. I felt like a film star in there. I'm just so glam. Amazing things they have. Soap dishes, toothbrush holders, scented candles, bits of dried flowers in a wooden block. Everything really. I bought:
Willow-scented candle – 30p
Frost-scented candle – 30p
Eight hot dogs – 35p
Tinned macaroni cheese – 40p
Small quiche lorraine – 78p
Two egg custard tarts – 52p

The quiche was a bit of a letdown.

On Tuesday Michael and me went to The Parkin Lot, Sophie and Molly Parkin's night at The Green Carnation. I don't mind it in there but it was a shame that the pints were off. And I'm not keen on disco, but apart from that I like that family. Sophie's always been nice to me cos she's a good person.

I've joined lots of market research focus groups and keep getting £75 a time to give them my views on things like smoking and other stuff. My views are worth £75. Shame I don't get that a time for writing this.

Me and Michael got back together after two days apart. I made him a cheesecake with a big M on it. Just from a packet like. Then I bought him a blue Mr Freeze ice pop. I ate that the other day though. I told him I'm not gonna change though. Cos the person underneath, where does she go? Does she slide by the wayside or does she just die?

YOU'RE THE CLOSEST I'LL EVER
GET TO DEATH

August 8th, 2008

01:41 pm

I have to go back to the hospital at 4pm. It's all very depressing today. Don't bother reading this if you're feeling sad already cos I'll only make you worse.

Last night I did a gig at quite short notice but still managed to text everyone in my phone about it the day before but not one person turned up. Does anyone know what it feels like to play to an empty room? And to think I turn up to the things that you do. Well anyone that received that message that I see in the next month I will physically mow down and leave for dead. I'm serious.

Michael didn't turn up cos he was out with his dull record-collecting friends the night before so I've told him I'm not going back to Kennington. I just sent him an email now and his reply was that he was so upset he's going home. Well, I'm glad. If people can't support me then I'm gonna make their life hell on earth.

Anyway, The Dry Bar liked us and they want to put us on again. And I got back to Leytonstone and I just wrote and wrote and wrote. Then I woke up at midday and had some ravioli on toast.

I bet I'll have to wait for ages at Whipps Cross. I'm sick of waiting in hospitals alone. I wish I had a friend but I've lost them all. And it's probably my own fault for drinking too much and telling everybody how much I hate them. But that's the way I feel sometimes, but not one person tries to understand me and be there for me.

I'm going back to bed cos that's the closest I can get for the moment to death. Unless today they tell me my time will come soon and if they do I'll be so happy. I can see no future for me.

HOW TO SURVIVE YOUR ADDICTIONS

August 14th, 2008

11:38 am

Whipps Cross Hospital has always been one of the less depressing hospitals in my view. As usual my consultant was running an hour late so I decided to explore. I was looking for people that looked like they were about to die cos I was hoping it would make me feel less like dying. I eventually found them in the corridor by the cancer ward. I felt quite sad and guilty for me wanting to be them and then I felt quite happy and decided that I didn't want to die anyway. Everyone was quite old though so I thought, "Wow!" Most people die when they get old so perhaps I don't have anything to worry about for a number of years anyway. I got out of the cancer ward fast then and went on a search for this weird shop where a very strange woman sells my kind of tacky jewellery. Big diamond rings, shiny earrings and jewel-covered handbags. Well, I found the shop but it was all closed up cos I think it only opens on a Tuesday and Thursday.

Back in the waiting room the opening ceremony of the Olympics was on and I couldn't stop laughing. It just seemed so shit and surreal and the TV was all fuzzy and everyone kept saying, "Oooh, that's so nice". Cos they're all friendly like that round Essex way and they're all over fifty in the cancer clinic so they can still speak English. Then the receptionist goes, "Oooh, it's just like E.T." And I looked at it and it was; it was just like E.T. And I laughed and laughed because it's alright when you're in a hospital, you can get away with acting out how you feel cos people are more worried about dying than you going insane. I don't think they monitor mental health at Whipps Cross anyway.

Eventually the young attractive homosexual Asian consultant called my name. The room was bright and my make-up was all caked and horrible. He asked me what had happened so I explained the story. I couldn't understand why he was asking me cos he had all the papers there. They had a massive file with my name and CONFIDENTIAL written on it. Then he said he was gonna discharge me. It's taken seven visits for them to say that but I suppose they've got to cover themselves. So that's alright then. I liked that hospital though. I wouldn't mind dying there in my seventies although I'm hoping to be enjoying my twilight years in Blackpool General.

SHOOTING UP SMACK AND
EATING A DWARF

September 29th, 2008

12:24 pm

I got a lucrative job posing for portraits in Buckhurst Hill. I found the job posted on the miscellaneous notice board in the Stratford Sainsbury's. I sat very still for two hours in a church hall while keeping my eyes fixed on a door handle. Most of the portraits look a lot like sketches of Myra Hindley so perhaps I do have a certain dangerous charm about me. Maybe that's why Michael puts up with me. If anyone else wants the job now it's alright and it's £9 per hour every Wednesday between 10am and 12pm.

I went away with my Mum over the weekend to a little place called Ross-on-Sea in Wales with her church. We sat at the dinner table with a war veteran who told me a joke: "What's the difference between the French and a slice of bread? You can make good soldiers out of a slice of bread".

I told my Parisian guitarist this yesterday. He laughed so that's alright then. My band played that Oxo Tower event yesterday called Down The Rabbit Hole. Three twenty-minute sets. We were amazing as usual. A deaf man has become our biggest fan. He said my lyrics were very good. He was lip-reading he said.

I got well fucking pissed after. We drank in the sun for a bit on Gabriel's Wharf by the river, then we rehearsed. Then we went to The Angel pub on Saint Giles High Street and drank more.

I eventually got back to Michael after buying everything up in the chippy. Like all the leftovers and burnt bits. They always charge me about £5 for the lot and they never give me a discount. I remember pleading last night. Dunno why cos I'm not that skint anymore cos The Soho Arts Club pay me loads but once you are skint it never leaves you. Like my Mum and her postwar rationing. She's very generous with her food though.

Michael got really angry when I came back pissed again. I can't remember much of what he said but I think he had good reason. Porno Steve had been round asking for me cos I'd arranged to meet him but once I have a drink I forget things.

JUST ME AND THE DRINK

October 16th, 2008

02:47 pm

I can't explain the way I feel about everything in my life at the moment cos whenever I try to I'm always misunderstood. Mainly by Michael. Everything's gone wrong. I suppose DJing and the Iraq are going really well but everything else is fucking awful.

My depression is sinking me and every day I wake up and I can't move cos I just want to die. And people who don't know suggest things like tablets and herbal remedies but they don't understand. But eventually I'll step out and get ready to DJ again and I'll be happy when I'm there but at 4am I'm back where I began and so I just break down and cry.
I don't know whether I should be writing this.

I always go back to Leytonstone when things get this bad because I'm a nightmare to be around and I just want to be alone and free from people's wicked comments about me. The sun always shines here. It's shining now through these big windows and the birds in the churchyard opposite the library are singing. So there is brightness. There is a future and I won't kill myself for anyone. I've tried to have a good time though, but I've failed miserably. And I can't think of anything more I can do to have a good time. I've done everything. Perhaps ecstasy or getting into drugs might be an option but I don't like the look of those ragabones on the street that have wasted their lives on all that. I just don't know what else to do. I'm so bored every day, I wake up and no matter what I do everything bores me. I like the drink though and that keeps me entertained for six hours at least. Just wandering through Holborn to Leicester Square, drinking half pints in every pub I come across. Not speaking to anyone. Just the silence of the afternoon and the clanking of the glasses. It seems to give me immense satisfaction. Immediate too. Not having to wait around like I do with my band. Just me and the drink.

IN THE DARKNESS OF THE PISS-SOAKED LIBRARY

November 3rd, 2008

05:51 pm

It's a bit dark in this library this evening. The lights keep going on and off. I'm going to have a chicken and turkey Subway sandwich when I've finished writing this.

I've been very busy doing my disco and doing my band in these last few weeks. Everything has become exciting again cos I have a new Schedule for DJing at The Arts. Well, I'm doing Tuesdays instead of Mondays. The reason for this being that I kept getting bored on Wednesday and drinking too much so now by me doing Tuesdays I'll hopefully be hungover on a Wednesday thus not craving a drink.

My band did another gig for Club Criminal on Thursday. They fucking love us. And it was a Halloween party so I was wearing this long black wig and witch's hat cos I'd gone as the Wicked Witch of the West. I threw the wig off and there I was in all my platinum glory. My sister couldn't believe it. She was there and she was amazed at how amazing my band are.

Then after the gig, this man from a management company comes up and tells me they're interested. And they were in their fifties these two men. Someone had seen us somewhere and told them about us. So there it goes.

Michael and I went to Camden last night for a Country & Western shindig. We like all that. It was freezing though cos we have to sit outside cos we're chain-smokers. I drank five pints of Guinness and then we went home. Back in Kennington Fish Bar I bought a battered sausage and Michael bought a massive chicken meal.

I was in Stratford this afternoon and this woman who stank of piss kept following me about. I don't know what it is with me and people that stink of piss. They're in love with me. Next time I see someone that stinks I'm gonna invite them to an Iraq gig.

IN THE ILLUMINATION OF THE CRUISING FOR PENIS GROUND THAT IS INTERNET CITY LTD

November 14th, 2008

03:48 am

I'm here again cos I don't come here often. I have a lot of time on my hands, but time spent on the internet is time ill-spent.

I've written things, don't you worry about that. I've been drinking, be sure not to worry about that. I've even worked out how to mix in new songs with old songs without a blink of the leg from anyone.

I keep hearing sniffing in this internet cafe and it's not me. Just like a long sniff as if it's cocaine or something. That's for them and it's probably poppers. I bet the other hand is wanking. And then he's gonna meet him round in Trafalgar Square, down a dark bit. He's gonna suck him off and then he's gonna put his penis into his anus, lubricant on hand.

Anyway, I'm thinking of a battered sausage and by God, I'm hungry. No battered sausages round here though. On Tuesday night I bought a pack of £1.97 smoked salmon from Tesco's and ate it on the bus. Just fingering each slice out of the plastic and after licking my fingers. I wasn't even pissed but working these hours does this to you.

I tell you what, I've never felt so lucky. Now I'm a full time DJ, all I do in the daylight is go round to charity shops and buy other people's unwanted videos, usually three for £1. Then all twilight I just sit around and watch them. I feel like what Marc Almond sang about in Bedsitter, apart from I'm loaded now. And I'll buy all this exotic food for Michael, like stir-fries in a plastic covering thing. It's mad... I probably owe a lot of money to those that donated to me while I was skint but bloody hell. My life is fucking marvellous, let me tell you.

Sometimes Michael goes mad though, gets sick of my weird sleeping hours and the drink that goes with the job. That place was packed tonight and to see what I do to people, drive them crazy on the dance floor the way I do, well that brings a wry smile to my face.

The owners like me so bloody much that I'm DJing on New Year's Eve. Cos I'm great.

And it's weird cos I don't have time to hold down any friendships but I don't remember having any friends anyway, hardly any... Michael, Father O'Brian... Erm, I'm struggling now.

Michael's decided not to spend Christmas with me. I don't think he likes my family, to be honest. My family are the best though. There's never so much fun to be had. They make me laugh every hour cos weird things happen when I'm with them. Like my Dad pissing through the letterbox, like my sister smashing up someone she thinks is a phoney, like me laying in the road and refusing to move. I reckon it's always fun.

I'm gonna go, buy some fags, a prawn sandwich and watch Smile TV.

BANGING MY HEAD, BEING COVERED IN BLOOD, GETTING HIGH AND GOING TO HOSPITAL

November 19th, 2008

05:32 pm

I came round when the paramedics turned up in their bright uniforms. I was sitting on the settee and blood was pouring from my head. I had no idea what happened. Michael was there in his Bombay mix-stained vest and the female paramedic spoke clearly to me: "You've had a nasty head injury. You've got to come with us in the ambulance".

Then the male paramedic said, "It looks worse than it is cos you've got blonde hair".

I just went along with it all. They gave me something that made me feel nice and high and calm, the same stuff they gave me when I broke my leg. I waited in St Thomas's hospital I found out later. A towel over my head. Then they washed my hair and cut some of it out. I didn't need stitches so I was glad of that. Or superglue. I've been feeling dizzy and forgetful ever since Monday morning when the accident occurred.

I was upset on Sunday evening after getting no text message back from Michael who was out with his ex-girlfriend. So I did what I do terribly and got pissed out of my mind in The Bar on Hanway Street. I heard that at one point I threw my coat down and started to dance. How unusual.

Michael hasn't told me what happened. He said I hit my head on the corner of the bathroom door but he won't give me any more details about my arrival back at the flat. No doubt I was livid with the rage I so often feel when my emotions are wrought because of outside influences.

There's still a load of dried blood in my hair cos it's too painful to wash. I DJ'd last night. It went well. I wore my red trilby with the giant safety pin in.

I've decided to give up the drink when I'm not working. I am not social drinking anymore. I'm a professional drinker. I don't get pissed when I'm working because I'm occupied.

I got some fan mail today. Someone said how much they liked reading this and how they wish they could hang around at my nights with me. That meant a lot to me. So thank you. I'll send you an email back and perhaps I can come and visit you for a few months or so. How would that be?

I'm back in Leytonstonia. The landlord's wife has cooked some proper Pakistani food and says I can have some when I get back. It smells well nice.

I'm DJing tomorrow night but I'm not doing this Friday cos Radio 4 record a show at The Arts every few months. Instead I'm DJing on Tuesday from 6:30-3am. I won't be drinking for the whole time.

INTERNET CITY AND THE PENIS MAFIA

November 28th, 2008

04:04 am

I'm here again and I feel obliged to talk to you. There's no wanking going on in here tonight or sniffing of any kind. It's a Thursday morning and a man is sweeping up around me. The people in here look like homesick foreigners. Well I dearly hope they get home for Christmas.

I saw my Mother off today. She's the best person ever. I know I went wrong in a lot of ways but it was never her fault. I messed up cos of my alcoholic father. The devout Christian that is my Mother has nothing to do with my downfall.

It was packed tonight in the club. Read back if you want to come along. I'm DJing tonight 7pm-11pm if you're absolutely desperate to see me. Otherwise fuck off.

I had a good night. I was wearing this really wonderful outfit. I won't bother describing it cos if you can't be bothered to be there then what's the point?

I went to see Hairspray on Wednesday night with my Mum. It was alright. I like my Mum and am looking forward to a roast dinner. I am especially looking forward to the Christmas pudding being set alight. My sister, Anne, will turn the dining room lights off and the room will go dark and then my Mum will hold the Christmas pudding while me and my sister will go, "OOOOhhhhhhhhhh". Then we'll watch telly for a bit. Then I'll wanna find my Dad in a pub and get pissed with him, then I won't be able to find him and then I'll give up on everything and then I'll start to cry like I've got no future anywhere, or something.

Twelve minutes left on this computer. My Mother asked me if I've got a long-term plan. She means to say that The Soho Arts Club is very strange to employ me. Perhaps they want someone younger? That will play the modern records that are in the charts... I tried to buy a chart single yesterday. Zavvi. Then HMV. They don't do singles anymore. I'm not bothered though. I did want that record though, that one from the Clarks advert. Not feeling adverse about anything though. Just happy, depressed, high, euphoric, depressed, sad, lonely, popular, strange, thoughtful, confused, manic, high, lonely, depressed, confused.................................

A BODY BAG FOR CHRISTMAS

December 17th, 2008

04:10 pm

I've been sitting in McDonald's in Leytonstone for an hour. Just watching things go past the window while eating a quarter pounder with cheese meal. I really like that McDonald's, it's so plush.

There's all these great things about Leytonstone, like The Sacred Heart shop that sells everything Catholic. There's two black women in there that are constantly saying Hail Marys together. Even when I buy something, they don't stop. Today I bought a Virgin Mary ring and eighteen Virgin Mary stickers.

Last night I DJ'd to a packed club. Tuesday night and you couldn't move in there. I think more people are going out now they know they're about to lose everything.

The fair in Leicester Square reminds me of happier days. Yesterday I had a dream I was in New York and everything was exciting and new again and I was happy.

I think I might disconnect myself from the world again. Try my best not to speak to anyone or see "Friends".

Last night I went to The Immaculate Conception Catholic church for a carol service with The Catholic Young Adults in London group. I went for a drink after with a Masters in Physics student. She was nice. Nicer than anyone I've met for about a decade.

CLEAN AND EASY TO SERVE, YOU DON'T NEED FORKS ANYMORE

December 26th, 2008

11:23 pm

I've got no time for all this me.

I bet you're all dying to know about my Christmas and how my Dad pissed through the letter box and how my sister beat someone up and how I lay down in the middle of the road shouting for the next car to kill me. None of that happened. My Dad has sat in the pub at the end of the road for most of the time and does so even when it's not Christmas. Every time I go out of the house and down the road I wave at him through the window. Sometimes he sees me, sometimes he stares at nothing, deep in depressed thought about God knows what. I joined him there on Christmas Day for an hour while Mum was cooking the dinner. I bought three sherries to which the landlord exclaimed, "I haven't sold a sherry in two years!"
"It's the in thing now. It's well in fashion in London," was my hip reply. Is it though? I like it. Reminds me of school days when I'd drink half a bottle before registration then escape to Werneth Park at 9:15 to drink two litres of White Lightning, all carried in my pink and purple Head sports bag.

Back to my Dad then. By him in the pub was an Aldi bag containing a can of processed garden peas, one tenth of a jar of crushed Ritz biscuits, some cheese and a can of evaporated milk. He said it was his hamper from his "ex-housekeeper". Anyway, he was happy with his lot and told me how he had a chicken boiling in the slow cooker. It would be done by the time the drink was done with. I wish I had that plan instead of the fried chicken plan whenever I get half cut.

I got back in time for the Queen's Speech. She didn't have my Christmas card up again this year. Perhaps it could have been in the back room. I'm sending one to that Princess Diana lookalike next year if I'm still here. I might be in with a chance of getting one back from her.

The dinner was lovely, made by my wonderful Mum. Anne lit the Christmas pudding and we turned the lights off and everyone went "Ooooooh". But the blue flame wouldn't go out, but then it was alright cos it did eventually.

I went to sleep on the settee after and just spent the rest of the time gazing sadly at the TV thinking about all the downfalls of late.

Y'know things come to an end. My job as a DJ may be wrecked, the addiction is killing me and I don't have that much money anymore.

But I'm not in Sudan, a walking skeleton trying to find water. I'm not on heroin or crack shitting myself in Falconberg Court. I'm not pregnant and I don't have AIDS so maybe things are alright after all.

TCP, CHIPS AND PROPER CANCER PATIENTS

January 9th, 2009

05:07 am

I heard about a ghost down my club and there's a lot of them cos I've seen them. I know most of you that read this don't believe in life after death. I can't wait to haunt you. Tonight I got my pendulum out. It's not one of those dodgy star ones cos that would mean I'm into Satanism and I hate all that stuff. No. So I asked the ghost a few questions and it went mad down there. Kept swinging madly and my fingers kept going stone cold. I know it's cold out but it was warm in there.

Anyway so it said it was a man but I didn't really know what else to ask it, but it kept saying that it wanted to tell me something. Left right, circle circle and all that kind of stuff. I gave up, too confused to carry on.

Every time I DJ when it's empty I see a shadow by the DJ booth holding a drink and it's like the shadow is asking for another. The bar used to be where the DJ booth is y'see. Anyway, I've got nowt more to say about it.

On New Year's Day I had my palm read. The woman said I didn't have much longer to live but I could change all that if only I could change my life. Well, some things are easier said than done.

My brother can't be arsed to appear to me to tell me I'm doing everything wrong, and if he can't be arsed to do that then I can't be arsed to do owt right. Does that make sense?

Maybe the childhood trauma will never leave me. Huh huh. Bollocks. I was never that close to him anyway. After all he never wanted to hang around me, even though he was ten years older. Maybe we all suffer from each others' traumas. Michael for mine, me for his and so on and so on and Soho. We all suffer from Soho if it gets you first.

I'm in that internet cafe again. The gay fuck place. However, the place is empty and silent. All I can hear are my own fingers on this cum-injected stiff keyboard.

I went to Ilford the day before yesterday. What a wonderful place Ilford is. I ended up in a cafe called Noah's Ark. Cheese and ham omelette, chips and beans and a cup of tea as always. "A warm and happy place." That's what the menu said. And well, it was. Once again, I was surrounded by cripples and the smell of TCP. This time the cripples on crutches looked like they actually had cancer or were dying of something terminal. Fantastic, I'm in the exact right place methinks. I feel better within myself already. Wonderful. Absolutely bloody wonderful. I feel warm and happy methinks; these are people that make me feel better methinks.

So apart from speaking to the dead and watching Sky TV and getting absolutely pissed every other night, I've not been up to much.

MY BAND PLAYS LAST GIG. METRO THURSDAY. 9PM.

January 18th, 2009

04:29 am

Here I am, writing from a place that will be dust in two weeks' time. All these places that I wrote about and all the places that I go on about in such a way I hate will be gone, taken up for some Crossrail link in the middle of Soho.

It's too late now. I didn't even bother to sign any petitions; think I signed one about The Astoria but I knew the jury had won. Knew those pathetic women with their scoop neck jumpers and their dirty fuckin trainers worn on the tube had won this war. I knew there was nothing I could do to save owt. Even if me and Michael had strangled the planners on the street, the Starbucks, Champagne Bar, Disneyland, Ann Summers, We Are Not Paedophiles, We Love Americans, Kill Soho for Protection and Gap people would come and kill everything.

The place where I am, it stinks of dead rats but fuckinhell I love it that way. It's well much better than that cum-stained keyboard five minutes down Charing Cross Road.

They say they're gonna pull down my rehearsal rooms as well. I heard The 12 Bar's going too but no one's got any proper confirmation.

Let's move on. Yeah, so easy to say. Too easy to say. Can you name a place that will welcome me in this part of town? You can put your finger up your arse and start moving it if you think I'd be seen dead in places like New Cross, Stoke Newington, Camden and all those other places that house people like you in the vicinity. I want centre of the city action. I want to move alongside prostitutes and the insane. I'll stick here until I die. Just like those old men that stick to a Walkabout pub just cos it was their favourite in their day. Everything's gone. And soon it will be me.

PURCHASING A GLOW-IN-THE-DARK PLACE IN HEAVEN

January 20th, 2009

04:28 pm

That gig went well. It was amazing. There was definitely something about The Metro. Being on that stage was so relaxing. I felt like I was singing on a cruise ship. Like being a Gene Pitney impersonator. Well it's a shame it's all gone now.

The 12 Bar and Enterprise aren't closing so that's alright then. I asked the man.

Back in Leytonstone my favourite shop is closing. The Catholic shop in the High Road, the one that's just packed with everything Catholic. Glow-in-the-dark Mary and Jesus statues, holographic pictures of Bible scenes, medals, Holy water, anointing oil, prayer books, 1970s birthday cards, bangles and even Communion wine and wafers.
The black woman that works in there just sits in a chair saying the Rosary.
I said, "It's a shame you're closing".
She goes, "It's a shame, it's a shame, it's a shame, it's a shame, it's a shame......"
It went on. She just kept saying it. So I said, "It's a shame".
This must have gone on for about five minutes. It was a bit like saying one of those Catholic prayers, just repeating like that. It was nice not having to think about what to say.
Eventually she said the Holy Mother had told them to close because of the recession. I thought she meant THE Holy Mother as in The Blessed Virgin but then I got the gist she was talking about the nun who ran the shop.

I eventually bought some postcards that depict Jesus with blonde hair and a six-pack. He looks quite erotic. The shop's last day will be on 15th February so I'll be in before then to catch some glow-in-the-dark bargains.

I went to Matalan after and bought Michael some Pierre Cardin underpants.

A ONE-WOMAN PROTEST AGAINST CROSSRAIL

February 16th, 2009

03:02 am

Just come out of the casino. Those bright lights and endless taps seem to drag me into constant desire. Michael had enough. Chucked all my stuff on the landing after another twenty-four hour drinking "binge". I'd call it more of a yearning.

And that was Thursday. I just left my stuff on the landing and slept with my boots and leather jacket on, only to get undressed, washed and made-up when The Arts Club DJing called me to do so.

I've been rehearsing tonight. Got a bit sidetracked and kept looking into the liquid amber remembering my dream last night: my brother was worried and telling my sister that I was about to die on the streets through drinking too much. It doesn't inspire too much surprise within my soul. I've been worried about my death for about a fortnight, much more worried than I usually am. This drinking seems to happen on a Tuesday and goes straight through to Thursday at 4am. 4am is the time it ends. Anyway, I'd say I'm not bothered but the dreams of my brother caring for me worry me slightly. He's dead y'know?

Michael told me to come home, that he had a venison pie cooked for me, but I just couldn't. I feel so alone. It's terrible that I hang around casinos but I feel alright at the same time in these places; flashing lights, constant refreshment, no day and no night. It's like a nice kind of purgatory. Catholic. Y'know? Everything's awful but something keeps me hanging on, asking for more coffee, more sandwiches, more tea, a Ginster's steak slice, a tub of Ben & Jerry's Phish Food. A place where everything's available but where you don't have to have any friends.

And Michael is left worrying about me at all hours. Sick of my stupid ways. I can't blame him. I can't write about my personal life here. I haven't got a gambling addiction. I just like the lights, the coffee and the food and have done for about a year. I've tried gambling but always lost. My alcohol addiction is enough.

For all of you out there that went on about how sad it was about The Astoria getting knocked down, I lay down in front of one of the pneumatic drills on Wednesday 4th February. I stopped the whole road. I was pissed out of my mind, think it was 9:30am. I could be dead. But here I am...

I'm barred from Carphone Warehouse opposite the casino. Apparently I went in there just before The Astoria incident and wrecked a display of phones. Then I shouted, "Try and sell me something! Go on sell me something now!"
I know I'm definitely barred cos I had a go at going in there the other morning but was stopped by security and so I ran.

I don't think my life is going downhill or that the alcohol is dragging me into oblivion. I'm just doing the things that unconsciously you all want to do. If I did it without the alcohol it would be deemed as madness immediately, but the alcohol covers my real intentions and so I'm saved but led to sudden death.

I enjoyed it. I very much loved it.

SIR TREVOR McDONALD WAS A BIT DULL

March 11th, 2009

05:17 am

I'm in that cum-soaked internet cafe again on Charing Cross Road. DJ'd. All went well. Played the records I'd been meaning to play. Got people chucked out who I didn't like the look of. Got people to stick around for hours who I liked as people. They did their usual human activities: snogging, dancing, talking and the like.
I didn't talk to them though. Always keep a distance from the people I'm working for.

Went to Terminal 5 the other morning. Saw it on the telly when it opened and thought it might have a 24 hour bar or pub. It did. Sat there for a few hours drinking pints of Amstel and going to a special smokers' paradise at half-hour intervals. Ended up talking to some prematurely wrinkled drag-type queen about her "Alburn" hair. Even met Trevor McDonald cos an Addison Lee cab had a placard for him. It even said "Sir" on. Just stood and watched when he got the cab. Couldn't be arsed with conversation. Was all a bit dull. The whole day of it.
Got fish and chips after.

Rehearsed on Sunday. As usual. Afterwards went to 23 Romilly Street. That's what they call the new Colony. Went there when I first moved to London though. 2003. When it was called "The Green Room". Huh huh… Not original. No wonder they've just kept it as 23 Romilly Street. Someone there was saying they'd read my previous diary. Well done. I always knew that was a work of sheer genius.
"I read it from beginning to end. You're a genius." Well it doesn't take a genius to work out what I am, but it might take a bastard to work out how much money they could make from me.

I sat in yesterday and the day before. Just sleeping and talking to myself. Watching telly. Reading a bit. The kind of stuff I do when I'm not drinking.

SAINT GEORGE, THE BEATLES AND PAKISTANI TAXI DRIVERS

March 23rd, 2009

10:18 am

I've been keeping my thoughts to myself lately. But then today I thought, what good is that?

So back in Oldham where all life begins, I feel a bit more peaceful about things. E.T. is by my side again and telling me what I should do. He is always right.

Last night my sister took me and my Mum to see a Beatles tribute band called Semolina Pilchards. Y'know, like the lyric. I'd seen them before on one of my many trips to the homeland. This time the venue was a bit like a WMC. But it wasn't. My sister said it had recently been renovated. The clientele were mostly National Front. They were all wearing those nylon bomber jackets with light blue denim jeans and red DMs. On the right-hand back pocket was the flag of Saint George. They had on various propaganda T-shirts. One had the slogan "Vote BNP". They didn't seem a bad bunch though but I was a bit worried about them mistaking me for a Pole.

They weren't there for the band. They just hang out in that place anyway all the time. I don't think they like The Beatles but all that peace and love can get a bit tiresome so I can understand that. The music in between was the best Northern Soul music played by one of the NF DJs. I go to a lot of Northern Soul nights in the Camden area with Michael. We do that on Sunday nights. But this man's selection was the best I had heard.

I fell asleep during the band cos I had been up since 1pm on Saturday and by this time it was 9:30pm Sunday. I heard it in my sleep though and it was nice.
I was too tired to follow my Mum's idea of getting two buses home.

The cold was biting and I could barely stand through exhaustion. We ended up ordering a taxi, a luxury unheard of if buses are still running round here. The taxi driver was a lovely Pakistani man who told us of the different parts of Werneth he had been living in for the past twenty-five years. He was comical too. Then he gave us lots of money-off vouchers for his taxi firm.

I'll be here until Thursday so expect more from me. I'm going to put my cheque in the bank now. It's nice to come back to the homeland loaded and successful.

SAUSAGES AND A SEVENTY-EIGHT-YEAR-OLD CROSS-DRESSER

April 20th, 2009

05:21 pm

I DJ'd at that new place on Holloway Road called The Gaff on Saturday night. It was a man's fortieth birthday party. You couldn't move in there though and I found it hard to believe how one man could be so popular. Maybe he's nice. I played rock and roll and punk but I did slip in Elton John's Crocodile Rock for his older relatives. People looked at me in dismay so I crouched behind the DJ booth and waited for it to end. I think I went back to some Lonnie Donegan after that.

Yesterday I rehearsed. I was wearing my red snakeskin trousers and Michael's Clash T-shirt. I feel the part if I look the part. Today I'm wearing a cardigan my Nan knitted. I still feel the part but in a teetotal way.

I popped into The Coach after. One of my acquaintances said something that insinuated I was thick so after going for a piss I disappeared out the back door and made my way to 23 Romilly Street. They had some entertainment on and I bought a Newkie Brown. "Do you want a glass?" No. I can get more in my mouth if I swig from the bottle and that's my aim.

I had only had a bowl of Special K all day so I went round and ate all the sausages and sausage rolls. Then I went upstairs and ate all the Pringles. I tried to get in The French after I had my fill but the man with the beard had decided I had well and truly had my fill so wouldn't serve me. Why didn't I realise? I thought. Molly Moggs. Perfect. That's the drag queen bar on Charing Cross Road. So off I goes. Another blonde Bet Lynch-type queen was singing the usual. A pint of Kronenbourg for me and the tragedy of life for everyone else.

I stood at the bar swaying and joining in. A seventy-eight-year-old cross-dresser and his wife stood nearby. They looked like they had been through a lot. He told me they had.

I stayed until closing time then went to McDonald's for a quarter pounder. I then flagged down a taxi and returned to Kennington. I walked past that pub The Doghouse and heard someone calling my name. It was my old Soho friend, Colleen. She was with Dave Ball from Soft Cell. We sat outside and I told her about the sausages and The French and then we tore Soho apart. "They're all bitter." "And what does anyone actually do?" etc, etc.

I was on top form with my endless anecdotes and fantastic wit and Dave was cracking up saying I should do stand up. Some people don't get it though.

I went back to my lovely Michael and to bed and was thankful I will never belong in Soho.

I LIKE YOU BECAUSE YOU'RE LIKE ME. YOU THINK TOO MUCH IS NEVER ENOUGH

May 26th, 2009

04:10 pm

This is one of my favourite pubs in Kennington. I only ever go to this one when it's 11am. I know I won't be on my own but I also know there will only be two or three other alcoholics in the pub. It's called The Black Prince and has the aroma of bleach. A smell I now associate with my early morning drinking sessions.

I went back to AA cos I didn't want to lose Michael. It was still as depressing as all the other meetings I've been to so needless to say I didn't go back and after six days sober I jumped off the wagon and woke up on the tube with a joint of raw meat. I think it was lamb or beef. The tube was pretty empty so I just threw it up and down like a ball. When I'd sobered up, the smell of the meat kept coming back to me and I couldn't eat anything for two days because of it.

Blackpool was nice two months ago. I have been meaning to write about Blackpool since then. I'd been out in Manchester all night with Nat and James and I woke up still pissed. It's bad that, cos that always means I wake up wanting a drink. So I got off the settee, put another layer of make-up on and got a £13 day return to Blackpool from Piccadilly. I drank coffee on the train and sat opposite a deaf and dumb girl. I tried to make conversation otherwise I would never have known. It was lucky for her that morning that she was deaf and dumb. Y'know what I'd be going on about. DJing, clubs, Wurlitzer organs, Bet Lynch, y'know.

The tower grew closer and closer and my stomach turned with excitement as it does whenever I see that great structure.

I went to the ballroom first. It was packed in there and all I could smell was tea and toasted teacakes. It was 1pm and a ballroom dancing party from Pontins were having an afternoon tea dance. I ordered a pint of Kronenbourg for £2.80 which I thought was very reasonable for such decadent surroundings. I sat at a table at the back near the bar and just watched the dancers. It was all synchronised. You couldn't just get up and have a go. You had to know the dance. Anyway I was sitting mesmerised for ten minutes just thinking about how lucky I was to be hanging around there on a Wednesday afternoon then an old couple from Birkenhead join me. They were at Pontins as well y'see. We have a chat about the old days and how he used to leave his wife in a pub so men could buy her drinks while he went on a crawl. That way he didn't have to spend too much. Cool I thought. I wondered if he thought that was what my man was up to. This couple weren't too good on their legs so I went and got them their tea and sandwiches.

"That's a man y'know?" I pointed to a transvestite on the floor. "Never," the woman replied. The trannies were funny though. One was dressed as a schoolgirl although she couldn't have been a day younger than fifty. But they knew all the sequences. The big organ came up as it does in The Tower Ballroom. I forgot all about that so when it came up I had tears in my eyes. Of happiness, mind. The drink gets me all emotional sometimes. But most of the time the drink is the only thing that makes me feel any emotion so when I feel emotion like the rest of you it's always a good sign. I'm still human.

After three hours sitting in the ballroom I thought it was time to go and get some more drink in less decadent surroundings. I chose Whittles, a favourite of my Dad's. My Dad is never wrong about where he chooses to drink. Me and my Mum left him in there last time we were in Blackpool so we could say prayers in the church opposite.

Anyway, in this pub I met another old couple from Preston. She was drinking sherry in this tiny ornate glass so I decided to follow. With another pint of Kronenbourg, mind. We talked about stuff.

Blackpool tower and Bet Lynch. The woman gave me a Polaroid of herself. No, not that dirty kind you're thinking. Just of her sitting nicely in the pub with a sherry. She put her phone number on the back and said I should call for a chat. I've tried calling that number numerous times in the two months since but it just rings. Old people like getting out during the day though and that's the only time I have owt to say.

A man joined who claimed he was gay and then said he wanted to be dominated. There was something quite dark about him. Grey skin, black eyes, y'know the sort. Smelt a bit weird too.

Time to go, no more drink. Always be aware of your surroundings and the people you're with when you're drinking to excess. I took a taxi to Harry Ramsden's on the seafront and had a lovely fish 'n' chip dinner. Bread and butter. Cup of tea. Lovely it was but then while I was eating, a sense of loneliness kicked in. The sky grew dark and I knew it was time to return home to my family. I left the restaurant and walked back to the train station. Through a deserted, cold, out of season Blackpool. Back up Talbot Road where the day had begun with such hope. I was hoping I'd find the peace I seek each day in Blackpool. I dream of Blackpool and think about retiring there often. I was disappointed I didn't find much.

WETHERSPOON'S IS NOT A PUB YOU'D SPEND A DAY IN BUT IT'S OK FOR FOUR OR FIVE PINTS IN THE MORNING

June 8th, 2009

01:01 pm

I had to wait ten minutes for this computer in Leytonstone Library so enjoy it while you can.

I started in Wetherspoon's at 9:30am. Met some of my regular drinkers. We talked about Ireland and voting BNP. Mind you, I voted Conservative in this election.

Got my cards read by my friend Bea last night. It was foreseen that drinking will not be the death of me so that's all alright then. I shall drink more tonight.

An Irish in Wetherspoon's said that women are all after the same thing. Money. I wouldn't mind some. I didn't do cloakroom yesterday so am well skint.

DISCOVER THE WORLD OF REAL ALE
DISCOVER THE LAND OF WHISKY

With slogans bandied around the place like that it's no wonder I'm an alcoholic.

"You're twenty-seven. You should have worked out what you're gonna do by now," said the Irish named Mick. I still can't work out what I'm gonna do.

I go to Wetherspoon's and I always reckon I'm gonna bump into my father. I miss my Dad. For his mistakes I have paid the price. I think I rang him up yesterday. I don't know though. I was so pissed.

This is beginning to sound like an epitaph. "Scarlet, She Liked A Drink."

I've run out of money though and that's why I'm here in the library writing this to the likes of you... I spent it all on gambling and drink. It's weird though. Whenever I'm out on one of my sessions I never meet a woman. I feel alone in that capacity. There's no woman I've met in twenty-seven years that is addicted to drink like me. Maybe they do it privately. What's the point in that? My addiction has never been private. Since it began I loved those three words: "I'M AN ALCOHOLIC". How can I write this well when I'm three sheets to the fucking wind? I have no fucking idea.

PUDDING, CHIPS AND GRAVY

June 21st, 2009

10:09 pm

I'm back in Oldham. I'm enjoying it very much and have just been to the chippy. I got special fried rice. Tomorrow I shall go to the chippy again and I'm going to have pudding, chips and gravy.

On Tuesday I am going to Blackpool. I shall write properly in the next few days.

BOOKS THAT I'VE READ THAT WILL ALWAYS STICK TO ME

August 5th, 2009

07:33 am

Taken from Aug Stone

Escort
Mayfair
Razzle
Penthouse
Essex Babes
Northern Birds

Erm, it's 25 to 8 and I can't be arsed… Gonna find somewhere to spend my casino winnings…

AN ALIEN, THE PROMS AND THE POLICE

September 1st, 2009

03:41 pm

I had to write an email to my drummer today asking him to leave Iraq. I'd threatened to do this for a while cos the whole band were receiving up to eight texts a day about him being a spy for MI5. It was getting ridiculous. Anyway, the texts and calls didn't stop coming so we decided enough was enough. If anyone is a drummer and would like to join my highly successful band, Iraq then feel free to call or text.

I went to The Proms on Wednesday evening. It was Strauss and Mozart. I was all alone but I didn't mind. Things are more exciting when you're alone. Anything could happen. Nothing did though. I just listened and drank Coca Cola. Afterwards I waited for the bus to take me back into The West End. I'd left one of my E.T.s at my club the night before y'see and needed to collect him. I saw a white Mercedes 1983 parked near the bus stop. It looked so lovely, like a car I would drive. I just kept staring. Wow, it was amazing!

I got stopped in Soho by one of those talent scouts looking for extras and stuff. I always get stopped by them. It's all a bit pointless. I'm not into extra work. I have enough on my plate. Anyway, I collected the alien, Alfie is his name, and then I whispered to him that we would have a nightcap in The Phoenix. Down there we sat and drank Kronenbourg, then some of my acquaintances joined. Then the vicar from Saint Anne's came in. I like him. I told him how the story of E.T. was the story of The Resurrection re-told.

I wasn't supposed to go back to my club but I did. I took The Phoenix with me. It was karaoke night. Anyway, I can't go into too much detail about what happened next but my friend lost her bag so we went back to hers cos we thought her neighbour might let her in. Unfortunately they didn't and then the police were called. I showed

Alfie to the policeman. They sent two cars y'see but in one car the policemen looked a bit bored. Anyway, they were about to arrest me and take Alfie to the experimentation labs when we made a run for it. I hailed a black cab round the corner on Bond Street and off I was. My alien and me were safe. Alfie doesn't want to go on any more nights out though. It was a bit much.

LIVER FUNCTION TEST, ALARM BELLS AND A BELIEF IN GOD

September 16th, 2009

05:18 am

I went to the doctor's today and asked for a liver function test. She asked how much I drank. I answered, six pints of lager and a bottle of wine. On a quiet night.

My birthday's coming up. I'm gonna have it in Wetherspoon's at 9am on a Sunday. No one ever turns up, so this time none of you will. My birthday symbolises a point in my life and now it's come to this.

The oriental doctor said I had another sixty to eighty years left. Wow! That'll do me. But I haven't been for the test yet. I've got to fast y'see. Like Ramadan. Brings me closer to God and lets them know how close I am to death.

Yesterday I went to Southend. A hotel close to the sea serves all pints at £2 a piece. The fire alarm went off as I arrived but it didn't bother me. At that price who can complain? Everyone else walked out cos it went on for twenty minutes. I just sat there looking out at the sea and sipping my lager. I love it when things go wrong. Like when everything's supposed to be calm and then wooo wooo wooo wooo wooo wooo wooo wooo wooo wooo wooo for twenty wonderful minutes. I think it might have even been thirty. I didn't care.

Before that I had been in The Wetherspoon's. It's an old Post Office and a postman dangles from the ceiling in a burlesque-esque pose. A man that looked exactly like Truman Capote propped up the bar alone and everything seemed like a glammed up Blackpool. I thought about getting a hotel. I don't quite have the money for that yet, so thought better of it. Why not spend all the money on champagne?

And so there I sat in Wetherspoon's with my £35 bottle of Moët. Oh the glamour sidled with depression was wonderful! I should have just taken the train to the end of that pier and jumped.

Instead I returned to London. Went to Stratford Gala Bingo Hall and had a game. A few to be precise. Didn't win. Then I got chucked out for being pissed. I'd finished my games though so all was well and I didn't feel bad about them. They were Jamaicans and I don't mind Jamaicans too much cos they all seem quite cheerful. I went back to Leytonstone and drank some Communion wine that I had bought from the Sacred Heart Shop on The High Road a week previous. It brought me closer to God and I prayed. And everything seemed alright again.

Now I'm in 11 Charing Cross Road with the gays. I'm drinking Fanta Fruit Twist and in the next few minutes I shall return to Leytonstone and join Wetherspoon's for four hours.

MUSEUM OF THE UNIVERSE, CORAL ISLAND AND THE BLACKPOOL CATHOLIC CLUB

November 9th, 2009

01:40 pm

I went for my liver function test this morning. It's one of those NHS walk-in clinics where they take your blood. I was number 50. I walked in at number 4. I knew it would be a hassle. I was really in the mood for a drink after but had a fry-up instead and a cup of tea in Wetherspoon's.

I asked the yellow man who's always in there if he'd had the results for his liver function test yet. He said they didn't get back to him. Perhaps he should get in touch with the patron saint of hopeless causes. I think that's Saint Anthony.

I've just looked up the symptoms of liver disease. I have a few of them. I'll be shocked if they tell me there is no damage. I'm hoping they tell me there's a bit of damage and that I have to stop drinking cos then I will. And then I'll write more and then I'll have more money and then I'll be able to get into designing my home and buying more E.T.s. Once you've been to Ikea or Harveys The Furniture Store a few times then what do you do? See, you can't drink. Well, I soon won't be able to. I visit museums and read books on my days off from the alcohol but I do get a bit bored with all that. I'll write this journal a bit more perhaps. I'm just thinking about the gap. All that time. What on earth will I do? I'll miss all those wasted hours.

Anyway, perhaps by some miracle they will tell me there is no damage and that I'm fit and all that, but I doubt it. I very much doubt it. I'll carry on as I am if that's the case.

My birthday party at The Arts consisted of two fights between my friends that don't get on. I knew that would happen and I quite enjoyed sitting down and not speaking, just watching it all blow up. I did a couple of karaoke songs. Then the taxi driver on the way home was arrested for not having a licence. It was all ideal.

After my birthday I went home for a few days. The highlight was Blackpool. Ten years ago I jumped the train to Blackpool cos I didn't feel like going to work. I went into the alien museum and the owner told me everything I needed to know about the universe and the human soul. It fascinated me but I was still quite young. In the past few months I started to think about what he had said to me all those years ago and so my main aim in Blackpool was to seek that man out in the alien museum. I did just that. He was now running The Doctor Who Museum but his other museum was round the corner. He opened it up especially for me. If you ever go to Blackpool you need to see this man. His museum is called The Museum of The Universe. I'd been studying a lot in these last three years about the New World Order, 2012 and supernatural phenomena. These subjects are quite vast but on my days off from public houses and public life in general I sit in my bed reading. I was speaking to the man for about an hour when he said, "You rang me up today didn't you?" He seemed to think that I'd booked an appointment with him but he didn't mind and just carried on telling me about everything that's going on and everything that is about to happen. At 2pm I decided to go because I wanted to check out the pubs and y'know there's nothing better than a Blackpool sunset. I thanked him very much for his time and told him I'd put a word in for him on Channel 200. I'm eternally grateful to that man.

The first pub I went to was called "Uncle Peter's". I just love that name. My Dad's called Peter y'see. It was nice just looking out at South Pier. Some rap music was on, which I'd kind of expect. Then Bing Crosby came on and the rain drove heavily against the windows and everything seemed perfect. Just for that song though. So after that I drank my half pint and walked to the next pub which was a sports bar. This place was terrible. Three men stood about, a bit like they do in gay bars in the afternoons, but these men weren't homosexuals. You can just tell y'know. I ended up with a pint in there cos in Blackpool the reoccurring phrase when asking the barman for a half was, "It's cheaper to buy a pint y'know?" Well, go on then. I wasn't planning to, mind, but I may as well now. I'm only here for the day hopefully.

The rain still drove at the seafront windows and they had some awful TV station called "Viva" on the various screens. There's nothing I hate more than TVs in pubs. Wetherspoon's ones are alright cos the sound is always down. I left a quarter of the pint, not wanting to be put through the latest Cheryl Cole single.

I regretted walking into the next joint. It said Karaoke Bar on the front and it looked pretty colourful from the outside. Inside it was all cold neon and loud gangster rap music. There must be quite a scene for rap music in Blackpool nowadays. I couldn't just walk out again. It was a bit unnerving but I walked to the bar and got my plastic half pint. I think there too it was cheaper for a pint but believe me, this was no place for a leisurely drink. The men were dangerous looking. All in their fifties in long black coats and gold jewellery. It was all a bit odd. I noticed a pole. Anyway, I just sat in a corner and drank up.

After that I was in the mood for the grandeur of the ballroom. I thought for a fiver it would save me anymore awkwardness. And Kronenbourg in there is only £2.80 a pint. This time however the BBC were doing some kind of filming and it was £12 to get in. I didn't bother and went to a pub called The Mitre round the corner. All the time I was trying to get into various bars and pubs which were closed for the season's end.

I sat down with my £3.26 pint of Kronenbourg. Four men sat on the table further along the bench. Old women with plastic laundry bags with pictures of Blackpool tower huddled together at the other end. Silence was upon this place. Maybe it was me. I began to tear my nails off before I realised what I was doing. Silence. £3.26. I actually should have got a half in here, I thought. It was £4.50 for a four-pint pitcher in the "karaoke bar". I eventually piped up with, "Are the illuminations still on?" A small conversation was eventually achieved but there was a sense of unease and so I left. Start again. And what am I actually attempting to find? The Blackpool of Bet Lynch, that is always what I'm attempting by these trips.

There's a pub opposite North Pier I think. I drank a £1.99 pint of something or other and wrote notes in my moleskine notebook. Y'know the kind of stuff you write when you've had a few. Something about a Turner sky, the ghost of Gene Pitney and a deflated birthday girl balloon blowing behind the red velvet curtains. Which it was. Then I watched the starlings migrate. Y'know, when they turn and dive and more and more gather and they're just flocking about so gracefully and it's like one black mass of a wave, and the sun was setting and I drank my pint and watched and that worked for me. I felt something, an emotion of some kind but I couldn't quite think about how I felt. It was something vague, but at least it was something.

When the sun had gone and the lights had come on I made my way to more pubs and attempted communication with people. None of it worked. The drink was making me feel uneasy and nervous and after The Blackpool Catholic Club I decided to call it a day. Drinkwise.

I walked along the seafront and popped in to see Gypsy Petulengro. They're the famous family. She didn't tell me anything that amazing, just to keep away from married men. I was confused about that cos I haven't got any interest in married men. I do look like a bit of a good time though. I suppose she might have got that from the red lipstick and glamorous outfit.

After that I went for pie, chips, mushy peas and gravy at Coral Island. I enjoyed that but felt a bit forlorn and melancholy as well as drunk. I walked past a place where bingo was 10p a game. I went in for that. The place was full of cripples and mobility scooters. Everyone looked terrible. This was more of the Blackpool that I was looking for. None of my numbers came up so I called it a loss after 20p and walked back through the lights, up Talbot Road and onto the train home.

WHAT JOB ARE YOU LOOKING FOR?

November 30th, 2009

03:08 pm

I was writing to my pen pal the other day. I spent most of the letter complaining about various things: my gig cancellation, getting sacked from Bloomsbury Bowling Lanes, drunk people, having to wait ages at the hospital, people that don't bother getting a job. I just went on. This was a two-thousand word epistle so it wasn't all doom and gloom. I got a letter from him in the middle of writing about various things that he would like to do when he gets to London.

I got so bored the other week, sitting round with a group of people and not saying a word. I suppose all these people have been to a university where they learn how to debate. I can never get a word in with those sort but with the banality of their conversation neither would I want to. I feel so nervous with groups nowadays. Not my rock band though, we all get on like a house on fire. My drummer has strained her hands though so is having a course of physiotherapy. We still rehearse though. I'm writing the best stuff I've ever written although the stuff I wrote ten years ago was borderline genius but now I feel I've moved into a new realm. But y'know, you've got to get out of bed in the morning and make yourself do it.

Iraq rehearsed yesterday in the room of death at Enterprise Studios in Denmark Place. Room number 11 is in the basement. There have been four mysterious deaths in that room in the last five years and one disappearance. Well, most of them died through heart attacks, one of them was twenty-one, the other was twenty-seven. Perhaps that room is popular with cocaine use, I dunno. The disappearance happened when one of them turned right down the corridor outside and was never seen again. Well, perhaps he just quit the band but they were all good friends and knew each others' families. I didn't find out how the other one died cos people started getting their equipment at that time. There's a plague pit underneath that room as well. Well, I'm sure it's quite a few feet under the room.

I wasn't affected by any of this and we managed to write three new songs. Mind over matter and all that.

People hate me more than they used to nowadays. I think it's my drinking. I'm not drunk today and I'm not hungover. Monday is usually my day for sobriety. I feel completely on edge on days like this. My heart feels all churned up and excited. I feel like I want to do a cross country run. Not that I'd bother with that.

PORN, PG TIPS, PENS AND PAPER

December 8th, 2009

02:01 pm

I've not spoken to anyone for two days now. Well, apart from myself. I organised it to be this way. I've grown sick and tired of just about everyone and their menial problems.

I'm in Leytonstone Library. It's as hot as a nursing home in here. I'm going to be visiting an old person in a home in Streatham soon. I might opt for somewhere closer though. It's nice round here.

I sent a Christmas card to The Queen this morning. It's so great, that. In the second week of January, just when you think she's forgotten, she sends you a letter back saying how much she liked getting your card. Soon's I see the envelope with the Queen's stamp on it on my "Go Away" mat, a flurry of excitement runs through. I even got an invite to Royal Ascot this year. I think she's trying to branch out to me. Who knows what kind of invite she'll send me this year.

I'm DJing tonight. Would any of you lot like to do me a compilation CD? I don't have the facility to download anything or that kind of knowledge. I don't even have a cameraphone. I'm still using a cassette Walkman. My needs are simple. Wetherspoon's, porn, PG Tips, Iceland ready meals (not exceeding £1), pens and paper.

Last night I just lay on my bed. 5pm. Then I fell asleep during the news. I have to watch the telly with the sound down though because of the interference. I woke up at midnight and wrote a letter to my pen pal about astral travel. Then I listened to the radio till 4:30am. Just flicking channels, trying to find something, I don't know what.

I couldn't find anything so stuck with Radio 2. Then I drifted into a disturbed sleep. I can't sleep in the dark anymore. This is a recent thing. It's not as if I'm scared of anything, I just find the darkness so depressing. So I keep my little gypsy light on and try so hard to dream. I always dream though. And because I wake up without a start, I drift into the waking hour slowly from the dream. They seem so real sometimes.

CHOCOLATE BODY PAINT AND POPPERS. LAND OF LEATHER TOMORROW 9AM. NO DECOY.

December 25th, 2009

10:09 pm

My family are downstairs watching telly. I feel claustrophobic if I'm too close to people for too long. Family or not. Perhaps this explains why the love of my life is also on his own.

These ruined streets are covered in snow. Even the snow doesn't make this place look any more appealing.

I've been giving the alcohol a rest as is the tradition with me every Christmas. My Mum got me in some Shloer and I've had a few glasses of that. I've been drinking coffee as well. I'm trying to be American. That's what Americans do don't they? David Bowie tried to be American once. I'm sure all great people go through an American phase.

Yesterday I went into Oldham Town Centre to buy some presents and meet my Dad in Wetherspoon's. I had a Pepsi while my Dad drank half a bitter and wrote my sister and my Mum some Christmas cards. My Mum had given him the Christmas cards, all with the same acrylic picture of Christmas carolling. We caught the bus after, back down to the pub at the end of my road. On the bus a middle-aged man kept shouting at an Indian woman and child, "Get back to your own country. What you gonna do about it?" He just kept repeating and repeating this. The woman eventually got off with her child and waited for the next bus. We got off at the next stop. Everything felt surreal. The twilight was reflecting upon the snow and I wondered whether I was really here, back where I began.

I was so tired but then I had to get ready to go to church. I sang the carols badly and loud as is my tradition at Christmas. Not on purpose like. I just can't sing hymns or carols. It's not my key. But I enjoyed it and I really love that church. I'd love to find a church like that in London.

When I got back my Mum made some sandwiches and cut up some pork pies and we had a buffet. They'd taken the picture of the Queen down from above the fireplace in my bedroom so after putting it back up I got into bed with E.T. and went to sleep keeping my 1930s lamp on. I still can't sleep in the dark no matter where I am.

This morning we went to church again and I sang more carols very badly. The sermon was ace and when I come back to London I aim to return to church. I've really been missing it without realising. All those sober people are so nice.

The Christmas dinner was delicious. We had chicken. Afterwards Christmas pudding and brandy cream.

I've been on the internet since then. I like this. It's a great thing for anti-social loners like me. I used to be mad on pen pals and am still mad about my only pen pal so this is a bit like that. I find friendships so difficult. People fall out with me all the time cos of things I say or do. Maybe it's the drink and my unreliability but this thing is so much easier for me. If I had a computer I wouldn't need anybody, only my pen pal for a bit of almost human contact.

I'm going to bed again in a minute. I had the most wonderful dream last night.

SING-A-LONG, CLAP, GET UP AND DANCE AS MUCH AS YOU LIKE AS LONG AS YOU ARE CONSIDERATE TO OTHERS

December 29th, 2009

09:34 pm

I'm trying to gather into bags most of the possessions I left in this house eight years ago. It all needs to go to the charity shop or to the landfill. What to do with drawers of make-up I know not. I've worn tons of the stuff since I was twelve. Always getting bored of a colour and buying more and more. I'm not naturally good-looking you see but I've never had any problems with the men.

I sit here with E.T. as I have for most of this Christmas period. As I said, this internet thing fascinates me. I keep wondering: what am I into? What do I like? Then I Google it. I've Googled my name loads of times but there's not much on me. I've Googled my pen pal's name loads of times. There's loads on him. Even videos. Wow!

I eventually succumbed to the drink on Saturday night. All the clubs were shut in Manchester so me and my friend hung around in Withington playing a game I made up called "Truth or Lie". It's a bit like Truth or Dare but in my version you have tell the truth or you can lie. It's up to you. That's like my life. I usually find lying works the best.

The next day I went to Withington Methodist Church. The service was good. Full of poetry. One about Christmas by Milton stood out. I'm sure you can look it up. The preacher spoke to me after. I told him about the Methodist youth club weekends in London I used to go on when I was thirteen. I used to love those. Just sitting in Battersea Park with a load of other teenagers smoking roll-ups. I didn't mention that bit though. I did say that Jesus was a bit like a punk. I was still slightly drunk but anyway, it went somewhere and he completely agreed that Jesus was a revolutionary figure. A bit like Maclaren. Huh huh…

Coming out of the church I noticed a pub. Now for those of you that are not familiar with the Methodist Church, they are a branch of Christianity that are teetotal. So I looked back at the church and made sure no one was watching and went quickly into the pub. It didn't really matter. I don't think I'll be back in Withington that soon. The pub was the kind I love, full of Irish navvies. I had a big chat with the barmaid. She was very Coronation Street. I told her this. She liked that. I gave her my card.

I made my way back into town after this. Back Piccadilly has always been a favourite place of mine. Mother Mac's is a pub that is rather dear to my cold, cold heart. Inside, horse racing was on the telly. I love the vague sound of horse racing in the background when I'm drinking. It reminds me that I've still got all day.

I got a bit worried about the amount of lone men waiting for their wives to finish with materialism. It was boxing day. If there's one thing I can't stand it's shopping. Anyway, that's me and that's why my clothes are always a bit crap.

I felt a bit awkward and so left to seek out my Dad in Oldham. I found him in the pub at the end of my road. We drank and then my sister and her boyfriend turned up and we drank some more. Then we went to another pub and played on the jukebox and had a game of pool. Then I got worried again cos I was three sheets to the wind and had to go home and face my Mum. Anyway, this I did although I can't remember much. I got in a bit of trouble the next day but she told me I'm too old to be lectured about my ways now. So that's alright then.

Did I mention that my liver is in perfect working order? I was absolutely shocked at this news two months ago. So shocked that I spent the whole day in Wetherspoon's drinking pints of Kronenbourg followed by Harveys Bristol Cream chasers.

I'm gonna stop drinking when I go away though. My pen pal said I've got to take more care of my liver cos it's important. I believe in him. He said I'm too pretty to be getting ill. Well, I'll listen to him. Yes, that's what I'll do. I'm honest with my pen pal.

I DON'T LIKE YOU AND I DON'T LIKE HIM. NOW FUCK OFF

January 4th, 2010

02:13 pm

I was glad to return to London. I feel a lot more organised and free here. I think, wow! I can do what the fuck I like and no one's bothered too much about it. I'll have to pay my rent soon. There's some things you have to do because y'know, I don't want to become a crack addict hanging around Sunset Boulevard.

I haven't had a drink since Friday 1st January. Now that was a lovely little session I went on. Wetherspoon's, Leytonstone for most of the day then to The North Star, a pub that could be in Yorkshire. In Wetherspoon's they had the horse racing on and y'know how horse racing makes me feel. Like I've got the rest of the day set out before me. That's a nice feeling. I turn me phone off and I'm no one's. I just sat there taking notes and the future looked wonderful. 2010! Wow! And I'm still only twenty-eight.

But then my peace is shattered. An articulate man opposite says I shouldn't be treating the drink like a boyfriend. He says he likes me because I don't swear but he'd hate his daughter to be sitting drinking on her own.
"My drinking has nothing to do with either equality or loneliness. I just like to drink."
I then should have said, "Now fuck off," but I hate having to have a fight.

He still carried on, saying my eyes looked so sad. I'd had my contact lenses in for two days and the mid-afternoon sun was still blazing through the large windows. I let him carry on and wrote down a lot of what he was saying. He told me about the dangerous men that lurk in The Walnut Tree in Leytonstone. Well I've seen plenty of red and yellow men and even met a man in the SAS in there but where is this danger he speaketh of?

He left eventually to go back to the wife that cooks as wives usually do. At last peace came clamouring back to me but the horse racing had disappeared and that meant most of my day had too. Night filled the place, and so did Matalan and Primark bags. Women with their halves and glasses of white wine. This wasn't my scene. As soon as the women arrive, I'm most definitely gone.

And so to The North Star, one of my favourite drinking establishments in Leytonstone. I sat with the jukebox and some young people playing darts. It was nice and I was happy with my pint of boyfriend called Kronenbourg.

I went home after going out for a cigarette and breathing in that terrible oxygen so the alcohol hits like it never used to. Not before the smoking ban.

In the safety of my room I turned on my mobile phone. People kept calling me wishing me a happy New Year. Maybe 1st January is the day for loneliness. Why would anyone want to speak to me? I was happy to speak though. I had a lot to say. Y'know, I just talked about bingo, money, a holiday I'm going on in June. I talked about my new-found happiness. Just about everything seemed rather perfect. And exciting, cos everything always has to be exciting or what is the point in existing?

LET'S SLIT THE DOGS OF WAR! WE CAN BE ANYONE!

January 10th, 2010

01:25 pm

So 2012 and all them predictions of doom. I will carry on being an alcoholic until 21st December 2012. That's when the New World Order is supposed to come about.

Yesterday I was on the piss again. I'm just Leytonstoning it nowadays, what with after the boyfriend dumping me. Michael, not the Kronenbourg. I wasn't too arsed about it. I didn't cry or owt like that. I made the choice. He stopped loving me years ago and I knew when he no longer wanted to hold me in those dark hours.
But still, I wasn't arsed. I just thought that if I write about it here it might make good reading material. My job is to entertain and I'm trying my best.

My pen pal made me break free from everything. How can one imprisoned have so much influence over another's life? I mean, he has no idea. He's made me realise how useless people really are. Y'know, menial problems and all that fucking crap.
Last night I dreamt of a car boot sale.

If you're into blogs I only read one. It's this man on death row in my pen pal's place in Texas. He's only my age but it's the best writing I have ever come across. Not that I'm putting the rest of you down but having all that time to spare, well it must make you better at something. It's written by Tom Whitaker. He's there because he hired a hitman to kill his whole family. He's branded a sociopath (not to be confused with the overused "psychopath").

If I did get a column then would there be someone to write it for me? I'd hire Tom Whitaker.

FIND YOUR WAY BACK TO WORK

January 14th, 2010

12:36 pm

I'm sick of writing about my sessions.

So yesterday I was hanging around Wetherspoon's after having a dispute with the telephone box at the end of my road. I was pretty stressed out about it y'know so I had to drink a few pints to calm myself down. This was 10:30am. Unusually I had been to bed for four hours. I don't usually sleep in those early hours of Wednesday morning when I return from the club, because I usually get pissed in the casino and carry on from there.

I was eager to return home after my set though. I wanted to find out if my pen pal had written. Luckily, he had so that cheered me up. He'd run out of paper though and was waiting for his parents to purchase some more so he'd written on the back of one of his fan's emails.

Anyway, back to Wetherspoon's. I drank a few pints of Carlsberg (£1.49 in the January sale). I talked to a few old men from the fair country (Ireland). Paddy said he was one of fourteen. Unlucky for him they named him Paddy but he seemed cheerful enough. I met him again some hours later but by this time he was bumping into things. He gave me an Allen key so I could bleed my radiator. How kind.

I got a text from Malik at five-ish and he said he was having a gathering in Claridge's to celebrate his birthday. I just thought, I have to go to this cos Malik always turns up at my events and I like Malik cos for me Malik is like watching television, like some kind of comedy. So I made my way to Claridge's, sobering up on the way with a bottle of Yazoo strawberry milkshake.

We had a right laugh in the bar there and Gordon Ramsay brought out the cake and it was nice. Then we got a taxi to The Coach. I drank a few pints of Löwenbräu there but I couldn't continue and everyone knew I couldn't continue and so I made my way home stopping by briefly at Molly Moggs. I like that place cos whatever state I'm in they never refuse to serve me. I then caught the tube home.

I woke up this morning surrounded by chicken bones and life seemed kind of perfect. I've just had a walk round Tesco. I never buy anything. I just like looking at all the things one can buy. I find Tesco a comforting place. All those frozen foods. Such variety nowadays. I always feel like I've just stepped into this age from another.

DRINK, GAMBLING, SEX AND SMOKING

January 19th, 2010

02:12 pm

Those are my hobbies, probably in that order. Well, no doubt you know that already.

My friends all went to The Intrepid Fox on Saturday night. Y'know, my young friends. People to do with my band. As soon as I arrived I had to get out. I really do like those people but The Intrepid Fox? I couldn't breath. Not that I was looking like I was having some kind of panic attack. I was talking to everyone about DJing and computer games and the upcoming gig. But after drinking my half pint it was time to disappear to the Phoenix for a bit of solitude at the end of the bar.

And this I kind of found. The Phoenix was full of smiling actors fresh from their musicals. So different from The Intrepid Fox. All those Goths can never get over the fact that they were beaten up at school for being miserable. All that isolation crap. They should have gotten over it by now. I wasn't beaten up after I took a hand grenade to a girl's head. No, I was just nicknamed "Psycho" for the next four years. Much easier.

This morning I ate ham, egg and chips in Wetherspoon's, my usual. And a cup of tea. Most unusual. Yesterday I lay in bed for twenty-four hours, hardly moving. Today I felt like my organs had sunk too deeply into my body and so it was time to go out into Leytonstone Town Centre again. God, I worry about this place now. I've created so many enemies around here. But the old people don't mind me too much and there's a man with a yellow-grey face that can hardly walk who I nicknamed "The Face of Death". Well, The Face of Death has developed a crush on me. I avoid him. I feel like death could be contagious. Well HIV is, isn't it? I feel like death is as easy to catch as a common cold. Whenever I see him I pace to the opposite side of the pub. But sometimes he follows me. I'll be drawing up future plans and all of a sudden The Face of Death will appear and offer me a drink. I decline his drinks. He was shouting about seeing his social worker today. Well, at least someone sees him.

I've been betting on the horses again. I'm gonna make it big on the horses this year. It's handy cos the betting shop is right opposite Wetherspoon's.

My pen pal sent me an email just now. I much prefer his letters. There's more love involved in a letter. Y'know.

JAMIE MANNERS AND ME
HANGING AROUND

January 20th, 2010

05:48 am

Well, I've had enough. It doesn't start with having enough. I love having enough. I've been in the casino all night, and I've won £2400. And now I'm happy. All my money's gonna be spent on my pen pal. It's strange not knowing whether he's happy. But most of the time I'm so happy I can't believe it. And it's unreal.

I used to look upon London and Euston and its marble floor and now all those dreams that I had are made.

Me & Jamie Manners, we rule. And here I am. You should never begin a sentence with and. But here we are.

Prostitutes hung around tonight. There were two of them at the coffee bar and one said, "You know what I just did? I just ate a bowl of Rice Krispies," and the other one said, "You pig!" Another one said to me in the toilets, "Don't use the hand-dryers because one of my clients is gambling out there, and he can hear the noise of the hand-dryers and it puts him off his game".

There was an old Chinese man sitting across from us. He had a coffee and an orange juice, plus a copy of Attitude and the Evening Standard. He spent the whole time reading Attitude and didn't budge from his seat all night.

Nothing else happened. That was it.

OH I SAY............

January 23rd, 2010

06:04 am

I am writing this from my bed in Leytonstone. Trevor the doorman kindly gave me his old laptop so you've him to thank for my endless updates of my extremely dull life to come.

What I'm worried about most with this thing is the fact I'll come home drunk and write a load of crap, slag everyone off, y'know like I do in internet cafes. It won't matter too much though cos I'll be able to delete it the next day if I don't spill anything.

I've been non-stop Googling again. I would still be seeking something now but I'm not allowed to access anything with adult content. I'm stuck with writing this instead. There's only so much you can do with this thing. I'm not tired again. I've been up for nearly twenty-four hours. Sleep only comes to me in blocks of twenty-four hours every alternate day.

I haven't had a drink for two days. On my last session I believe I may have been barred from Leytonstone Wetherspoon's. I dunno though. I'm in one piece and haven't lost anything of value so I can't have been that bad. But they wouldn't serve me after the twelve hours. Well, twelve hours they may have thought but they have no idea that I'm always fresh from the casino session as well as two cans in my room while I sit and wait for 9am.

Apart from the drink there's not much to report on. I went to a pie and mash shop in Wanstead today and had, you guessed it, pie, mash and liquor. It tasted nicer than my usual liquor. I loathe the taste of alcohol y'know.

I did my DJ set this evening. Well yesterday and the day before. You know how hard I work. When I don't drink I write down every song I play in a little Hemingway notebook. Just out of interest like. I'm genius at DJing now, if you catch me at the right time with the right crowd. Y'know if someone's having a hen party I'm not gonna start playing "Some Girls are Bigger than Others," but I haven't seen a hen party at my disco for around two years and I've had a fascination with that song for the last month or two. When our Ste goes, "Send me the pillow, the one that you dream on, well I still dream oooohhhhhhhhhh," well that one always goes out to my pen pal. I think he might need his pillow though. It's cold in there.

CAN I KILL YOU NOW OR SHALL I TALK A WHILE?

January 25th, 2010

01:47 am

The only writing that I admired on the internet was always mine. And now I'm stuck in my room. All I ever think about is me, because that is all that is.

All there is is you. Well, that's an obvious statement. The other day I wished I was dead. I was thinking of hanging myself on the door handle. That was the only thing I could see but y'know, my pen pal said how much he wanted to be with me and that was the only thing that stopped me. I was gonna do it with a tie. Hot pink to be precise. My friend said to always call him when I felt suicidal but as usual, I had no credit. So sleep was the closest I could get to death (as usual). I thought about admitting myself to Whipps Cross Mental Health Unit, walking in and saying, "Section me please, please". But in my bed I thought about my club and how I save everyone three nights a week with my amazing taste in music. I wondered what David, Debbie, Steven, Scott, Cilla and all them would say. Y'know. They'd just tell me to carry on, for their sake. Well, it obviously wouldn't be mine.

And so the crowd get younger and younger. And some ask for the Top Gun soundtrack and some ask for Dirty Dancing. I have neither. Just sit there in my booth. Having a marvellous time, mind you. No matter whether I'm drinking or not. It's like watching telly. All those people with their careers. Fuckinghell. A career. I never expected music to be mine.

That fucking slag of a careers advisor at school. I said I wanted to work in the music industry. She said that Setons would be more my thing; that's the main factory in Oldham. A body bag factory. Production line and all that.

"Get realistic."

"Yes you need to be realistic," my Mum replied at the final "careers interview".

I don't blame my Mum. She's cool. She had no idea what I was capable of. Bringing up four children and setting up on her own to avoid my alcoholic father... But that fucking "careers advisor". I mean how many other people's hopes has she killed?

GRINDING ON WITH YOUR DAILY BORING FUCK

January 27th, 2010

10:10 pm

It's fascinating to find out what addresses those you're interested in have got, what they're doing and suchlike. Even if they're not on the Fascistbook you can still find out stuff on this thing.

I find when people leave me they don't do well for themselves. They end up with that dull kind of woman. Children. Stuff that bores me completely.

Cos at first when men go out with me they have all this ambition. And that's why I like them. Men are supposed to have ambition. Women just want to live off it. Well, that's what I reckon. Soon's a man finds a woman they're off in some other place. Grinding on with their daily boring fuck and day job. It's always completely gone. Soon's they reckon they've found "the one," that whole procreation crap kicks in. They're providing then. They become sensible. No more madness with Scarlet West. No one I've known recently has found love. This is purely an observation I've made over the years. I've never had any female friends so I can't comment on their whole menstrual palaver.

I sat in a pub in Essex for most of today, overlooking London and you lot and your tedious lives. Nothing struck me. I just drank pints of Peroni. That was the only decent thing on tap. I'm not a bitter person. Those at me disco last night were though.

Spitfire all over the piano at the end of the night. Bloodyhell. I love my club and I love my bloody great job. Johnny Vegas came down. Now he's a good friend of mine from years back when I was DJing for the drink. We talked for a bit about them rotten days. I played a load of Northern Soul for him cos that's his favourite. Alwynn

Davies always used to say that I'd be better off with Johnny. Well, it would go alright. Just getting hammered loads of nights. Having drunken sex and all that. We'd have a great time. He trained to be a priest though and when we talk we mainly speak theology. Y'know I did a nun's course when I first moved down here, in Hammersmith, at the convent. Sister Francis still prays for me. I doubt it's doing much good.

I pray every day for my pen pal. I've just been watching the video again of that divine man. I do believe that he's the man for me. I'm completely and utterly obsessed with him. Soon's he walks free he is mine. I will give him everything. I will give him absolutely everything.

REASONS YOU'RE SINGLE

January 31st, 2010

11:35 am

It's great this is, doing what the fuck I like whenever I want to do it. Well nothing's changed, I just get to write it all down now.

I arrived back in my room fifteen minutes ago with a skull in a plastic Sainsbury's carrier bag. I kept getting it out on the tube and shouting, "I've not lost my head, I'm just out of my skull ha ha ha ha ha!!!" No, it doesn't make sense.

The human skull is now on top of my wardrobe where I keep my bottles of Communion wine, Harveys Bristol Cream and cans of Boyfriend. It's empty today though. I've drunk the fucking lot. All I'm left with is a carton of Del Monte Fruit Burst (Caribbean flavour).

The skull came courtesy of the bouncer. We have a right laugh me and the bouncer. Not in a sexual way though. Just a laugh like. My pen pal used to be a bouncer. It takes a special man to make a good bouncer. I've learnt that over the years, going to clubs, working in them and everything. It takes an even more special person to become friends with a bouncer but as soon as you're the bouncer's friend you're made for life. And protected. As long as it's not some second-rate club bouncer.

I do have to say one thing on here though. Like I'm not used to saying this cos I don't get nervous about gigs and things. That drummer that my band has, well, she's only been to the audition and she's had hand strain ever since. At first I thought she might have been wanking someone off too hard but it turns out it's more serious than that. Anyway, so she's just gonna turn up at the gig on the 6th and do it. No, not wank someone off, don't come down for that sake. She's just gonna play for the first time on the 6th. I'm not exactly shitting myself but when you don't know how something's gonna turn out then it's best to think the worst.

Y'know the whole recession was caused by Americans thinking positive. Well, fuck that. Think the worst.

My pen pal still thinks the best. And I hope for the best for him. In October we will be together with only bulletproof glass separating us from consummating our relationship.

A FREEZER FULL OF ICELAND DINNERS AND A CIGARETTE

February 2nd, 2010

05:03 pm

I don't believe I'm wasting my time on this thing even though I'm only leaving the house to DJ and rehearse. I have a freezer full of Iceland dinners. The traditional types are my favourite: beef stew and dumplings, roast beef and Yorkshire pudding, toad in the hole. Those sorts. I did go a bit mad with a purchase of spaghetti bolognaise. I don't think I can even spell that. I'll eat that only when I get desperate.

I was reading an interview with the director of my film and he said the best advice that he had ever been given was by Michael Palin who offered the wise words of "Just keep doing what you're doing". I was thinking about this through lack of much else to think about and I thought, "Wow! That's good advice".

Only if you like what you're doing though. If you don't like doing what you're doing then you need to think of an alternative but you don't want to become homeless. Then again, no job, no home, no worries or so the saying goes. I'm not keen on the cold though.

I've been swearing too much in the last entries. I'm not apologising for that. You can blame that articulate man I met in Wetherspoon's on New Year's Day, liking me cos I don't swear. But it's not really me. I only start swearing when I'm pissed.

It's good I can go back to the lectures at Gresham College in High Holborn now. I never had time to find out what days they were on before. Do you remember I used to go to them all the time years ago? Financial regulation, accountancy, the culture of Mongolia. I had a right laugh. Anything to do with banking and the world of finance in general holds a great fascination for me. Tomorrow I'm going to the lecture at 6pm entitled "Is Lloyds the McDonald's of the Insurance World?" If there's wine and salmon after I'll be well onto it.

Having no structure to your own education is the best way to go about learning different things. Organised education is for lazy bastards I reckon. You should just learn about what you're interested in and fuck the world of work. And why is it so important to own your own property? That I can never understand.

I just rant on here now cos I'm not leaving the house. I'll leave the house for the lectures though so I'm sure something of interest will happen that I can report on. I don't wanna get barred from Gresham College though so I'm gonna be careful there. I used to meet really fascinating men there. I went for the fellas as well as an education y'know. The red wine after is about fifteen percent. And the silver service staff in their smart black and white uniforms top up your glass every time you take a sip. Then when the wine runs out I say to some half pissed suit, "Do you fancy going for a drink?" I check the wedding finger first. I wouldn't want anyone having an affair.

So that's my plan for tomorrow. I'm gonna have my last fag now, then toad in the hole with gravy. I don't like stuff that's not wet.

INCEST, EX-OFFENDERS AND
A FRILLY TUTU

February 8th, 2010

02:37 pm

The gig went well, thanks for your concern. My new drummer is ace. She wears these ear protector things all the time. Even when she's not playing. It's quite a look. I'm going to get her some Russian military ones for next time though.
Here was the set:
London I
Crime Time
Demons, Outlaws and God
Alcohol and Cheap Hotels
Castaway
Museum of The Universe
Now World Order
Texas Calling
Space. Division. Time
Escape Route

If you didn't catch us this time, our next gig is on Sunday March 28th at Tommy Flynn's in Camden.

I'd stuck to my no alcohol two days before the gig rule so when I came off stage I was desperate for a pint. My old friend James Bryce-Walker bought me a Kronenbourg then I went out for a fag. Everyone was congratulating me and we even got paid. Some of our female fans had made I heart Iraq T-shirts. Our female fans have very nice breasts.

I stuck around to watch the other bands and chat with the fans. Michael came and talked a lot about a new shirt he'd purchased. He got a lot of whistles from people when he brought me my water on stage. I think Michael is such a good person. It's a shame it's not worked out but my lifestyle isn't permitting relationships at the moment. I've a whole lack of interest in all that crap now. Mind you, when my pen pal gets out I'm sure I could fit him in.

Afterwards me and Michael popped into my club and we had a bit of a dance to Get Into The Groove. No matter how many times I hear that track I still love it. After a few bottles of Tiger I took Michael to The Phoenix Theatre Club. It was alright in there. All the actors were there and high from their musicals.

When I woke up in the morning I fancied another drink so I strolled up to Wetherspoon's (Leytonstone branch). I drank more Kronenbourg and talked to a couple of old men that sit at my table in the window. I couldn't be arsed going to the betting shop so I told one of the old men to put my bet on while he was putting on his. I did a £3.10 each way. That's my usual.

As the twilight came I started chatting with a woman who was working on a wordsearch puzzle book. She told me how her father was also her grandfather and then I noticed that she had no fingers. She told me also that her feet were webbed. She was quite a spirited lady and we had a bit of a laugh about it all.

By 6pm I started on the cocktail menu. I had a Wuwu and a Frilly Tutu. They're not real cocktails by my club's standards. They're just a load of different coloured bottles of WKD thrown into a pitcher with some ice. It does the job though. I always finish off the session with a cocktail pitcher. £5.95.

At 8pm I had had my fill so went home to bed.

SITTING HERE, WAITING FOR FUCK ALL TO HAPPEN...

February 16th, 2010

10:56 pm

I couldn't put the jukebox on in a certain pub. Just couldn't, like. Eight-year-old boys were playing pool with their fathers. I am lost with normality.

I left my Father, pissed in the pub on the corner but I continued to follow in his well-trodden footsteps. The only difference between his alcoholism and mine is the fact that I write mine down.

Today he cut me off mid-sentence; no one had said anything in that pub for over five minutes. The silence was draining me. Dad said, "Stop waffling". Before that I had said,
"If a man was stripping then he would lose all his appeal because he could be anyone's and if he could be anyone's..."
I was talking in reference to a male stripper they are having perform on 26th February. Troy was previously seen in Coronation Street. I remember that episode, being a fan. That builder that got off with the black-haired barmaid at The Rovers. He was the window cleaner or something.

This morning I went to my Dad's house. Jesus and Mary were in the window, an Islam pamphlet too, propped up for goodwill. The heat from the gas fire started to melt my make-up so I took to the kitchen. I started on the washing up. I'd just done my nails the day before so I was pretty pissed off but my Dad can hardly stand nowadays so that awful love for him kicked in.

After I did the best with the kitchen, we left the house. My Dad and I speak little. We have jokes though. The one we use most often is: "You can't still be thirsty!" Ha, ha, huh huh... We laugh each time one of us says it; usually at hourly intervals.

My Dad's like me though. We don't like people too much. Like my lyric, "The clever never talk about it" (Demons, Outlaws and God). And we also love that "Those that do, know. Those that can't, teach". This afternoon we took a short cut across a derelict factory site. There's loads of them round here. Along the way I told him the name of every species of plant that the council had planted beyond the perimeter fence. Not that there was a perimeter fence anymore. This lot was planted in 1987. I know because I have a fascination for plants and bushes that Oldham council grew between 1976 and 1988. The council used certain plants in the Oldham vicinity y'see. I made an effort to find out the species of the whole lot. I was bored. Anyway, I left my Dad in a drunken state. He was about to kick off and as much as I love him, I don't want to be associated with all that cos it gets me into massive trouble sometimes. I booked a taxi under my real name with "Britannia Cars" and went off to my sister's part of Oldham.

I hadn't had enough so went off to a pub on the main road. It was the kind of pub where men have wives so I couldn't have that yearned-for conversation. Those men sit at the bar and talk football. I know they're waiting for 7pm so the whole thing calms down and the baby stops crying. And only then will they return to the female.

I mean, I can't blame them. No wonder my Father took to the pub. Children are too loud.

Phil Collins kept following me around after I left that pub. Another half, alright, another plush or threadbare corner and another half. Still Phil Collins.

I had to do the jukebox in a pub called The Honeywell. Child-free this pub and men only. And my selection?
Del Shannon – Runaway
New Order – True Faith (meant that one with the blue eyes whole thing, but forgot the name cos was pissed)
The Beatles – Lady Madonna
David Bowie – Ashes to Ashes
Joy Division – Atmosphere

"Don't walk away in silence."

I sat it out but no one cared about a song I played and being a professional I'm used to that. That lyric came through close though. James growled at me, "People like you, find it easy, walking on air". And I thought, yeah, everything for me has been a bloody breeze and now I'll walk away in silence although I never got the opportunity to air any of my breezes through lack of living people to talk to. Abandoned too soon and all that palaver.

The song stopped as Joy Division songs have a penchant for doing. The noise began, the payphone was ringing. I heard words. Contractors. Barred. Landlords.

"I'LL JUST HAVE HALF"

March 5th, 2010

02:34 pm

I've been on the piss since Wednesday. It all started off innocently as these things do. A screening of London in the Raw at the NFT. It was a shockumentary about pubs and clubs in London in 1967. After seeing that I got a thirst on so went to The Players underneath The Arches of Charing Cross. After that on to my favourite casino off Piccadilly. Just drinking pints of lager and shots of Sambuca like. In the morning I still wanted more so went to The Camel pub in Bethnal Green.

After a small nap in the afternoon I popped out to DJ. I wasn't really there. It was like I was seeing everything from outside my body but I functioned and so I managed it. I kept licking my E.T. that I keep behind the DJ booth. I dunno why.

This morning when I woke up, my first thought was one of suicide. It's always that way after a two-day session. It passes though, but for hours I'll just think about how I'd hang myself. I wouldn't want any of that kinky sex business though. That would be terribly embarrassing.

I've got a lasagne doing in the oven now. I've got the shakes on. That's always a hassle.

On Wednesday I wrote a song called Nihilism. It was Leo Washington ages ago, he said this journal is very Nihilist. I do believe in God though. Not morals, but God is always there.

My insides are killing me. Everything feels bruised. I'm struggling to walk. I have to DJ tonight, 7-11pm. It will be alright. I'll turn up. I'm off the drink now for another couple of days. I'll go to be with Michael. I do love him. He's the only person I've ever loved. I just look at him sometimes. I could look at him forever. When I'm on one of my sessions though, that's it. We have no contact. I only ever see Michael when I'm sober now. He's the only man with the joy of seeing me sober. Everyone else just sees the rippling reflection.

When he comes home from work I put something in the microwave for him and make him a cup of tea. It's odd to have these two separate lives. If I didn't have these two lives I would be so bored. Neither one nor the other bores me but I have a need for variety.

Somebody said to me the other day that my belief system is fucked. The fact that I'm so bloody awful to people. Will I ever get what I truly deserve though? Some people find me so amazing. More people think I'm bloody terrible though. They always say I'm a user. I guess I am. I'll use people for entertainment. If anything goes wrong with them I won't be there. I won't turn up when I've arranged to. Sometimes I'll be not pleased to see people when they've made an effort to turn up to my disco. That's cos I want to be alone some nights and just get on with it. Most of the time I'll be happy to speak to a few friends there. If it's a non-drinking night it makes it go a bit faster.

So that's me and how I feel today.

THE DANGER OF DEATH

March 8th, 2010

02:51 am

I haven't had a drink since Thursday. So there goes the epistle to the pissheads out there.

I woke up today believing I was choking. I was swimming in a mud sea. Bodies were drowning me. After what seemed like days of struggle I pushed all these dead bodies down and managed to scramble to the top of them, climb over them all. It was a very brown sea. Bodies just everywhere. I saw a ship and they saw me. When I got on board it was a bit like a caravan. There was a Northern woman offering me tea and toast and it was the 70s again. Then still in this dream I vomited out all this dry noodle and sweetcorn stuff. It was a bit like a half done Golden Wonder Pot Noodle, chicken and mushroom flavour. I had to help it out with my hands cos it didn't flow the way vomit usually does. I hadn't been able to drink for days. Y'know. Water.

So that was the dream. Here I am in bed, can of Kronenbourg by my side. I fucking hate the stuff now. Gonna start drinking something else. Thing is, I started off on White Lightning, then Strongbow, then Stella, then Heineken, then red wine, then Löwenbräu, then rosé, then white wine and now Kronenbourg. That wasn't all tonight. I'm talking about fourteen years here. I've had certain drinks though. The alcohol is a constant but the brand, well that doesn't mean a thing. There's no soft cell with a woman like me.

I get bad hallucinations when I drink a lot. That's one of the side effects of drink, I hear. Someone will come into my realm, end of my bed or wherever I've ended up, and talk plainly to me. I will reply. Usually the apparition that arrives is that of a young boy, sixteen or so. He will either be talking of his suicide or murder. Each one different-looking though. They will say the house that I'm residing

229

in had something to do with all that. Never here though, never Leytonstone, never this fine suburb.

Just all those inner places though. Y'know. Leytonstone feels sparse compared to Bethnal Green. The amount of spirits, trapped in this city. This city will not trap me. As soon's I'm dead I will be gone.

"I JUST GOT INTO THIS CLUB. ASK HIM, HE KNOWS EVERYTHING. HE'S BEEN SITTING THERE FOR THREE YEARS, LIKE."

March 16th, 2010

06:51 am

My pen pal wrote to me yesterday. He's had his death sentence overturned. Well, that's the power of prayer. He may be free soon and one of the first things he's gonna do is visit me. We'll have such a laugh, I'm happy about all this. He's on the move from Texas death row to the county jail now. I believe they have tellies there.

On Saturday morning I rang The Samaritans. I tried to ring around a few of my friends first but they weren't in. I quite like having a chat with The Samaritans. I can be more self-indulgent. All they want to hear about is me. This woman sounded a bit posh though. She was trying to make me say I was suicidal but I kept saying, "No, I'm quite happy, I just want to stop drinking".

I told her that I find it difficult to stop when I'm working as a DJ. We went through all the options. Well, the only option. I stop DJing and find myself another career. But I like DJing and I'm not gonna stop. London needs me three times a week. In the end she says, "I don't know what we can do to help you then".
It was alright for her to say that to me cos I wasn't suicidal so there'll be no blood on the hands of The Samaritans. I do often wonder why they work on the line. I really couldn't be doing with listening to self-indulgent suicidal people all day. I probably brightened up the banality for her.

I've rang them a few times before. They're okay for a little chat, y'know, when your friends are not answering or are busy. You know I never answer my phone so if any of my people need me for any reason, I won't be available. The Samaritans are alright but you can't talk about pop music or your favourite things though. The tone has to be a depressing one. Otherwise they'll think you're wasting their time.

I've been having bad dreams all night. Dreaming is your conscience trying to come to terms with what you do in reality. I must be doing some really bad things.

My sister seems to have this idea in her head that I'm working as a prostitute. I know some of you are on The FascistBook. Well, there's a really great picture of me on there lying beside a puddle. I mean, I'm fully clothed. I can imagine if I was half naked you might wanna make certain valid connotations. Maybe it's cos I'm lying down.

I believe in free speech and that I have something more valid to say than most people. If my family disown me for bringing shame upon them then so be it. Always say and do what you wanna do. This is not Pakistan.

"SHE KNEW THAT BOB MARLEY WAS DEAD BUT SHE DIDN'T KNOW THAT ELVIS WAS"

April 6th, 2010

10:46 am

I've been busy but when I've not been busy I've been in bed. Last night I stayed awake for too long and watched too much porn. I also searched for another pen pal because my pen pal who's not on death row anymore has stopped writing. I think he's got himself a girlfriend.

My search led me to find an Oxford educated psychopath. One afternoon he went on a killing spree. It's so funny what he did. He started off by killing his Jewish next door neighbour, then went to the corner shop and killed two Indians, then went to the Chinese takeaway and killed the staff in there and I lose track after that. He didn't like foreigners apparently. He's not good-looking though. I like writing erotic letters y'see.

I was in the pub by 9:30am yesterday. They've changed the staff in Wetherspoon's again. I don't mind that though. They don't know about me so that's alright. I write all my best songs in Wetherspoon's at table 23. I sit in the window.

I must go to Coral today to pick up my winnings. Sometimes it's difficult to find a Coral. I should start using Ladbrokes instead cos there's one at the top of Dean Street and also next door to The Montagu Pyke on Charing Cross Road.

I've been asked to DJ at the top of Centre Point in The Paramount. That's cos I'm good. I'm a top DJ me. I think that's the thing I do the best. I drink well too. I wonder when I'll die? My suicidal thoughts keep coming thick and fast. I don't know why, I'm more or less content.

Some eighty-five-year-old man in the pub asked me to have sex with him the other morning. It was in Wetherspoon's. He said the urge never goes away. Well, I thought it did. "You'll have to make do with masturbation," I said.

"It's not the same as a real woman," he replied.

"It's less hassle and cheaper though." I think he thought I was a prostitute. That's a common misconception about my drinking alone.

I'll have to have one of my days out soon. Maybe Frinton-on-Sea.

IF MEN LIKE HIM LIKE WOMEN LIKE YOU, WHY DON'T WOMEN LIKE ME?

April 22nd, 2010

02:22 am

Have done with, is my usual observation. People don't like me and I'm willing to have done with people.

I've had nothing to say for ages. I'm satisfied.

Monday: Cinema, I will go to see whatever is on, usually between midday and 3pm.

Tuesdays: Bingo, main session. Elephant and Castle 13:45. DJ 22:00-03:00

Wednesday: Day off. Pub crawl ensues.

Thursday: Internet. DJ 22:00-03:00

Friday: Shopping – records, clothes. DJ 19:00- 23:00

Saturday: Acting class, Charles Verrall 11:00-13:00. Private party beyond 21:00.

Sunday: Sleep ages. Rehearsal – 16:00-19:00.

PSYCHO AND THE
ALFRED HITCHCOCK HOTEL

April 29th, 2010

04:33 am

I don't understand why people get so fascinated by me. When this happens, which is often, I always regret speaking. The only reason I'm compelling is because everyone else is so damn dull. I'm so sick to death of going through my stories. I've got it all down to a crappy art form, telling the stories of my past to a captivated audience.

Today I had my liquid breakfast in Wetherspoon's. I was running a bit late cos the man that lives downstairs had been stabbed by my acquaintance and my acquaintance spent ages explaining the reasons behind this. "Cos he's a cunt" was the prevailing one. All I could think of was cigarettes and the pint, so after half an hour of sorting out the whole commotion and after the police and paramedics arrived I drifted onto Leytonstone High Road and into The Walnut Tree.

I sat there and drank. Hanging around on the gambling table. I asked for some tips and went to Coral. I put on a £3 bet. Four horses this time. No idea how they did, like. I've always forgotten I've put on the bet by 4pm. I have so many Coral betting slips scattered around my room.

My criminal friend came in at 11:40am. The one that bought me the roast dinner a while back. I couldn't speak to him though cos he was with his wife. Y'know women. They never want to be friends with me. It's cos I fascinate people like.

Anyway, I was bored and lonely and I didn't know what to do cos I was looking really good. I'd bought a new red lipstick after rehearsal a fortnight ago called "Digital" and I was wearing that. It makes me look even better. I tried to talk to people but they just made their excuses about "work" and departed. I just sat there looking out into the awful sunshine, and the people with friends were all going past the window. I thought, this is why people murder. I'd do the same.

I'd had enough. The smell of food does my head in when I'm on one. I departed and caught the bus to Epping Forest. I went to that forboding place, The Alfred Hitchcock Hotel. The weather seemed to turn when I got there, all grey and I looked up at the place and thought, yeah. Empty. The hotel's just like the one in Psycho. Which is strange cos that was my nickname at school. I sat in there and reminisced about winter. The forest was covered in snow and the open fire was ablaze last time I was upon the place.

The awful sun came back again. You can't tell in there though. It's so dark. The little Irish Catholic woman was behind the bar. She didn't mind me. Just carried on after serving me the Staropramen. I sat outside for a bit, by one of the bricked-up cellars. It's always like they use the bricked and boarded-up parts of the building to store the bodies. I sat there a good two hours just thinking about things, glad that I could be alone and there was no chance of anyone bothering me.

I always reckon that when my looks leave me it will be a blessing. I'll just be mistaken for an old whore instead of a youngish one.

I sat at the bus stop after four pints. I got on the first bus which was going to Leyton. I remembered a nice pub near the Cash Converter place. Hanging baskets outside, brass on the wall. The name escapes me. Anyway, there I went. It was nice in there. Dark and empty. Can't remember much else after that. Woke up here a few minutes ago. I'd been watching funeral videos on YouTube again. Why do people video funerals? For the most part it's so the relatives in Australia can have a nosey at what went on. I bet they never expected to get so many hits and me commenting though.

They discourage pen pals at Broadmoor because they reckon that it only encourages psychopaths that have not yet done the deed to form writing relationships with their idols. I'm sure I'll find a way.

THE SMELL OFF PISS AND DEATH MAKES ME FEEL ALIVE (FOR NOW)

May 19th, 2010

08:38 am

I just got all my money ready to pay the landlord but then they went into a special room off the corridor. I think it's Ramadan cos they took their shoes off before they went in. Him and wife like. I'll leave them to it. We don't want a repeat of that time I fell over that man in the 24 hour supermarket who was praying on one of those magic carpets. The Muslims don't bother me though. After all, the white people hate me more. Problem with every other race is that they all believe themselves to be so righteous. I don't mind the blacks too much but they always have a look of sadness in their eyes and let's not forget, they hate me too, just cos I'm white. But there's no chance of me getting a council flat so there's no need for that look anymore. Having a past as dreadful as theirs must be a difficult crux to bear.

The whites don't like me. The working class don't like me cos I don't work as much as them. The middle class don't like me cos I drink and read The Sun and don't bother with education. The upper class don't like me cos I don't know enough about dressage. I give up with the fucking lot of them.

I turned my phone off for three days the other day. I constantly thought about hanging myself or going "missing". Well, perhaps constantly is a bit much cos I made it out to Palace Bingo in Elephant and Castle Shopping Centre and had the most wonderful steak and mushroom pie, carrots, roast potatoes, green beans and gravy meal. All for £2.

It made me slightly (but not that much) happier hanging round Palace Bingo. You hear all those chesty coughs and you see all those people that have only got six months. You can tell they've only got six months (it's that funny colour they go). It's good to see. I felt well after that. The smell of piss and medication. I don't mind the smell of piss too much but medication, urgh…

I could imagine being unhappy if I didn't have much to do but I've worked out a schedule now (see previous entries). Sometimes I'm sober for three days. God help you if you meet me when I'm off on one though.

I'm off on one today. It's 08:30 now and I'm heading to The Walnut Tree in Leytonstone. I'll be there at 09:20-11:45. I'll put on a bet at Coral once I've seen the tips. £3.10 each way. My usual, then I won't bother claiming for weeks, then I'll write up in here how much I've bloody won. Am I repeating myself? That's what people like me do. I hope I die soon. I'd put a bet on that any day. I won't give you the odds cos that's illegal.

HARD, ROUGH, MIDGET, VOYEURISM

May 24th, 2010

10:12 pm

I woke up this morning with a load of fag burns up my arms. It upset me a bit but after five pints and a few Harveys Bristol Cream chasers I felt like doing it all over again. I even bought a shot of blackcurrant Sourz. Tasted like Ribena it did. I knew I hadn't been self-harming cos I'm not a Manics fan. I just fell asleep with a fag in hand.

Cos it was sunny I thought about vitamin D and how it might be quite crucial that I get some. So my plan was to sit in Epping Forest drinking cans of Kronenbourg. I passed the charity shop on the way there. It's run by a Christian organisation called REMAR. It's for people coming off drugs and alcohol, a bit like that Amy Winehouse song. I spoke to the woman working in the charity shop for a bit. I told her how much I wanted to come off the drink but working in a nightclub, y'know it's difficult. She told me that I should become a radio DJ. That's sane. And I was speaking to a radio DJ in The Coach at the start of my bender the previous day. John was his name. He worked for Caroline, Radio 3, Capital, Talksport and the bookies' one, Turf. He was alright him, and he caught me at the start. The best time.

I took heed of what the nice lady said. She talked a bit using those phrases that only people that have come out of rehab use. I had to let her down gently, edging out the door backwards. The cans of Kronenbourg were warming up. I stood outside the Co-operative funeral directors' waiting for the bus. The tiny coffins were still in the window. It disturbs me that one of them is engraved with "Oswald". I got upset about this again as I had the previous week and I rang on the bell again (as I had the previous week). I just want to tell them to remove that small coffin out of the window. They never answer though. God knows who would remove the body if someone just pegged it like.

And so the bus came and it dropped me off opposite The Alfred Hitchcock. I couldn't go in there today though cos I was in the previous night and I'd caused a bit of a ruckus if that's the term to use. I'm sure it'll be alright in a few weeks. You have to let the dust settle, or failing that, just wait for some bar staff to turn over.

The sun was turning that nice orange colour by the time I lay in the grass. Nothing mattered and I thought about the world ending and how much happier I'd be if other people didn't exist. Well, I love Michael. Apart from him I wouldn't be bothered if no one existed. Relatives are alright though.

He came to my disco on Friday. All quiffed up and looking divine. I even played "Young Guns Go For It" for him. I'd do anything for Michael. Absolutely anything. The more I think about him, the more in love with him I am. He doesn't read this so I'm safe to say that, otherwise I'd be crass.

I fell asleep in the grass after a bit. I woke up in the twilight and I could tell that the dogging had begun. I'm not into syphilis so I scrambled up and staggered home.

YOU WERE MY BROTHER, AND THEN YOU DIED. YOU WERE TWENTY-THREE, I WAS THIRTEEN.

June 14th, 2010

12:39 am

I met a group that just happened to come down to my disco a fortnight ago.
It was the first group of people that didn't mean any harm and it felt weird. I was doing my hate look when they all came up to me. They said that my DJing was the best they have ever heard.
"Obviously New York," I replied.

Anyway, they didn't mean any harm for people so young with their lovely looks;
"I love Morrissey."
"Ooooh I know Morrissey, 'Piccadilly Palare' aye? Or do you want 'We Hate it When Our Friends Become Successful' eh?"

Jacob Graham and Jonathan Pierce just said, "Wow". I didn't say owt cos I didn't know who they were. I just played Elvis and bits of Morrissey in between.

I'd watched a band called "The Drums" on Jonathan Ross the previous week. I thought, "Uhhh these are well good". I hadn't seen a band in ages that impressed me. I felt quite bad cos the lead singer was stealing epileptic dance moves from our friend Mr Curtis. I felt upset about that and didn't bother to think any more.

I took note of their name: The Drums.
Anyway, it's the best thing that's ever happened to me. No one likes me. No one ever, but these people came down to my disco and loved me. For the first time ever. It's given me faith in new music. The lyrics are dire. I'm not bothered about that. The opening one is the

best though for The Drums: "You were my best friend / But then you died / When I was 23 / And you were 25".

Well, the amount of people I have seen die in front of my eyes, I can relate to that. But the rest is as bad as an early Suede record. It's just nice that the kids are listening to a band that's mad on Orange Juice, Cure, Smiths, Camera Obscura and naturally, Joy Division.

I'm ageist, I know.

Jacob Graham and Jonathan Pierce asked me if I could DJ for them, afterparties, and so I said, "Alright, as long as I get a yellow budgie with a green head".
They said, "Alright".

Then I don't think anything more about it but I get this email from Island Records saying that The Drums love me and they want me to DJ for them, and what's me hourly rate and stuff. So I tell them £100/hour. PA for MD of Island comes back to me saying that's cool but what budgie would you like? The Drums spent ages looking up budgies and are mad on the fact that I should have a budgie.

Should they bring this rare bird down to Heaven and put it in the backstage area for me? Fuckinghell. I wasn't after anything. I gets down there and everything's alright.

The budgie's coming to me address today but that night gave me such faith.

I put a £10 bet on in Ladbrokes next day. All on one horse. I won nothing but still haven't stopped laughing.

When death is close, laughter isn't far.

I COULD BE ANYONE. ACCEPT MYSELF.

June 23rd, 2010

08:22 pm

I haven't written cos this fucking computer hasn't worked. God knows, this will all be lost.

Sometimes I look out of this window at the Asian children next door. The oldest child is on roller skates, the other one is on a small bike and the next one up is on a BMX. It reminds me of my childhood. They just circle and circle. It's a bit like "As Tears Go By". I've felt suicidal these last few days.

The man in Molly Moggs wouldn't serve me anymore. I said thank you and went to McDonald's. I didn't mean harm.

On Sunday I ended up in that strip club I used to work in, just standing there, at the bar like, watching an Eastern European on the stage, spreading her legs. After she finished I put a fiver in the pint glass. I got a taxi after that.

I've been on the piss for a couple of days and how I wish I could stop all this shenanigans. I thought seriously about jacking the band in. It gets me nowhere and brings me down.

I don't mind DJing but that brings me down too. I just don't know what I'm supposed to do.

Yesterday afternoon I went to Leytonstone Boating Lake, but it was too busy and I felt awkward cos it's a well-known dogging area.

I came back to my tiny room and then after this thing didn't work I tried to stamp on it. Completely sober but so upset with my lot and this life that I've been dealt. It sounds stupid and it is cos I could be my sister who has to look after mentally ill people who put their fingers up their arses and wipe it on her. I could be my Grandma or Grandad who worked in the cotton mills. I could be my Great Grandad who died at The Battle of The Somme.

Me go bed now.

SIX MONTHS FOR THE PRICE OF ONE SECOND

July 19th, 2010

12:57 am

Sometimes I just have these visions. And it's weird like cos most of the visions happen, y'know like within a few months or within a few years.

I just keep having this reoccurring one of me sitting in the bar of a really posh hotel, well it's posh anyway. Five stars. I've sat in the bar of a five star hotel before so it's nowt new. But in this vision I'm buying the drinks. Well I never. (Done that before.)

Today I went to The Soho Festival. It was one of those fundraising events. There were a lot of old men from the merchant navy around so perhaps it was for them. Then again, it was in the grounds of Saint Anne's church so perhaps that nice Father David Gilmore took a bit and helped the Soho community a bit more. He's good him.

After going to all the stalls, I stood around, feeling awkward. Why do I always feel so awkward? Even when I'm drunk I feel awkward. I always feel like I shouldn't exist.

I bought a book and five birthday cards from the stall run by The Phoenix Theatre Club. I knew it was just stuff Maurice was gonna throw away though. He makes me laugh. He never recognises me though.
Some people did though. There were a few there. They said, "Hello Scarlet".
"Hullo," I replied, with a glazed look in my eyes.

I'm sure I've got that weird disorder. I don't recognise faces and I never remember names unless I've known them for at least six months and even after six months it all goes a bit dodgy. There was a girl working behind the bar at my place of work. She popped in last Friday. She goes, "Scarlet, ooh it's so good to see you again!"

I smile and goes, "Ooooh you've changed your hair again".

"No, my hair's been the same since I left. You don't remember me do you?"

Well no, I didn't, but this girl had worked with me for six months. We'd been hanging around the casinos together after work too. We'd even had a sober afternoon at the cinema. Anyway, what I'm saying is my face and name recognition is shit. Don't take it personally if you're on the receiving end of my blank face.

I had to leave that festival anyway. I felt at odds with it all. I went to The Coach and the emptiness was exactly what I needed. People that aren't paid to take my money don't like me and people that pay to listen to me, well, they don't like me either. Bar staff, however, most of the time they pretend. And that's alright. I sometimes bore them with my anecdotes when there's no one else around.

I'm sick of foreign bar staff though. Whenever I try and explain Blackpool to them they get really confused. Or whenever I have a little joke or tell one of my anecdotes, the confusion escalates. I choose to go into pubs when it's dead. Often I won't enter unless there's three or less people in. When the midday sun is shining through the windows, well, that's my favourite hour. As long as they don't do food. That's one thing that fucking annoys me about pubs. Fucking food. Go and eat if you wanna eat but don't destroy my senses with the smell of food when I'm doing liquids only, cos it just makes me feel sick when I smell it. However, as soon as my twenty-four hours is up I'm onto the solids. Not in a pub like. Halal chicken is the usual for me.

So that's me and my thoughts for now. I'm just gonna stare at those red double deckers passing the window for about an hour until I drift off. Smoke a few Marlboro Lights. Listen out for Big Ben's chimes in ten minutes. It's more exciting south of the river.

PLEASE DON'T CRASH AGAIN

July 25th, 2010

05:48 am

My band did a gig last night. It was alright, like. I didn't bother publicising it cos we hadn't had that many rehearsals since getting the new drummer. He's alright though; called Joe, comes from South Africa. He brought down these really glamorous women. And they had lovely personalities too.

I got my first camera/video phone the other month. I've taken to filming pissed people when they're unaware. Not when I'm DJing like, cos that would be against the rules. Just when I'm on the bus or waiting at bus stops. There's nothing I hate more than pissed people. I'm gonna make a YouTube channel for all my findings.

Right, that's it. I haven't written much because my internet keeps disconnecting and I just wrote another six paragraphs before and now it's all lost. The only thing that stayed was those first two. Does anyone know why this keeps happening?

I mean that's the main reason why I don't bother writing anymore. I've never lost anything on a library or internet cafe computer so why do I keep losing everything on a laptop? It just disconnects.

Anyway, what I was saying in brief was: I was wondering why women go out in packs wearing skimpy outfits. I was wondering why I always see them go home in the same pack at the end of the night. I was wondering whether they send a text message to the men they fancy and I was wondering if they wear jeans and T-shirts when they go out on the date.

Is it to do with sex? I don't reckon so. Women seem so needy. They always want children, and I overhear conversations a lot. All women talk about is men. All men talk about is how much they hate women. Well, men talk about records as well but it upsets me that men have such a low opinion of women but then again, so do I.

Women just seem so desperate. Even the lesbians. The lesbians try and come onto me and I'm like, well if you were a man and you started stroking my hair I'd fucking give you a kicking.

Just about everyone gives me the creeps to be honest.

I remember, I didn't write half of the stuff above, I was just writing about the shit in a doorway of Denmark Place and how it knocked me sick. Then I was writing about how you get free electric devices like microwaves and laptops if you get sterilised in China. And so does the man. If he gets the snip like. And I was saying that's really great and how they should do that here cos this country is too packed.

TO BE DELETED

July 28th, 2010

11:32 pm

I quite enjoy watching close-up footage of people falling out of the World Trade Centre. Well, I don't enjoy it that much but it does fascinate me.

I also look up people in coffins. It's weird how many people put their relatives on YouTube just lying in the coffin or "casket". It only happens the other side of the pond, naturally.

A young girl put footage of her stillborn baby on there. Perhaps she wanted the world to share her pain. A problem shared is a problem halved and all that. After 190,000 views she won't be upset anymore.

There's this really funny video when one of the people that lower down the coffin falls into the grave before the coffin does. I found that so hilarious. I watched and watched it over and over. It was like Hot Chip. It was real though. The mourning women went mad, beating their breasts like some kind of pre-historic apes.

The blacks video funerals quite often. The wakes are always quite funny to watch. There's one where they have a dance-off. It's so bad. Well y'know, it's funny.

Then there's one member of a black gang that wanted to be standing at his own wake. He knew what he was involved in was dangerous so he made his funeral plans when he was eighteen. He was shot at twenty-three and you see him standing. Track suit, shades, ha ha! He just stands like a weird pale black waxwork in the corner and everyone's eating the buffet and having dance-offs around him. You can look all of this up on the YouTube.

Perhaps if I wasn't exposed to young deaths in my early life I wouldn't be obsessed with it all now. Maybe I'd take death more seriously. I kept seeing cement mixers today. I always feel like it's my brother waving. I saw how he was crushed by it last week. It was on the news about cyclists and blind spots and turning left at traffic lights and then it all came back to me that that was how it happened. Then I saw a bicycle smashed and I wondered what his body must have looked like. I thought, well I'm glad he didn't survive, I'm sure he's happy where he is. Manchester Royal Infirmary worked on him for two hours. I shouldn't be writing this here. I'll probably delete it tomorrow.

Today I went to the theatre. I much prefer going on my own cos then I don't have to have a discussion about how it was. It was shit. La Bête, Comedy Theatre, Joanna Lumley and Niles from Frasier. Don't bother.

THE ICE CREAM VANS IN OLDHAM
HAVE BANGRA CHIMES

August 16th, 2010

06:54 pm

I think my Mum's gonna make me some dinner in a bit so I thought I'd write something while I'm waiting.

I'm back in Oldham. I had a wedding to go to and a baptism. It's done now. The wedding was a lavish affair. It was in a big hotel with a massive swimming pool. No church was involved. They just had the ceremony in one of those rooms where they have bows on the chairs and flowers everywhere.

I think God should be involved in a marriage though. I told Michael and he agreed with me. So when we get married we'll be doing it in a church. We're going on a romantic holiday next month. We're staying in a posh hotel in Bournemouth. I love Michael so much. Sometimes when he's sitting there watching telly I'll just stare at him. Aaaah… I'm missing him.

Me and my sister went out in Oldham town centre on the piss last night. We started off in a rock pub called Whittles but the music in there is quite loud. While I was waiting at the bar, a man wearing shorts comes up to me and says, "Will you go out with me?" He was hammered. I said no and walked away. When my sister got back from the bog she said I should have arranged to meet him on Friday.

My sister's a bit cruel like that.

A man that stank of piss paced around the place for the duration of our visit. He was wearing an ancient suit pinned with war medals. He had a long greasy ponytail and was wearing a baseball cap. My sister informed me he was a regular.

We decided to sit outside in the smoking area when the stench became too much. Out there we met one of my sister's old school friends. He was called Vincent, soon to be Vanessa. A pre-op transsexual. He stank of B.O. but I felt quite sorry for him. He'd had a brain injury and his face was all over the place. He was articulate though, once you heard past those mongoloid tones and saw past that contorted face.

We decided to move on when the man in the shorts started to bother me again, saying it was his birthday. We went to a much more civilised place, a place that made me drop out of college: Jackson's Pit. Now this is one of Oldham's more bohemian establishments. An art exhibition was happening and a few bands were playing. My old friend Rick was there. He was playing in two bands. I remember Rick from when I was fourteen. He used to busk outside Littlewoods and I'd always give him 10p or something. I had quite a bit of money back then. My cigarette dealing business was booming, 8:45-9am I'd be lurking in the toilets doing the deals and taking the cash. 9am registration. 9:15 through the gates and into town straight to Manchester Central Library to get on with my own education.

Anyway, I've digressed. I got to know Rick and would spend many evenings smoking cannabis and drinking White Lightning in his council flat. It was nothing dodgy like. He never fancied me.
He'd lend me books to read and we'd talk about God a lot. More of the Buddhist type rather than my favoured Catholic one.
So it was good to see Rick again in Jackson's Pit. He sang well and hadn't aged. He has a child now. That's how people grow up I suppose.

I'm getting sterilised soon. It's something I've always wanted to do. I have my E.T.s y'see. I don't like children, I don't even like looking at babies. They look too squashed and red.

My dinner's ready now. Some cold meats left over from the baptism, a jacket potato and cauliflower cheese. Top. Totally top! And Corrie's on twice tonight. This is the best day of the year so far.

WHY DON'T YOU WRITE SONGS ABOUT FOOD?

August 28th, 2010

12:56 pm

My band played the trendy Proud Gallery on Tuesday. It was a bloody awful gig. I'm blaming it on the rest of the band cos they were out of time. I just stood there on the stage feeling awkward and embarrassed. I had to carry on though and so I did. It got better by the last two songs but the other eight were atrocious. I'm writing a bad review of my band. Yes, that's what I'm doing.

When we came offstage people were polite and they said they couldn't tell it was out of time. I was straight out of that building though and on the tube to Soho. I sought solace in a bottle of wine and a few Sambucas and DJ'd. I played a load of 80s pop cos I needed a lift after having to sing that depressing music I write.

I'll have to stop writing here cos my computer keeps disconnecting. I'll try and write in an internet cafe next time.

The next day I went drinking around the East End again. I sat in the Shakespeare in Bethnal Green Road and played my favourite Morrissey songs on the jukebox. Jack the Ripper was on there. There's a nice pub on the same road called The Misty Moon which used to be a Wetherspoon's. It's very odd. It has all the same fixtures and fittings but it doesn't do raspberry Sambuca spritzers or have those signs up everywhere about the deals that are on. And I miss the watered down pitchers. They're the ideal thing to drink after a session.

I'M AN ALCOHOLIC COS I'M JUST SO FUCKING BORED

August 31st, 2010

10:58 am

I was just watching Heir Hunters on BBC One before. I must have seen so many episodes of that, it's really starting to bore me now. Retired boxers that own pubs are interesting though. I don't mind them.

I don't know what to do today. I'm limited with my choices. I suppose I could do one of the museums or galleries but I'd rather have a game of bingo and a cheap pie or Wimpy lunch any day. I want to be on my own today. I'm finding people more and more difficult to get on with. I don't mind Michael though. Michael's not keen on the kind of food I eat. We were going to go for a game of bingo on Sunday but time drew on and we missed the session.

We ended up in The Dog House having a chat with Dave Ball and drinking pints of lager all afternoon. Dave was with two lesbian friends. They seemed a bit addicted to cannabis. It becomes a terrible thing that. I meet so many people nowadays either addicted to coke or cannabis. What ridiculous drugs to end up with a passion for. I'm glad mine is alcohol. At least it gets me out of the house.

Mind you, I popped into AA at Whipps Cross the other week and some of them were saying their drinking got so bad that they couldn't leave the house. They all seemed a bit messed up. Like woe is me. One Irishman piped up: "My name's Paddy and I'm an alcoholic and I'm just so fucking bored". He was swearing ten to the dozen, going on about how bored he was and how he wished something would happen even if it turned out to be a bad thing. I completely agreed with him. I mean, I had no intention of giving up, I just wanted something to do on an evening where I'd had too much drink the day before. Some people's misery is appealing to listen to. It's like listening to a story on Radio 4, but everything's real. I'm sure some of those alcoholics fabricate stuff. You have to go to a meeting at least once a week. Some go every day. They like to share their stories but some of it is an ego trip. I think, how many different meetings do they go to, retelling their "My Booze Hell" story? I can't say much though. These journal, Facebook and Twitter updates, they're just the same. All this internet crap is just a big wank off. It's like having sex or masturbating in front of a mirror. Yeah, where am I going?

My acting classes start up again soon. I love September. It's like a fresh start. I'm back at school and this year I'm gonna try harder.

THE JOYS OF STREATHAM AND BURNING DOWN YOUR OFFICE BUILDING

September 13th, 2010

09:11 am

I haven't been out on any two-day pub crawls recently. When I'm sober nothing that exciting seems to happen. Everything ticks along nicely. I'm not a manic-depressive or bi-polar cos without the drink I always feel just right. But being just right is also a bit boring. I'll try and go to bingo when I'm feeling like this. I might go to Streatham Bingo today cos I've got some vouchers. It's lovely in there. It's in a theatre that was built in the 1920s. It's all art deco inside.

Last time I went, the manager introduced himself to me. I told him my usual was Coronation Bingo in Elephant and Castle. He explained that his was a much smaller operation. Then they started playing: a can of Carlsberg for a line and a bottle of wine for full house. Yes, I saw, this was much smaller. Sometimes the temptation to drink is there when I'm least expecting it. But, as usual, I didn't win. I'm always hoping I don't win cos I don't want to shout out and have the rest of the bingo Mafia give me dirty looks.

I'm glad it's September again. I can go to the cinema during the day again now. I can't stand groups of young people. I find sitting in Streatham Odeon and being the only person at a screening really exciting. I can put my feet up over the seat in front. I have to sit near the front anyway cos my eyesight is so bad.

Wimpy Bar is opposite The Odeon. I usually go in there before. You can get a cheese and ham toastie, chips and a cup of tea for £2.99. Sometimes I get one of the burgers cos Wimpy always does the best burgers. I get the one with onion rings in. No chips though. Just a milkshake or sometimes a cup of tea. I'll catch up with my texts at this point. Now that was a good invention. There's nothing I hate more than having to speak to people on the phone. Unless I'm pissed. I'm always grateful for any company when I'm pissed.

There's a Heart Foundation shop further up from Wimpy. I usually finish off the day in there. It just sells books, videos and CDs. I look through all the CDs and most of the time leave empty handed. I've got most things worth having in my DJ bag. I'd be better off downloading stuff now but I don't know how to do that.

Each day I get more and more scared of all this modern technology. I've been keeping this diary since 2003 and it's been simple enough to do. I've got MySpace, Facebook and Twitter accounts. I don't like all that though cos it's messed up my attention span. I'm sure it's done the same to other people's.

Well, I'm gonna write to Sandy, my new pen pal now. She's in prison in Texas for inadvertently killing three people; she set alight her office building. If I had to work in one of those pointless things ever again, I'd do the same. I told her that I completely understand why she did it. I hope that made her feel somewhat better. But now, like so many other incarcerated ones she has found Jesus. I've been looking for Jesus but I haven't found him in church. Seems he still likes hanging round with criminals like he did all those years back. They are fascinating people though so I don't blame him.

BLACK COCKS AND ELECTRO
POPE MEETINGS

September 18th, 2010

05:16 am

It had been ages since I went out to a club that was not my own. A club called "Bedsitland" seemed proper. That song meant a lot to me in November 2002. Although mine was just a room.

Highbury and Islington has always been a place I remember spending a few hours in when I first came to London. Two years later I got my demo played down there from my first band, "Do or Die". I'm sounding like a Vietnam war veteran now. It was an empty Tuesday night in the warmth of August 2004.

Tonight I returned. It hadn't changed and I was glad. I hung around as I had in 2003. I talked to Rat-tail Reece. Y'know, that one with the plaited hair. I used to mention him a lot in my previous diary. I always used to say you could tell it was a club that I'd be into if he turned up. I found out later he'd been mad on the fetish scene. That's not my type of thing. All those lot are a bit dull. But every time I saw Rat-tail Reece he'd be taking pictures of every woman in the place. Flash. You would never see him get the camera out but. Flash. He would never hold the camera up to his eye. Just flash it from the side of his long leather coat. Forever alone, like me.

Anyway, he told me there was nothing worth photographing and I didn't see a flash bulb go off all night. He said the club was out of date and I reckon he was right. Synth pop is 2002. That's why I'm in a heavy rock band.

A lot of the people were overweight. I always try and do my nails and make sure I'm not too overweight. I don't mind people that are overweight though. Cos there was this really anorexic girl that smiled at me and I smiled back and told her I liked her leopardskin top and I pointed at mine and said, "You're well cool".

She looked back at her group of five friends while I had my head turned towards the bar and then she rolled her eyes and grimaced at me. I turned back quick you see. I know when people are not really trying to make friends with me.

I later saw three of them taking drugs in the toilets. I hate people that do drugs. I don't think it's right.

A few people that I met once in February 2003 kept coming up to me. Poncing fags. They hadn't made much of themselves. Those types of people ended up as F.E. teachers. Those that can't. Well, they teach. A few of them told me that they'd lost their jobs. Everyone seemed to be having a hard time. No matter what the job, they'd lost everything tonight. Flats, boyfriends, girlfriends, friends to suicide, friends to heroin, friends to crack, friends to rehab. The only thing that remained was this 80s electro mixed in with stuff like Ladytron, Ladyhawke and The Vichy Government.

I drank a few bottles of San Miguel. I choose a drink and stick to it and tonight that was my choice. Half an hour before it closed I had a bubblegum flavoured vodka shot. £3. It was the best part of the night.

I got the bus at three-ish. There was some black kids on the top deck of the bus that were parading their penises about. But it was alright cos they were at the back of the bus and they were just showing their penises to the other top deck of the bus behind. They had some tarty white girls with them. I don't mind white girls but some want to be black cos they all like that Rihanna and every time I saw her before she got beaten up, I wanted to smack her as well.

HARVEYS BRISTOL CREAM
WAS ROTTING MY TEETH

October 8th, 2010

03:14 pm

I've been sitting around, watching telly and going to pubs lately. It's been alright.

My Mum came down to visit the other week. We went to see Dreamboats and Petticoats, really good seats like. An old man sat next to me and said on his arrival, "Oh, I am looking forward to this. It's going to be a riveting show".
"Yeah so am I," I said.
Anyway, three minutes into the first number and he had his head to his chest and I wondered whether he was dead. He woke up for the interval though and then came back with a loaf of bread, a bottle of milk and a plastic cup of coke. Then the show started up again and he fell asleep again and then he woke up for the last number, walked into the aisle and started doing the twist. Thing is, everyone else got out of their seats then and started doing the twist too. Even I started to do the twist and I rarely dance. Wow! That man is an inspiration to us all. Hang around on your own and do what the fuck you like. That's my theory anyway.

I went to Harrods the other day and had an afternoon tea complete with a glass of champagne. Bloodyhell, it's boring in there so I won't be doing that again. I'm gonna stick to bingo and dodgy pubs.

The next day I hung around with the woman whose Dad is also her Grandad in Wetherspoon's. I went to a few pubs about the vicinity in Leytonstone. I tried to contact my other obese acquaintance. She's a nice girl but smells of piss and cheap perfume. I buy her Coca Cola when I see her cos she doesn't drink. You can't drink on the tablets she takes. Anyway, my obese friend stood me up and I thought, well I'm not even good enough to be friends with the mentally ill nowadays. I think then I sank into a morbid mood cos I read a few scrawls in the notebook I carry around. I'd written down an argument I was overhearing in real time. Then I can just make out, "I've wrecked it all". Oh yes, I guess I could have. What I don't know, but it was more wrecking myself than anything else. And oh, I did enjoy the process.

I'm going for my liver function test in a week. One every year. It's come round quickly this year. Last year when I got the everything's fine result I celebrated with eight pints of Kronenbourg and a few Harveys Bristol Cream chasers. I don't know whether I'll be as lucky this year though. I'm not as good-looking anymore so what goes on on the outside is symptomatic of what's going on in the inside. I hope something is wrong. I hope they make me quit cos I would then.

I think I'm only alright cos I don't drink spirits. I don't drink Harveys Bristol Cream anymore either cos I reckon it's no good for my teeth.

I like being with Michael though when I'm sober. That's the best thing.

COVERS FOR STRIPPERS
October 16th, 2010

09:11 am

I keep hearing the couple from the flat below playing out their sexual antics against a wall. Fuckinghell, it worries me.

A woman wearing nipple tassels came up to Michael tonight while we were sitting in a bar watching her strip. "You know where you spent last night," she said into the microphone.
Huh huh, I just laughed. She was older and uglier so I wasn't arsed and I knew that Michael had gone to bed after I'd finished with him. Plus I'd have smelt that vile perfume within the flat when I got back.

That's what these awful jazz clubs are, they're just covers for strippers. I reckon burlesque is sexist. Why should women be pretty when they want to get off. The sexiest women are in Wetherspoon's Leytonstone on a Friday night. At least you know they're gonna put out. Or anywhere in Oldham. In a bar of course.

I rang 5 Live when I got back, explaining how I didn't mind prostitutes or women that put it about but how I couldn't stand women in high heels. Generally.
I took a lot of stick from everyone but just kept going on about me broken leg and that how these women have an unfair advantage on me. And me alcoholic y'see? I couldn't wear them, me just fall down anyway. I got nowhere.

Michael don't mind me not wearing high heels though. Sometimes he makes me meet his ex-girlfriend and she wears them all the time but she's not a patch on me and my good looks. She's alright though cos he always insists on inviting her to my concerts and she always turns up.

I've got a bottle of Lambrini in the fridge. It's 09:10 now so I'll open that and get to acting class by eleven.

PURGATORY. THAT'S LIFE

October 23rd, 2010

12:32 am

When I'm suicidal I start looking round the room. The blind rope is doing a lot for me right now. I'm thinking how could I tie it so it would really do me in. What could I tie it to? A chair, a door knob, what did Ian Curtis do?

I dunno. This drinking depression hits me hard. I should have blacked out by now but I haven't cos I had to work. Michael's asleep. He doesn't understand all this nonsense.

And that's what this is. It makes no sense. Why do I feel this bad? Why am I an alcoholic? I fucking don't know. Half the time I wish I was dead and the other half of the time I can't believe that a person as great as me can actually exist. But right now, this moment and for these few hours I don't want to exist. I want to get back to where I was once from.

And that's not Oldham. I want to die. Nothing tonight made me down. The club was packed. I played all my favourite songs. I drank Tiger beer.

I've got nothing to live for. Every success I've had has meant nothing. If only I could catch that cancer. One in three catch the cancer. I must be the only two in one that's chasing it. I wish death would catch me. I feel so cold. All the time. People's feelings. I don't care when I beat people up. I punched some people in Valentino's the other night. That's the cafe on top of Greek Street. They deserved it. I'm hoping they'll catch the cancer sometime soon. Mind you, living in this terrible purgatory that most call life is worse.

A BIRTHDAY TO NEVER REMEMBER
ADVENTURE STORY

October 30th, 2010

08:20 am

I went to my favourite casino tonight. Met some models. They were quite dull. Models always are.

I DJ'd beforehand. There were some women dressed up as nurses. They looked like they'd bought the outfits from Harmony. They copped off. They danced in front of the booth all night, snogging different men. It makes me laugh. People seem to have so much fun when they're wearing a uniform.

I caught the tube home. That was about an hour ago. It's always nice to catch the tube at this hour. I don't like it when it's busy.

Last night was my birthday. Me and me sister went to St Moritz. Gaz's Rockin Blues. It was absolutely crap. It's not what it's cracked up to be, that place. We got so sick and bored of the people that we went to my place of work. Dorian was there so I sat in a booth with him while me sister danced. He was with his family too. We talked about families and cracking up, depression and highs, stuff like that. A few arseholes came over and tried to pick fights but I'm quite confident now with me method of grabbing people in an arm lock and punching their face senseless. All the staff say is if anyone pisses me off then it's alright to do that.

Me and me sister went to Valentino's after. I wanted to check out whether I was barred and thankfully I'm not. I had a smoked salmon and cream cheese sandwich with a few Monster Munch on the side.

I flagged down a black cab after that. Drank a bottle of Lambrini when I got in. My sister just lay there on the settee. I stared blankly out of the window. It was dark. I watched the cars passing on the main road and listened to Big Ben's chimes every fifteen minutes. As time drew on, the aeroplanes started to pass above. I like the aeroplanes.

We went back out to the pub round the corner at midday. I played Silver Machine by Hawkwind on the jukebox. My sister wasn't keen. She drank Britvic. Me, usual, Kronenbourg.

For rest of story start again. Like one of those adventure books.

I HAVE SOUL LOSS AND
I WISH I WAS DEAD

November 6th, 2010

07:14 am

I have a lot of terrible images that I keep trying to block out. If you google it, it's "Soul loss". I wish I was dead. I keep wishing I was dead. All the time I wish I'm dead.
Apart from when I'm with Michael though.

I'd die tonight, happy in Michael's arms. In anyone else's, there is harm.

I stand firm in what I said. Y'know I wish the cancer would catch me. I look closely at every fag. I go to the fridge, I look at every single can of Heineken. But the trouble with me, I can't be arsed drinking and I can't be arsed smoking. I simply don't have the time.

08:54 am

why does no one like me?
I struggle. With people. I know no one likes me…
Well to be dead would be a joy. But to not have to talk to anyone and just be me… I'm knackered.

BLOOD AND GORE IN TELEPHONE BOXES

04:15 pm

I've been searching ways to stop drinking. I've even gone so far as yoga for addictions. Nothing has brought me to the light. When I'm hungover I have the best intentions. I mean, I'm a nice person with the hangover. Michael loves me with a hangover if he doesn't know I've been drinking the night before (well, the previous two nights as is always in my case).

I even feel nice with a hangover. I'll sit down and get stuff done. I remember when I was at school, the most productive days would be the hungover ones. I'd enjoy me paper round if I was hungover, just strolling along listening to my metallic blue Sony Walkman (R.I.P.). I feel so satisfied with a hangover.

I'm getting another paper round soon. For the three years I had my old paper round I thought a lot. I still think too much but having a scenery going past while you're doing it is magic.
I remember the door numbers, the different kinds of letterboxes, the smells of mince and potatoes cooking in the old people's flats. I remember the sunsets. Well, mine was an evening one.

I used to walk and think of my brother and how he was killed. Sometimes I'd chant Hare Krishna and light a jostick in people's gardens.

It doesn't take much to throw you over the edge and perhaps that did. Well, the dead brother, not the paper round.

My acting teacher once told me, "Those that do not move forwards will go backwards". My acting teacher, Charles Verrall, is the most fascinating man I've ever met. He just seems to know everything. He told me once that drinking was contagious. I've never been drunk in front of him but I was talking to him about my addiction.

I was talking about The Coach and Horses on Greek Street, Jeffrey Bernard, Francis Bacon and the rest of the contingency. My only inspiration comes from getting out of my head among the drunks. Why does nothing else inspire me as much?

I used to like getting out of my head with famous drunks but now whenever I sit down and drink I just get the dead ones. Hallucinations y'see. My hallucinations under the drink are fascinating. Disturbingly so. Sometimes I see people with their skin all off. Like demons. And they start talking to me. They tell me things. I've been barred from many a pub from talking to people that no one else can see. Sometimes they appear just as I do to you. Sometimes it's children. They appear as they died.

I wonder whether I'll get sectioned from writing this. I mean without the alcohol I'm fine. I wouldn't mind going to some clinic or other. "Away for a while," as that NHS consoler put it. I was just grief-stricken like. You know, my boyfriend rang me up and dumped me over the telephone, from a public call box. His pips went like. And then all that raw meat business afterwards. Staunch vegetarian, he was. Just coating the phone box he used in blood and gore. No one's crossed my path since. No one needs to. I'm awful now.

My faith in love and human life has been lost and that's why I am this way. They can use this as evidence if I kill someone. At least it will give my diary the attention it so truly deserves.

WOULD ANYONE CARE FOR
AN AFTER EIGHT?

November 8th, 2010

12:52 pm

I've been laughing all morning. A change is as good as a rest as they say.

It started off when I saw a car number plate with a silver playboy sticker attached (I'm back in Essex). Oh I dunno, but why?

Then I went to Tesco. Big Tescos never fail to crack me up. I don't buy anything in the one in Leytonstone because I don't need anything here. I looked at the Christmas confectionery section and saw some After Eight mint sticks. I just imagined handing them round with a coffee after a dinner party. Oh God! I just couldn't stop laughing at the thought. Then I remembered how my Mum has a special gold rack for After Eights. Y'know like a toast rack. Then I saw you could get Tesco's own brand After Eights. I imagined wrapping them up and giving them to someone as a Christmas present. You could also get Tesco's own brand After Eights but with Turkish Delight in them. Now what you wanna do with them is put them in my Mum's special After Eight gold rack and that would surprise your guests! Maybe even make them puke. Not many people like Turkish Delight. Me? Well I can take it or leave it.

Back in Tesco I saw they had a selection of frosted jellied fruits that were made to look like slices of oranges and lemons. That cracked me up even more. I was just standing there in the aisle, doubled over, tears rolling down my face. Security had to be called. I was led out for being drunk. The irony of this is that I'm sober today.

I've been up since 7am. I had a shower and washed my hair and made an early start. I set off for Hollow Ponds because it was raining. Hollow Ponds is an amazing place at the top of Leytonstone. It has a boating lake and all the trees are hollow. It's in Epping Forest. I often hang around there. I feel happy there. I had a bacon and egg sandwich from the Lakeside Diner, a can of Pepsi and a cup of tea and sat there watching the rain and the car drivers.

I feel a lot happier than I did. Thanks for your concern.

SPREAD BET ON PIGEONS.
KENNINGTON-LEYTONSTONE

November 11th, 2010

02:07 am

I hadn't drunk since Friday. I had immaculately saved a dinner from the microwave oven when I explained to Michael that drinking wasn't in my nature anymore; I had gone through last night's DJ set struggling but not touching a drop. Sober for three days for the first time in about two years, with no reason to be. I mean, there's nothing I need to do. If there's something that I need to do, I won't touch it. It was just all that suicide stuff. Anyway, he says, "Let's go to this new pub".
"I don't want to ruin your life by becoming sober. It just makes me suicidal," I says.

Eating. Silence.

So I watch the Jack Duckworth documentary and off we go.

Fantastic pub it was too: The Old Red Lion on Kennington Park Road. It was a bit like my place of work. All old furniture and fascinating knick-knacks from house clearances.

I used to go when it was the old place, when it opened at 11am and had a blind and deaf dog called Daisy; the unmarried mothers would go in with their sleeping newborns. Mother's ruin a year ago in there was a pint of Carlsberg. I'd speak low about my life to them and they'd talk loud about theirs, and the rotten men that undid all their dreams. Never ever waking the baba. The babies were comatose but my Father and the ones that went before him were given alcohol, so it can't do that much harm.

Now it opens 4pm-11pm. Things change.

Knives and forks were spread out in the side section of the pub, the one that used to be graced with a pool table, three fruit machines and a dartboard.

I'm worried about the trade in this place though. It was such a wonderful establishment back then and it still is now, although I wonder where the women went with their prams in the morning. It's dangerous to drink at home. I never see those downtrodden women around Leytonstone. It's so peaceful round there. People have plenty to do. There's something that inspires me to do absolutely nothing round here, not cos there's fuck all to do, but just cos there's something that paralyses me. I don't know what it is.

Here, you can hear Big Ben every fifteen minutes and see The London Eye and all that Southbank/Embankment in close perspective. But the water tastes vile. The best thing going round here is Michael.

BINGE DRINKING IN TECHNICOLOR

November 25th, 2010

10:32 am

I've been wanting to go afternoon drinking in Walthamstow for years now. I never got round to it cos I worry about the bus journey back. It takes fifteen minutes from Leytonstone and that's fifteen minutes too long if you're too pissed.

Anyway, on Monday I got round to it. I hadn't been drinking for a few days so I was feeling a bit too normal. First of all I passed by The Chequers on the street where the market is but it seemed too busy. I'm not used to busy pubs but I'd started this session a bit late in the day. It was 2pm. I walked down the road and went to The Cock Tavern instead. I couldn't have dreamed of a more run-down dodgy pub. It was full of swearing locals. I should have had a tape recorder. The way they were shouting and swearing was extraordinary. There was a boy with them of around eight years old. It wasn't school holidays but then again, perhaps he was suspended or expelled.

I sat in the corner near the window with my half pint of Stella. Horizontal blinds covered the window. In the opposite corner were some over-eighties. The woman among the men must have been around eighty-five with jet black hair and blonde highlights. She was wearing sunglasses, drinking from a pint and looking really pissed. That's me if I get that lucky and pubs still exist.

I didn't want to linger in The Cock for too long cos it was all getting a bit loud and violent and I didn't want to get glassed. So I left and found an amazing pub next door to the old cinema on Hoe Street. The Victoria. A chalk sign outside read, "Sky Sports. £2 a pint. 12pm-12am. Mon-Fri". This seemed like my kind of pub. I'd passed it a lot before I developed a drink problem. You have to go upstairs, it may seem a bit daunting to most of the general public. This bar used to belong to the cinema. You used to be able to see the screen from in there but not hear the sound. Like a viewing gallery. So up those lonely stairs I went. There were five men inside, all in their fifties and sixties having a bit of banter as is popular in these parts. The landlord said, "What can I get ya princess?" That took me back a bit that. In twenty-nine years no one has called me princess. The landlord was Scottish though. Anyway, I ordered half a Foster's. One thing I notice about these kind of pubs is the fact you can only get Carling, Stella or Foster's. But I'm not fussy when it comes to lager. I hate Carling though. You might as well be drinking water for all the good that does.

The landlord and the men went back to discussing how to store Guinness but not before the landlord gave me a copy of The Daily Mirror to read. I was writing stuff in my notebook about The Cock cos I would definitely have been glassed if I'd have gotten me little green book out in there. Anyway, me writing was unnerving the landlord a bit so I sat and read The Mirror. I'm not keen on The Mirror though. It's like an upmarket version of The Sun. I much prefer The Sun. At least they've got politically aware women with their breasts out, which just shows you can be intelligent and have sex appeal too.

Anyway, I spied a jukebox next to my table and asked the landlord if I could put some music on. And so I chose. I was limited because it wasn't one of those new ones that have just about every song ever on it.

Gene Pitney – Backstage
Elvis – I Just Can't Help Believing
Tony Christie – Avenues and Alleyways
Del Shannon – Runaway

It was good in The Victoria. I got talking to some of the locals about Manchester and drank a few more halves that then became pints and before I knew it the sun had set and my afternoon drink had turned into an evening session.

I popped by The Rose and Crown once I had exhausted The Victoria. This pub was actually what I had come to Walthamstow for. It's a lovely old Victorian one. All carvings, tiles and mosaics. All restored to its original state. I got talking to some bearded men at the bar about CAMRA. And then the landlord gave me a tour of the building. There's a theatre at the top and an art gallery at the side. I don't usually like arty pubs but this one was top.

After that I popped by The Goose before catching my bus back to Leytonstone. There I met an ancient woman that really stank bad. She looked a hundred and fifty years old with crepe paper skin. I felt like Sarah in The Labyrinth, discovering all these strange characters that might help me get to where I need to be. Anyway, this woman was bitter about life, I forget her name. She kept swearing and seemed very angry, but all there in the head wise.

The smell got too much for me and so I left for Leytonstone. No more pubs for today. I cleaned my teeth and washed my make-up off. Then I sat up in bed and drank my last can of Kronenbourg while writing a poem about snow and stabbings in Oldham. The next morning I went to the library and emailed my masterpiece to The Oldham Evening Chronicle. I doubt they'll publish it.

Jeremy Kyle is talking about binge drinking this morning. There's a man on who drinks six litres of cider a day because his gran and grandad died. Fuckinhell! What a ridiculous reason to drink! You can't blame another person for your drink problem you wanker! Or circumstance! I drink cos I like getting pissed. I know it makes me suicidal sometimes but the drink has made me so happy in this last fortnight. And the hangovers have been of the most relaxing, introspective and calming kind. Wonderful news eh?

Oh, and another thing. He got his liver function test back at the end of the show and it turns out he's done no long-term damage! Cool, I'll carry on then. Just sticking to lager though.

SKIPPING SCHOOL IN WERNETH PARK

November 28th, 2010

02:55 am

Once the advert ends I'm returned to my journal experience.

Well, alright. Here I am. Is this an experience? I'm no Jimi Hendrix but this is a bit crap.

I'm sitting in the cold and dark. It's not damp though cos Michael took the mildew off the windows today, although he's mad on keeping things clean so I don't notice those kind of things.

There's a Mini Tesco about to open round the corner here in Kennington. Thank fuck for that. Those men in the 24 hour Costcutter hate me and I hate them. They're all on drugs. I know. They're all on cannabis. Every time I'm sober and don't buy drink, they raise their eyebrows and exclaim, "Why no wine today?"
"I can't drink every day y'know? Otherwise I'd be a right problem."

It's 2am now. I might watch a bit of telly. If you've got Sky then I like watching these channels/programmes:
Landscape Channel
Caravan Channel
BEN (TED Talks only)
Alba
S4C

What does my head in is seeing these really boring women every year that advertise Boots products. They put me off. As if the office party is the highlight of their year. I often see those kind of women going home on the tube when I'm going to work. They sometimes have on really dirty trainers. I don't mind women not making an effort but when your footwear doesn't go with your outfit, quit your job.

And the same kind of women advertise Dove products. And now Dove are trying to get men in on the act. Choose my DAD PLEASE! He's normal! For Oldham.

Tomorrow I have to rehearse.

I tell you what is weird though: sitting as I do, night upon night, not conversing with anyone other than to say, "Yes," "no," or "maybe".

It gets awfully lonely. But then when people come and speak to me, most times I hate them for it. But on a rare occasion I'm thankful. But then again, only if they're a person worth speaking to.

I used to be grateful of someone to speak to when I'd spent the whole day in a bush in Werneth Park as I did. I hated school so much. I used to meet a lot of strangers around those parts, I can tell you. Although they weren't dodgy paedophiles. They were just headcases from the local asylum and friendly criminals from the local bail hostel. They didn't do me any harm anyway!

Pen pals from Select Magazine stood me in good stead. Well I hope my Dad's sleeping well. I hope he survives my visit. I hope my sister has forgiven me for being a crap host and writing down our personal lives in diary form. I hope my Mum's arthritis hasn't gotten any worse.

I don't hope anything for me because I know that my visions for myself always become reality.

A WOMAN IS STABBED WHILE THE AIR
HANGS HEAVY LIKE MULLING WINE

December 7th, 2010

10:50 am

I can never bear to go back to this page if I've been up all night and then written an entry. I think I was being sexist in my last entry. I don't want to read it but then again, I don't want to delete it.

I don't like reading text messages I've sent either. I only delete them all when I'm pissed. And I only ever listen to my voicemails when I'm drunk.

I feel like I'm wasting my life. I'll live intensely for about three days a week and not sleep. I'll dress up in my furs and take everything I may need in my handbag. You know what I do. Sometimes I stop to go back to work but when I'm in this manic phase, work is a joy. All the colours seem brighter and people seem so nice to me.

Then after three days the bad comes but I don't want to go into that.

I will try and leave the house today. I need to collect my jumpers from Leytonstone and bring them back to Kennington.

On Sunday night I was looking up at a block of flats and I started to get a vision of a woman being beaten up by her husband. The next morning I heard that a woman had been stabbed to death by her husband in the block just at the time I was looking up. 7pm. What's the point in me getting these visions if I can do nothing to stop the deaths from happening? There's other ones I've had too. I woke up in the middle of the night on Tuesday and I couldn't get this woman out of my mind. I hadn't thought about her for ages but the next day I rang my Mum and she told me the woman had just died. Anyway, what does all this matter? No one would believe me. I know you're all "intelligent atheists".

279

I was speaking to a book publisher in an artists' community in Kennington on Sunday afternoon. Getting a book published seems pretty easy. It's all quite straightforward. I don't see why more people don't do it.

I played with my band on Wednesday. It was in a very small venue called Anam in Angel. £4 for a bottle of lager! The band before us were an X-Factor style vocal harmony group. Dreadful. Absolutely dreadful. They were called Holah. Holah! with a "!"

I knew it was a mistake to play there as soon as we turned up but I always feel as if Criminal Records might give us a deal or whatever the new thing is nowadays. I'm getting on though and the band hasn't sounded that good lately. I think the new drummer from New York has improved things for us. He's making us more in time.

I don't know what to make of everyone staring at me when I'm on stage though. I don't mind it but I don't think people particularly like us. I can tell by the way they look. And then the sound engineer always makes us finish when we've got three or four songs left to do. They only let us play for about twenty minutes nowadays. We used to get longer in the old days.

I always thought that if you did something for long enough and kept on turning up on time then success would be yours.

Anyway, we're going into a proper recording studio soon and then we're playing St Moritz on Friday January 7th so you know. I've been doing this band for eleven years so I might as well carry on till the end of days, which if the Mayans are correct may mean I only have to bother for another two and a bit years.

AND ALL THESE PEOPLE SEEMED
SO FRIENDLY AND NICE

December 11th, 2010

05:38 am

I started work at eleven tonight. I couldn't move from the settee. I'd been there since eleven in the morning. Telly was on but I slept with my face towards the back of the settee. Closing my eyes shut tight, I stayed there for as long as I could, all stiff and curled up. It reminded me of those depressing days past. I didn't want to go tonight. I had a terrible feeling about it all. At 10pm I had to. Contact lenses put in. A thick layer of make-up applied.

My palpitations began as I walked through Soho. My hands were shaking and all that malarkey.

I was right to be worried. The people kept telling me how crap I was but I knew that I wasn't. I played a wonderful set, a tried and tested one, but I think they just wanted some Kanye West. I've seen his name in The News of The World but I couldn't tell you what he looked like or sounded like.

As usual some people thought I was good and kept holding their fists up to me to which I'm supposed to hold my knuckles out and crash my knuckles into theirs. I don't understand all that. If only they could keep every part of themselves away from me I would be happy. I don't mind shaking hands with people if I'm introduced first but that's as far as it goes. Don't touch me if you don't fucking know me.

They all expect me to be dancing behind the booth and lifting my hands up to inaugurate them in some soft sense of the word. I refuse to do all that and so they just keep coming up to me calling me miserable and bored. But I'm neither miserable nor bored. But once they've said that to me I'm both cos I know what kind of people they are. The members are wonderful people though. They truly appreciate what I do.

One man kept posing shooting himself in the head when I was playing The Clash. Heaven knows what he was after. He'd obviously not been before.

Then while I was doing my Northern Soul section the wankers kept asking me for some other genre that I'd been playing for the whole previous hour.

And just what to do? What can you do?

Well I didn't know but just stuck to the usual set. The thing is, I don't want to do the same predictable set every night, but even if I play something slightly obscure I'll be inundated with requests for Lady Gaga while playing something different.

The members, like I said, they like me and I like them. It's just the rest of them that have never been to a proper club before.

When I left I was talking to my friends outside for a bit but a group of men were saying I looked like a bag lady. I knew I was looking really glam. I was wearing my black fur coat, turned up jeans and DMs. God, that really did upset me. I only had my small handbag with me too! I said to them, "I'm gonna go home and kill myself because if people like you exist then there's no hope for a future in this country".

With that I walked quickly down the street and onto Whitehall where the N155 came quickly. Driving past the defaced Parliament Square a man in front of me was talking to a girl called Scarlet that used to be called Sarah and his name was Michael. And then another twenty-nine-year-old woman piped up, "I'm called Sarah as well!" "That's my name as well!" I said. And all these people seemed so friendly and nice. And we all talked about how we'd changed our names because Sarah was the name of 1981 and everyone was called Sarah when we were at school.

We all talked about Ireland too and how we all had some connection with the place. Well, I suppose most people do. They were Catholics too. Everything seemed fine again.

CAN I BORROW YOUR MOBILE PHONE
TO RING MY SOCIAL WORKER?

08:54 am

Someone once told me no matter what you do, just don't stop writing. I've been trying to do other things but nothing has had the affect that these pages have had on me. And the fact that I'm not private about anything.

So Wetherspoon's the other day:
"I've not seen her sober yet."
Two old men were talking about me. It's amazing how sharp my ears are when I know people are talking about me.
The yellow man came over to my booth then and posed the question, "Can I borrow your mobile phone?"
"What for?" I said.
"To ring my social worker."
I lent it to him and he did just that. A few minutes later she was in The Walnut Tree having a meeting with Steve, the yellow man. I overheard talks about debts and how much he could pay off, etc, etc...
I moved to the window seat, knowing that my ears were the only parts of Steve's dignity left.

A dishevelled Irish man with a full head of black hair in his seventies sat opposite. He wore a tweed blazer with some pins on from some political movement. Asleep. On the next table, mind. There's a lot to be said for Guinness. Men that take that drink always look quite well. The sunlight poured onto us both and he sat up and grimaced once every five or ten minutes while taking another sip.

I glanced up occasionally at the flatscreen. The tuition fees protest had kicked off for the last time. Whitehall was on fire and I wondered about my bus stop that evening. They were due to vote that day. I knew they were going to vote to raise the fees.

Two heroin addicts sat in the corner. I'd bought a year's worth of mascara from them last month so they knew not to bother me again with their wares. They specialise in black mascara y'see... I overheard the heroin addicts talking about their fostered out children and how they longed for them back, how they'd change and all that.

It turned eleven and one by one the Irish men got up to go. O'Neill's up the road was just about to open. I only go up there when I'm absolutely gone but I wasn't on Thursday. I felt alright cos I was only drinking alcoholic ginger beer.

I overheard one of the men on the next table as he was getting up to go. The men asked him if he wanted to meet for a drink on Thursday. "No I'm on antibiotics," he said.
Struggling with his crutches while reaching into his blazer's inside pocket he pulled out a small white plastic bottle and declared, "Holy Water. I shall be healed".

That was the end of that then. I got my roots done which cost me £60. Usually it's £37. Anyway, that was that. I drank coffee and watched Live Coronation Street when I got home which was the biggest treat. Then I went to work and thought about sending in a few episodes I'd written. Only for myself. And if only I could play the character I'd written would it ever be shown.

I couldn't see anything through the steamed up windows on the N155 home. No one seemed bothered. Arsey middle class girls spread their legs over the seats and ate chips while the cleaners and workers had to stand up on the top deck not wanting to disturb the fuckers. I got a seat though. I dunno how. I found a migrant and sat down. I didn't want to disturb the fucking vile middle class fuckers either. We all know our place.

I JUST WANT TO DIE A LEGEND

December 15th, 2010

05:07 pm

I feel wonderful when the veil lifts and the colours become incredible. This seems to have happened today. I've been puking up all day cos I ate an out of date Christmas turkey wrap this morning. In between that I've been lying on the settee drifting in and out of sleep but it's lovely how amazing I feel. I'm so excited right now. I feel like this is some kind of amazing time like New York in 1979 or something. I feel like in a few years' time I'll be feeling warm and nostalgic about now. If I survive, that is.

People can't get into my club after midnight nowadays. It becomes too packed. I never move from the DJ booth when I'm in there now. I DJ'd from 8-3 last night. If I'm not drinking I'll make sure I have a cranberry juice and a Coke before I start. It's been nice these last few days. I've enjoyed doing my DJing. And I've got some new French records so it's been nice to play those.

Everything's coming together but my health is deteriorating again.

I bet just as I've done something of extreme importance for the future of art and literature I'll die suddenly. But it won't matter cos I don't care for money, I just want to die a legend.

SHE WAS A LONER AND
WE WERE WORRIED

December 17th, 2010

05:37 am

Now Co-operative Funerals are the first interactive moving advert that comes whenever I log on. Bloodyhell. I sure am a target audience. But I don't have enough money for them. Well, I've not saved.

On Monday the doctor will send me for tests, cos that's the usual thing to do. I hope I'm terminal. It will be lovely knowing that at last I'm going to die, hair all out but wearing that longed-for Bet Lynch wig.

As I said, fighting cancer? Why bother? I certainly won't.

As for my funeral plans, well I've given up my body to the human tissue organisation. Upon the notification of my death, they will bring round one of their silver vans to take away my body. They'll put my body in a freezer (like E.T.), then the experiments and dissection will begin. Wow! Just as it would have happened to E.T. if he had died.

I DJ'd tonight. I'm so cold all the time. Is that one of the first signs of dying? And being so nonchalant and happy with arseholes? Well, that must be the second.

I haven't seen a doctor yet.

"He was a loner." That's what they say when a killer strikes.

It's just lazy journalism. The term most overused when you're sick of people. And mostly it's your girlfriend that has made you a bit depressed so you've gone on the rampage with a shotgun. I can understand it. So don't worry, I'll still be writing for you.

If I'm still alive.

HOLDING UP FOR CHRISTMAS

January 13th, 2011

01:52 pm

Going back home for Christmas was more traumatic than usual. The snow was deep and the streets surrounding my house had become even more desolate and eerie. You could hear water gushing from the rows of steel-locked terraces. The council hadn't bothered to turn the water off and now their pipes had frozen and burst.

Most of the street lights were out. The moonlight reflecting upon the snow was the only thing to help navigation.

My Mum was good to me and took me for an all you can eat carvery. I think it was £5.99 for two. Well I piled my plate up I can tell you. Not as much as some of the other people in the restaurant. The Bridgewater it was called. It's on Manchester Road. My Mum had a voucher from The Oldham Chronicle. It was good to look around the restaurant and see the people of Oldham again. They look so different to people anywhere else in the world. They have certain hairstyles and wear certain clothes and their faces look not similar but just different. I can't work out what it is about them. They're not inbred, cos I've met inbred people. Although they probably stick to having children with other people from Oldham so in a way they might be inbred. But it's a big place. Soon most of the world will be inbred, with all this artificial insemination. That's wrong. It's against God.

I walked up the hill to visit my Dad on Christmas Eve. His house was freezing as his boiler had broke. He was drinking from brandy glasses filled with straight whisky and he smelt pretty bad. He was going on about how The Pope was a Nazi. He was talking about the prostitute, Pamela, he hangs out with. Then he kept saying he was like Jesus. Anyway, my sister came round and fixed his boiler. I had a can of Grolsch I'd bought from the corner shop. I bought him six cans of cat food too. I felt like my Dad might have benefitted from some food. The fridge and cupboards were all empty. He just had a few condiments on the table. But I'd got him a selection of cheese and biscuits for Christmas so I didn't want to spoil his surprise.

My sister fixed the boiler. She's good like that. I suggested we call a taxi and take him down to The Royal Oak, the only pub in the whole area that's still open. My sister held Dad up as I put his arms through his brown crombie. The driver beeped and taking each arm we walked him to the taxi. In the pub he sat in his usual seat and my sister kept making these snowmen on the shelf behind him sing, the kind of things you get from 99p Stores. It was funny to look at him sitting in front of these jolly singing snowmen. He kept frowning and rolling his eyes. He looked so old and embittered by the world. He looked older than his Dad looked at ninety-five, so thin and frail, hands all bone, smooth and pale.

I think my Dad bought about five whiskies in the hour we were there. Then we found he couldn't stand up so we had to call the taxi again. This time we had to get a few of the locals to help us with him. He was a dead weight. It was like carrying a corpse. We shoved him head first into the back of the taxi and he lay down and started to go to sleep. We propped him up as best we could and we were lucky that the Pakistani taxi driver was a strong chap or else we would never have been able to get him out again. Back in his house we slumped him down in his armchair and my sister made him some coffee. He was stone cold but he was still alive.

We left him in the chair with the heating on and we went up to Oldham on a pub crawl. I didn't get too pissed. My Dad had done a lot that afternoon to stop me even thinking about the joys of alcohol. I spent Christmas Day worrying about whether my Dad was still alive. I kept thinking about him sitting dead in his chair, and memories came back of Christmasses in the 80s. He'd be a lively drunk, smoke a few cigars and then fall asleep. My memories of those Christmasses are happy ones. Anyway, I didn't want to ring him up or go up there to check cos then Christmas Day would always be the day my Dad died. I waited until Boxing Day to phone and ask him if he was going to church cos it fell on a Sunday this year. Thankfully, he was still alive and he seemed alright although he kept the conversation brief and couldn't tell me which pub he'd be in after church so I guessed he might want to be on his own.

He came over to my Mum's house that afternoon. He'd still not had a wash. No amount of air freshener I sprayed around him made any difference. Even with a hanky full of my Vivienne Westwood Let It Rock perfume pressed against my nose I could still smell it.

My Dad used to smell of Old Spice and Imperial Leather. Anyway, this is what happens with chronic alcoholics. They just stop caring.

I was in Oldham for eight days this Christmas. With every shop assistant, barmaid, bus passenger and passerby, I just kept thinking, "How can you do this, how can you live here all year round?" I mean, where is the excitement and where is the freedom? Then I realised how wonderful my life truly is.

A DEAD RAT AND THE
WONDERS OF WANSTEAD

January 18th, 2011

10:55 am

I was in The George in Wanstead the other Monday morning. I'd bought one of those telephone directories where you press a letter and it automatically pops up on that page. It fascinated me because when you don't sleep things like that do fascinate.

The bouncer from my club had bought me a cigarette case with a built-in lighter too. You press a button and a cigarette pops up, then you press another button and a small green blowtorch type flame rises. I just sat there on the empty top floor with these gadgets, utterly enthralled by them. I took alternate sips of my raspberry Sambuca spritzer and pint of Kronenbourg and glanced out at Wanstead tube station. It's so lovely round there. Everything seems just right. I want to make friends with the whole town and buy a big house there. Everything is so calm and just so. I wondered how these people had made their money. How do you end up living in a place as nice as Wanstead? Well, I planned it all out. If I just hang around Wanstead then I'll end up living there. Some sort of osmosis will occur.

I sat and wrote some lyrics to a song I'd been working on. It's a song about a man losing his child, I mean his ex took the child away to live with her. He's been quite upset about it. She just used him to have the child you see. All he wants is to see the child now and again. Women are heartless sometimes. I don't think many of them realise that men have emotions too. Men seem to be getting more depressed nowadays. Women still use them because that's in their nature.

I wasn't getting anywhere fast with the lyrics so I made my way to The Cuckfield. On my way there I saw a dead rat, just on the pavement. God, that fascinated me more than the automatic telephone directory. I just knelt down beside it looking closely, trying to work out how it had died. There was no sign of blood. It looked like it had died quite peacefully. It couldn't have been there long cos Wanstead's streets are always immaculate. A girl walked past. "Look at that," I said pointing at the dead rat, but she ignored me and walked on. Some people stop and smell the flowers and all that, but I much prefer the stench of death.

The Cuckfield had a notice on the door saying that the kitchen was closed. Wonderful news I thought. I can just sit in these wonderful surroundings with my half pint and stare at all these successful people walking past the window without the groups of smarmy estate agents talking loudly about their shitty lives.

After sitting there for half an hour a man came in to fix the fire exit door I was sitting opposite. I asked him about his job and what had broken the door. He didn't seem too interested in engaging in conversation and just answered the necessary. I knew when to stop with him.

After half an hour the workman left and the pub was silent again. I saw an elegant elderly lady outside looking confusedly up at the pub. I smiled and she walked in and asked the barman if they'd found her gloves and scarf on New Year's Eve. He told her they hadn't and as I was listening to this I remembered that I had a pair of real lovely gloves I'd found the previous night. They were black leather with a fur trim. I called her over and offered her the gloves. She tried them on but they were too tight. Oh well.

"Have you got a cigarette though," she asked.

"Yes, I'll get you a cup of tea now you're here," I said.

"Oh, no, no, I just want a cigarette. Y'see I'm not supposed to be smoking." She spoke with a West Coast Irish accent and her face was all made up but not overdone.

"Well, I'm about to go for one so you can come with me if you like." We went to the beer garden out the back and she asked about my life so I told her stuff about my work. I asked her about hers and she told me that she was staying with her daughter in Wanstead but she thought she'd overstayed her welcome and she was getting lonely. I felt sorry for her, she seemed so nice. I think she had the start of dementia. I don't think she would have bothered talking to me if she hadn't the start of dementia. I mean it must have seemed like I was going to rob her the way I offered her tea and to come outside with me. I wanted some company too and the company of strangers is always my preferred option.

She left after half an hour and I left shortly after. A group of mothers had come in with their posh prams hoping for some lunch and I overheard them saying they were going to The George. So, no chance of me going there. I took the bus to Ilford and went to the Wetherspoon's there. That one's called "The Great Spoon of Ilford". It was rather a big place. Nothing to report on there. I went back to the Irish pub I'd been to before. I found it quite friendly in there last time and the jukebox was cheap. They'd just got Holsten Pils on tap. I like that one. I put on all the Morrissey songs and tried to get on with my lyrics but still nothing was happening with them. You can't write lyrics while listening to Morrissey. Time drew on and then I noticed a mother and daughter come in with shopping bags. I knew it was time to go.

I caught the bus back to Leytonstone and arrived just after 4. I went to my favourite pub, The North Star. I sat at the bar while they scraped the Christmas paintings from the window. I was solitary once again but then after twenty minutes the rest of the regulars turned up and we talked about rock bands and Morrissey for a bit. Then I realised I'd had enough to drink so I went home. I found a letter marked NHS shoved under my door. This is it, I thought, this will tell me I'm dying! But it didn't. It said I was alright.

THE TROCADERO (CANTONESE STYLE)

February 8th, 2011

11:16 am

A film crew stopped me yesterday as I was walking to The Trocadero on Shaftesbury Avenue. The cameraman had his camera on his shoulder and it was right up close to my face. Then this presenter said, "Can we ask you a few questions?" I was shocked, totally shocked. I just shouted "No" and ran. I kept running until I reached The Trocadero then I ran inside and up the escalators. I was all hot and nervous then. Anyway up near the cinema there weren't many people around and I felt safe once again.

I don't know what sparked that reaction from me. Had they met me drunk I would have answered all their stupid questions in my nonchalant way. I'm very shy y'see. I don't like people looking at me.

Anyway I decided to go and see the film Hereafter as it had been produced by Steven Spielberg and Kathleen Kennedy. They're the ones that worked on the E.T. documentary in 1981. This film was all about death and life after death which are subjects that appeal to me greatly. Part of it is shot in London. I always love when I see London on the big screen and then I think wow! I live here and I'm part of this wonderful film that is me.

The film was excellent. I believe the critics didn't like it but critics are bitter atheists so that's them. I loved it though. It was a bit of me it was.

Afterwards I felt all lovely and light in my heart and so I went to my favourite Chinese restaurant, Mai Tai on Charing Cross Road. £3.80. Yes, it's top in there. I got a nice big teapot of green tea and some pork sweet and sour (Cantonese style) and some special fried rice with a nice bit of lettuce on the side.

I find it's always best to keep your favourite places to yourself. People always do my favourite places down. Or if ever I take anyone to my favourite places they'll always complain so I only ever go to The Trocadero and Mai Tai alone. I take my Mum to Mai Tai but that's different cos I know that my Mum would like it. She always wants to go to a classier joint but I say with my appetite that comes and goes I'm not paying £20 for something I'm not gonna eat. I always eat the whole lot in Mai Tai though. Even when I'm nauseous and hungover.

I remember when they used to do the Channel 5 Pepsi Chart Show from The Trocadero. They used to introduce it with something like, "All the way from London's Trocadero… It's The Pepsi Chart Show!!!"
It sounded so cool. And you used to be able to see all the metal on the escalators and it looked all modern and futuristic. So I think that's why I like The Trocadero.

Of course, it's all full of European tourists and it's been like that for years. I always see those really uncool ones in there with backpacks and scarves. They look like exchange students. But they make me look like I'm the height of fashion so I don't mind them.

When I was working for MORI polls I was on my way on the Central Line and it was about 8:40 in the morning and I got to Liverpool Street and I just started to cry. I got off and went round a quietish corner in the tube station and cried for a bit. A few people saw me but they just walked on. Then I thought fuck it. I'm not gonna bother with these stupid working hours anymore. I'm not like these people. We're different breeds. So I went straight to Tottenham Court Road, across Leicester Square and into The Trocadero. I don't think I even bothered to phone in sick. I played on the dance machines and the twopenny sweepers. Then I saw one of the most amazing films I've ever seen. It was called Pavee Lackeen, all about an Irish traveller girl. I sometimes find myself thinking of that film. It always seems to come back to me.

LIGHTS FOR STE WEST

February 13th, 2011

01:57 am

Looking up at the skyscrapers surrounding the flat whilst smoking a fag. I always do that. I just think blank thoughts for quite a while.

There are three tower blocks that I gaze upon. Tiny lights are on in various windows of the three tower blocks. I wonder upon the tiny lights, try and look into them. What scenes are they illuminating? I wish I had a telescope. I ponder upon how many people are lying dead in there, undiscovered.

Then there's The Strata Tower, the tallest residential building in London. I look at the lights on in there and it all looks so clean. Energy saving perhaps. There will be dead people lying undiscovered in there before long. Suicide and loneliness happen to the best of us.

A fox on the street below is doing that strange mating call. But perhaps it has lost one of its own. Foxes feel sorrow too.

Dreams of my brother have become more real as if he's trying to contact me in some peculiar way. I rang my Mum up the other day to tell her. My grief has gotten me at last. After sixteen years... I think I'm a bit pissed off that he died. My Mum said that she and my sister have all been having these peculiar dreams of Stephen of late.

I dreamt that he was still alive. Everything always seems so real. I dreamt that my Mum got it wrong and she identified the wrong body as being his. Then he came back from wherever he had been after all these years. And me and Stephen were just hanging around in clubs and stuff, and we both looked so fucking cool. Well, he always did when he was alive. And he always liked to be called Ste. Not Stephen. He thought it too close to Stephanie.

It was his body that she identified though. And he's gone.

SOUTHEND I LOVE YOU

February 19th, 2011

03:01 am

I sat in Hamilton Hall. That's Wetherspoon's in Liverpool Street. I was totally bored.

Michael had this big job on, well y'know a government thing.

I just kept seeing Southend-on-Sea Victoria. It kept coming up on the screen. And I kept thinking I could go there.
So I did.
I went. It cost me £15 for a day return. I just wanted to go to the places and the pubs that I had done before.
I sobered up once I had arrived. Then I heard "Motorcycle" by The Manic Street Preachers. Then "Every Day is Like Sunday" came on. And I said to the woman or was it a man? I still wasn't sober enough: "I only came in here for the music".

There wasn't much to buy. I wanted a hairbrush with my name on the back. You could open them up and they had a mirror on the inside. There was some kind of Christmas tree with them all on the outside. I told the man that I was called Sarah or perhaps Scarlet but there was none.
I said I liked the name "Joyce". No one's called Joyce anymore so I took that one and paid 50p.

Next door was the teddy bear shop. I'd already got one of my E.T.s an England football kit. Then I saw a teddy bear's British Army kit. I bought that. It was £12.99.

I then found a WHSmith and purchased a Jiffy Bag. Wrote c/o my sister's name on it. I had two 97p stamps on me.
She texted me yesterday to tell me that she had received it.
I walked down the High Street. I was after the seafront pub, the

hotel that I remembered the other year, the one that couldn't stop yelling. That alarm.

A black woman stopped me. She was holding a clipboard. I answered her questions and then she led me to a shitty office off the seafront. She'd asked me if I liked chocolate and ice cream. I used to like both. It's weird, I like neither now. But I told her I liked both.

I spent an hour eating Magnum ice creams while she questioned me about my "taste experience". I saw the locals of Southend: mothers.

Eventually I got my £3 Boots voucher. I walked into the nearest pub. That was O'Neill's. I bought half a Grolsch and explained to the barmaid what had happened. She was not impressed.

I drank that half quickly and walked down to the seafront. I found a seafront bar that I was vaguely familiar with. It was the same pub where the alarm had gone off a year and a half before. The Royal Hotel.

Couples in there were kissing and cuddling. It was strange to see. Michael and I don't do that kind of thing in public. Urgh, kinda vile.

I left and walked for a while. I found an arcade and played on the dance machine for a bit. I'm totally bad at dance. I think I put about £3 in. I didn't get any better.

Then I saw the penny sweepers. I got a load of change. Well a quid in 2ps. I won a few but then I saw a poor gypsy girl. Well I bet she had more money than me in bloody benefits! But I gave her all my winnings. I think it was £2 in 2ps.

Then I went to a bar next door. It just played 80s music. I bought a pint of lager, can't remember which kind. They had all these fluorescent lights up and the landlord had photographs of his baby above the bar. I remember thinking, well I wouldn't do that if I was you, you never know who's gonna kidnap your child.

I got the train after that. Sat in First Class and then got off in Stratford. Then from there went to Leytonstone. Then got a Kentucky Fried Chicken.

SOHO TO BUS STOP IN ALDWICH

03:53 am

It's amazing that I'm able to play my favourite records ever.

It's weird that I'm able to do that as a job. The owners of my club, well, it's their club. But basically they let me do whatever I like with music. Every time I arrive, I have a brief look around and try and work out the people.

I have loads of different records, depending upon what mood I'm in. Sometimes I'll just play my favourite songs but that never does anyone any good. I'll tire of those after three. I want to make people happy. Even though I've heard the songs loads of times, I still want to make people even more happy.

But then I'll still throw in my favourite records. I believe they're called "Curve Balls".
Mogwai or Wire then?

Thursday's the worst day for going home. I never drink on a Thursday. I DJ from 10-3. As soon as I walk to the bottom of Frith Street there's always some dodgy foreigner chasing me. Not from my disco though. Just a dodgy man that comes out of the middle of nowhere.

It happens every week. Well, I think it's a waste of money paying for a taxi but I'm going to have to do that. Every Thursday.

AND SO TO BED...

February 27th, 2011

02:50 am

I must stop writing this journal when I'm three sheets to the wind.

I don't really feel like writing when I'm anything less though. I sit and watch telly all day. I'm not too drunk tonight. Must go bed.

Somebody said that I wrote the wrong thing the other night but I re-read it and they misconstrued what I'd said. Other people will too.

Must go bed.

Sat in Leytonstone pubs for two days, Wednesday and Thursday. Got to work alright though. Did a blinding set. Ears are killing me. Constant earache from my job. It's right inside my ears, quite painful. Constant loud music is doing nowt for me.

GONGS, GANGS AND GUNS

February 28th, 2011

10:44 am

First time I've written this journal sober in ages. I hate getting pissed on Sunday nights so try to refrain from drinking on that day. Sundays are lonely when you drink. Couples are everywhere. I hate couples. Me and Michael are different though. We don't go around looking annoying.

I've deleted the last few entries of this journal mainly because they were unreadable. I'd written in broken up sentences. Pissed people tend to write in sentences that don't link together.

I'm mad on all this internet stuff like Facebook and Twitter. People never listen to me in real life because I can't speak. I was in The Blue Posts on Berwick Street on Saturday night before my shift. I was talking to the barmaid and I was stuttering and my eyes were darting everywhere. It's getting worse this whole problem. I'm a bit better when I've had a drink. The stutter turns into a slur. I feel so nervous around everyone sober and I go all hot and shaky.

I'm alright on stage though. I feel quite relaxed up there. Even when I'm at my acting class and have to improvise in front of the rest of the class, I still feel quite relaxed. It's like everything slows down. Real life is such a chore for me.

I'm having a gong bath tonight. I got talking to a holistic therapist in Leytonstone when I was on my travels. I didn't meet her in the pub, I just walked past her shop as I was on my way to the pub and thought I'd pop in. I told her about my drink problem and she said this therapy would be really good for me.

You lie down and she plays these big gongs and it opens up your chakras and Kundalini energy is released. The NHS has failed me so these alternative treatments might be my only chance of survival. I've been reading a lot about esoteric traditions and the mystics. I'm probably trying to find enlightenment but I don't go much on cliches. I always find enlightenment when I've had eight pints, a raspberry Sambuca spritzer, a bottle of wine with a Harveys Bristol Cream chaser. I feel alright then. Kind of dead. So why do I have a need to survive? It's that turning yellow with liver disease like The Face of Death at Leytonstone Wetherspoon's. Alcoholism drags on for years. Liver disease is no quick death. The yellow people really give me the creeps. And then being connected to all those tubes with a colostomy bag. Kidney dialysis, diabetes, amputations. This is the real reason I can't carry on.

I'll stop writing this journal if I find peace cos then I'd have nothing to write about. I'd only be able to write about the wonders of nature and pretty flowers. Right now I'm sitting at my dining room table with a bunch of dead daffodils in a vase. I wouldn't want to look in the mirror every day watching myself fade. My eyes would be so bitter and cold and that would be the worst thing.

So how've you been?

ONE FLEW OVER THE WALNUT TREE

March 4th, 2011

11:22 am

The gong bath on Monday was really good. It's a bit like travelling through the universe at a million miles an hour and knowing absolutely everything. I'd highly recommend it. It costs £50 for an hour but it's well worth it.

It didn't cure my alcoholism though. Well these things take time. Tuesday was a busy night at the club. A girl said a nice thing about it on Twitter.

I went for a pub crawl around Bethnal Green and Leytonstone the next day. The Dundee Arms in Cambridge Heath Road is one of my favourites for afternoon drinking. The way the light is an orange glow in there.

So then onto Leytonstone. I sat in The Walnut Tree (Wetherspoon's). I haven't seen The Face of Death in there for over a fortnight now so I'm guessing he might have died at last. The asylum were on an outing again. The men paced up and down shouting out every now and again. Their carers sat in a corner with pints not caring. All this pacing about was making me slightly nervous so I left at four and went over to The Sheepwalk.

I put two hours' worth of Morrissey on the jukebox. Basically, every Morrissey song they had. No Smiths, just Morrissey. I play too much Smiths at the disco. Not many people know the Morrissey songs. He's not everyone's cup of tea I suppose. I don't think he was anyone's pint of Kronenbourg in The Sheepwalk either.

After two hours I made my way to The North Star and put on all the Morrissey on the jukebox there too. Well, I couldn't do all cos The North Star's jukebox is too expensive. I thought I'd get all my drinks in at once before they stopped serving me. I got a Cinzano, double Harveys Bristol Cream and a pint of Kronenbourg. Leyton Orient started playing on the telly after a bit. They were playing Arsenal and the pub was packed. Really good atmosphere like. Orient played very well I thought, even though it ended as 2-0 to Arsenal.

When the game finished I made my way back to The Sheepwalk. I don't want to get barred from The North Star. I really like it in there. It's impossible to get barred from The Sheepwalk though. I put some more Morrissey on the jukebox when I got in. The place was filled with the tinkers. I'm sure they don't really hear the music. They speak so loud. Not before long a brawl among the tinkers started. Glasses were flying. It spilled out onto the street. There were loads, then another two dozen came running down from The Walnut Tree. The wonders of mobile phone technology. Anyway, it was funny. I was watching it all with great interest, cushioned by my drunkenness.

I went home after it had died down a bit. Went straight to bed. Fully clothed, contact lenses still in. I was out for the count. I woke up with that strange sense of satisfaction and relief. Made it through another session. It's strange when you drink so much, you stop getting drunk but you still keep needing it.

OSWALD, CALIFORNIA, APOCALYPTIC MEETINGS, I'M SCARED NOW!

March 19th, 2011

01:25 am

The moon seems to be getting closer to The Earth which is a sure sign of the magnetic things making more earthquakes. See, the moon does something to the tide and that's why these natural disasters happen.

It's so simple when you have a proper look. I feel like a child when I talk about disasters. I don't contemplate any loss of life.
A disaster will strike California tomorrow. I hope my prediction is untrue. I dunno whether it's on a faultline.

I got my Gold Cup today. I got a tip but I knew it was going to come in. Long Run it was called. I was very proud when it did. I know that I have a gift for just thinking and all my feelings become reality. Please don't let the earth move in Cailfornia, Lord!

All that I've wanted has become mine. Which is really strange. It seems that I only have to picture something in my head and then whatever I have pictured becomes reality.

I've pictured Wanstead, as small as it may sound. A five bedroomed house in Wanstead. No children. Just a house and a Jaguar. Dark green. Emerald. A Jack Russell called Oswald to keep me company. A whole network of Alcoholics Anonymous meetings too. And I drive to them every day, every single day. And it's lovely. Life is mine again.

A WELL-DRESSED SOMEBODY
ON THE SOUTHBANK

04:32 am

The daffodils are blooming again.

I watched the ITV London News on Tuesday after the main news in the afternoon. It talked about a well-dressed woman in her fifties being washed up on the shores of the Thames. She was found in the morning, opposite The National Theatre. They made a point of saying she was washed up opposite The National Theatre. As if, what could be worse? Well, making a point, saying she was well-dressed too.

I reckon she was a suicide. I don't half speculate me.

I wanted to check out the white tent as seen on the news. I decided to take the one tube stop to Waterloo, do my own investigation by looking at the detectives' footprints.

I started thinking on the way. I thought about what I could do round those parts, y'know Southbank. I thought well, I've never been to The London Aquarium. So after that thought, I just thought like: well, I'll go to The London Aquarium.

The posh girl said it was £19.80 to get in but it was £12.30 if you booked online. I went away for a bit and looked into the river. I saw a dead dog floating along and thought Fuckinghell, I could be dead soon, just like that dog. I don't have facilities to book online. I went back in and the girl was surprised to see me again. I said I'd pay the £19.80 and so I did.

There were lots of fish in the place. I was only really after the turtles. There was a blue light about the place and plenty of people. A calming whale sound plays as background music. It was quite hot though.

It wasn't calming though. There were lots of people on dates, then there were lots of families and then there were lots of Americans. There were a few Chinese too that kept taking flash photography. The Chinese don't want to miss a fin. Huh huh…

The children did my head in. They kept screaming and banging their hands on the tanks. Parents did nothing to stop them. Staff did nothing to stop them either. I felt sorry for the fish, turtles and sharks.

I waited until a diver was feeding the sharks and a talk was happening. I ran round two corners, into the rainforest part and talked to the several terrapins. Their faces reminded me of E.T. They looked at me and shut and closed their mouths in unison. One of the terrapins sat on a rock. The biggest one. He looked me in the eye while I looked him in the eyes. He let out the biggest yawn I have ever seen. I took it personally and moved on. I was talking to them about the earthquakes that keep happening and how it is affecting the terrapin race.

I left the Aquarium then. I gave £1.50 to the Help the Turtle Fund. I walked out towards The National Theatre to try and find that white tent that I'd seen on the news earlier. A police car was leaving The National Theatre car park. There was no sign on the bank. Only footprints in the sand and six marks, as if a jolly holiday had taken place.

THE PLOUGH AND HARROW
ON LOVELY STONE

March 23rd, 2011

04:08 pm

The blood was smeared across the brass railing that people rest their hands on to steady themselves. It had dried from the night before. The place smelt metallic as blood does. Someone had had diarrhoea; blood mixed with shit. I won't describe the kind of venue this is. The Olympic site is nearby. I chatted to the local brothel workers. The brothel creepers were nearby too. Everyone was a strange shade of yellow.

The Irish made lewd jokes about my friend without thinking twice. "You're loose. At your age you're loose." My friend didn't mind. She was Irish too and this was all part of the craic.

Beforehand I had been in Wetherspoon's where I had met my newfound Irish friend. You must come with me to The Plough and Harrow she said.

She'd hit her head the other week.

I sometimes feel like I'm in purgatory with this addiction of mine. These are not the kind of people I want to be socialising with, but their downtrodden lives fascinate me, much more than all those boring media types that I meet in Soho. For them it's all about a career, a steady family, money and mortgages. I find that kind of living dull. These prostitutes and alcoholics live for the moment. Or the next drink. This way you need never contemplate a future. It's dangerous and boring at the same time. You can only think about one thing and that's the drink.

I always believed that the company you kept reflected on your life. On how your life would be in the future too. Well, I've been keeping extremely bad company and when I sober up it scares me to think I could end up as incontinent and diarrhoea-stricken as the people around me.

I can't get pissed with the Soho people anymore. As I said, I can't speak. People find me boring. I don't like company when I'm sober apart from Michael's. I can't have a drink. This week I was drunk from Monday afternoon to Wednesday evening. I've sobered up now, feel alright, just drinking tea.

I WONDER AT THE WOMEN IN LEYTONSTONE SEX CLUBS

March 30th, 2011

11:08 am

Here I sit in a Wonder Woman outfit. Nothing to say, nothing to do. It's the beginning of a dismal day.

Police cars scream past and red double deckers screech to the stop outside.

The homosexuals upstairs continue their forever argument. If only either of them had an alternative place to go. Perhaps to grow even. I've heard of a sex club in Leytonstone for men that can "let that inner girl OUT". Perhaps if he got dominated he wouldn't scream anymore.

I don't reckon that's right though. You either like someone and want to be with them forever or you don't. I want to be with Michael forever. He never made me change my alcoholic ways or any ways I had.

The people that surround me complain and complain and complain. I often write letters to Wetherspoon's enclosing a receipt (someone else's). Mr Wetherspoon then sends me a reply with a sorry note and a voucher for £20. So many satisfied customers y'see, they don't mind about the few disgruntled ones. They'll shut them up at any expense. You can try it too. Even if you go in for a half, try and find a family's receipt. Usually about £20.

The people nowadays are after money, and money is pointless. I used to walk around with the old lyrics in my head that go:
"There's nothing in this world that I need.
There's nothing in this world I will take."
That's it. If you go around this world with that in your head there's

definitely nothing you will ever get. But you will be happy. I was oblivious to what thought could actually create. Money never bothers me too much. I reckon that's why I've always got enough of it now.

I've changed my ways and I can feel more now. I used to just feel happiness. Now I can feel things.

THE PORCELAIN GUN

April 8th, 2011

07:58 am

I love the calmness of the early morning drink, I love the silence. The rattle of the air conditioning units settles my mind.

I see no sense in night life; have no understanding of it. They play in front of me in their overexcited ways. It's the same old peculiar notion they go through. Chatting politely for one hour, becoming demons the next.

The real reason I write is the reality of my job. I feel so awkward when I'm at work, the only way of getting through is with drink and I don't want to be the drunk. Although I am not the drunk now. I am an alcoholic. Never getting drunk but forever topping up.

For my pastime I like listening to the murmur of refrigerators, for it is of a lower frequency than my tinnitus. The only real sound that I hear in the pubs at this hour is the tinkle of my diamond ring upon my pint glass.

I was sat in The Great Spoon of Ilford the other morning when a man came in and parked his mobility scooter in the booth next door. His friend came in three minutes later, staggering with this terrible cough, then they both coughed. In between talking about the weather they spat into their handkerchiefs. Ten minutes later another man came in and complained about how long it was taking to dry his clothes on the line. These people have all day, like me. We contemplate the dull lives we lead.

I decided to leave. Went into another well-known Ilford establishment called Jono's. Bought a pint of Holsten Pils. Seems to be the only place in London that does that on tap. I found a quiet corner. Well I had the whole place. The barrels were being rolled into the cellar.

They echoed around like the familiar sound of a tube train beneath me. An argument broke out between three people I hadn't noticed sitting in the corner.

They looked dodgy, in black suits like Mafia gangsters, but this was Ilford. In their fifties and sixties with cockney accents and crosses. It was as if they'd been to a wake but this was far too early. This was 11:30am.

The argument died down so I kept on writing. A shadow appeared above. "What are you writing?"
"A letter to me sister." I showed him the page of the letter to Sandy the arsonist in Texas.
"Oh." He walked out to the smoking area.

On Friday the DJ in this place is called "The Doctor" and on Saturday the DJ is called "Hard 2 Handle".

I sat and wondered what this place would be like when packed full of the dancing desperate.

Foster and Allen's "A Bunch of Thyme" played. The same old man came over to me: "They used to always play this after a big fight at a wake and everyone would calm down but I saw you in and thought the lads should calm down anyway y'know? This wake's been going on for three days".

April 17th, 2011

10:13 am

I glance upon an object and ponder upon the memory forever.

For this five minutes it's a slot machine called Quid Vicious. £50 jackpot apparently.

A man dances around the place dressed in denim asking the other dead eyes if they remember John Denver.
"John Denver was from Limerick!!"
"No," a man in his seventies replies, dead eyes and wearing kipper tie and a 70s tweed suit, "he was from Roscommon".

In the distance within the same pub I see a mist of cigarette smoke.

Wow! I think just wow! This reminds me of the old days.
I shall update…

THIS IS HOW THE OTHER HALF LIVE, WITH A DWARF THAT DRESSES LIKE E.T.

April 22nd, 2011

05:25 am

My Mum came to visit for four days. I couldn't drink because I couldn't let her down and show her the woman I have become. Exactly like my father. I was miserable without the drink but I didn't want the drink while she was here either. I need to have the wrong company to drink and she is so perfect. I couldn't upset her.

She told me that she still looks upon me like a child. I was the youngest. She said I still seem like a teenager. I still feel like a teenager. Will I ever grow up?

I have plans and I do believe I've mastered them.

I wanted to show my Mum Wanstead; my dream. And so I took her to The George (Wetherspoon's). A yellow man was in the pub. He shouted at me as I walked in, "I know that face".
"Uh, I'm with me Mum. She's coming in now." I was awkward. I went stiff like a cat caught between two dogs.
"You're looking so much better these days. Last time I saw you you were away..."

He started to go on but luckily my Mum is a slow walker and I drove her to a seat that was far away from the yellow man.

I felt guilty and strange all day about what he had said and I was even more nervous about what he was beginning to say.

I feel sick about my lack of memory and my pissed up times. All I know is that I forever wake up in my own bed, fully clothed and listening to The Good, The Bad and The Queen or Depeche Mode's latest album. There's always a pen in the bed or still resting between my fingers. My notebook is always there too.

The early sobering up hours of the morning are spent trying to decipher my own handwriting. Sometimes it is genius. Sometimes it's shit. Sometimes I can't decipher it at all.

Sometimes I'm still writing when I sober up and my madness turns into perfect prose.

Me and my Mum went down the river the other day on a cruise boat from Westminster to Greenwich. When we passed the posh flats she said that thing that has become a mantra her whole life: "THIS IS HOW THE OTHER HALF LIVE".

I used to get so pissed off with that saying. It's as if no one could ever move over the halfway mark. This is our lot, that is theirs. We can look but never ever move over to that side. We shall always look and laugh and be jolly with our lot because at least we're not starving in The Third World.

What's all this about anyway? Social mobility scooters? Well I don't know about that. I don't wanna be hanging around with posh people on Saga holidays. All I want is no friends, a room full of E.T.s, a Jack Russell called Oswald and a four bedroomed Victorian house in Wanstead. No children though, but I wouldn't mind a dwarf that I could dress up as E.T. every now and again like. I could keep him/her in my spare room.

BASILDON AND DOUBLE PIE AND MASH £2.80

May 10th, 2011

04:41 pm

I went to Basildon yesterday. Alison Moyet and Depeche Mode used to live there and that's mainly why I went. I saw some pictures of it on Google image search and it looked like my kind of place: all concrete and 60s model of the future architecture.

It was a hot sunny day. I would have preferred it to have been dry and grey so I could be trapped in a void, not knowing where the sky began and the concrete ended. Instead people were smiling and I ended up feeling alright, like I was twenty-one. Happy to be away once again from everything and everyone I know.

The shops were all of my favourite kind: 99p Point, Poundland, 99p Stores, then all the bargain clothes shops which are usually Indian owned and selling the kind of stuff amateur porn stars wear. I don't wear any of that kind of stuff but sometimes you can get something quite emo. I forget I'm pushing thirty and I'm just drawn to fluorescents and tacky stuff for teenagers.

There were four charity shops I came across. In Cancer Research I bought a pair of sandals for £2. In PDSA I bought a whisky glass for my sister with her name on it. I don't think she drinks whisky though, but it was only 20p.

I found a Pie and Mash Shop and sat down in there for a bit. They had an offer on of two pies and mash for the price of one so I had that while listening into the innocent conversations about fly-fishing. The smell of bleach reminded me of vomit and early morning pubs. They were cleaning the floors because it was 4pm. I still managed to finish my two pie, two mash meal and so had a cup of tea. I felt alright again. As I said, I felt really good. I always feel good when

I'm on my own and without the drink for a few days. The last time I'd had a drink had been Saturday and it was now Monday. I was doing well.

I gave the nice grey-haired woman a 20p tip and went on my way. I hung around the new shopping centre for a bit. That was nice too. I had a look round HMV but they don't sell many CDs any more. I looked at the modern equipment. Novelty I-Pod docks and other equipment I don't have a clue about. I remembered my New Year's Resolution to learn how to download music, but I still can't be arsed doing it. I'm being left behind.

I went to Primark and had a look at things. I bought some tacky £1 jewellery and a £1 pair of polka-dot sunglasses, a Cherry Coca Cola lip balm as well. I'd left my last one in a pub somewhere.

I walked back to Basildon Railway Station. On passing the market I saw a group of people in their early twenties posing by the Basildon Market sign. Yes, it was a group of Depeche Mode fans. They had a little tape player with them playing Depeche Mode. It seemed odd. I went up to them and told them I was a Depeche fan too. They got so excited, in broken English and with everyone talking at once. I gathered that they had come from Oslo and were here for some sort of electronic festival that Depeche were supposed to be playing at as well as Erasure. I told them I did a disco in Soho and to come down. They all got so excited again so I wrote down the details and hopefully they should all be coming tonight.

I was laughing. I said goodbye and caught the train back to Fenchurch Street. That was my day out without drink.

An acquaintance of mine said that I go round depressing everyone so I haven't bothered to write for a bit cos I'm quite happy sometimes but happiness is really boring to read about. I'm entering a stand-up comedian contest but don't tell anyone. It's for the best female newcomer award. I have to do five minutes. I'm quite good at that, stand-up comedy.

SOAP AND GLORY, GYPSIES AND PSYCHOPATHIC TENDENCIES

May 14th, 2011

03:47 am

On Tuesday I went to work wearing a leopardskin pillar-box hat with a slight veil. I had dyed my quiff red. I was also wearing a Frank Usher (transvestite specialist) sequined top and a leopardskin pencil skirt. I looked rather fantastic. I get so bored with looking at people in Soho and the dullness. It's not what it used to be.

On Wednesday, life had killed me. I hung around Leytonstone still in the same outfit with the hat too. I sat down in The Sheepwalk and played Morrissey again for two hours. I fell asleep and dreamed of Michael. Some Gypsies woke me up and asked if I wanted to buy some Soap and Glory products. I had a look at what they had to offer. There were twelve of them. Products like. The two gypsy girls worked out a price beforehand. £20 for these twelve products. Wow! I thought. Wow! I gave them a £20 note and they gave me the twelve products.

I put them onto the table and tried each item, apart from the face scrub cos I wasn't going to interfere with my make-up. They all worked well. So that was that.

The Morrissey stopped and I started to get hungry so I went to The Walnut Tree. I sat at table number 1 which is the booth that I usually settle in. I fell asleep once again.

The manager woke me up and asked if I could do with anything. I bought a roast chicken dinner and a cup of tea. I only know this because I found the receipt in my bag. I was sitting at table number 1, my usual table, the one with all the pictures of Hitchcock directing Psycho.
Quite bizarre how my nickname was Psycho at school eh?

My phone has gone. No doubt been stolen by someone worse off than me. Well, I tell you what, they can bloody have it. What do I want with a phone anyway? No one wants to speak to me and I only want to talk to people if I'm three sheets to the wind. So that's that.

MUDLARKING

May 22nd, 2011

04:53 am

I should have written about this sooner but it took a few days to sink in.

I was found on the banks of the Thames by the riverboat police. I was dipping my feet and walking about in the shallows. On a Wednesday I generally go to a seaside venue such as Southend. This week I didn't have enough money and the Thames was just there.

Anyway, I was drunk and an arrest was made. An ambulance was also called and they injected me with that usual saline solution, topped with a slight dose of morphine to dull me. It really sorted me out. Michael had to be called for. They asked for him because I was wearing my wedding and engagement ring. They also asked me my name which was a confusing situation. I could only remember the name "Scarlet West". They had to get out my debit card then. Then they thought I stole a load of cards with the name Sarah Crosby on. I still had no clue who Sarah Crosby was. I had her name on the casino cards as well. The policemen and ambulance people kept asking me who Sarah Crosby was. I gave them my business card and asked them to come down to my disco. The name "Scarlet West" is on my card (naturally).

Michael turned up, looking gorgeous in his immaculate grey suit. He sat in the back of the ambulance with me while they pumped that perfect cool saline into my vein. They gave me lots of water and I felt a lot better.

I kept repeating, "Ooooh, I'm in trouble".

Michael and everyone else said I was not. They all said I was troubled.

Hum… Troubled…

I don't feel troubled now. I feel alright.

I AM DROWNING…

05:57 am

It's very difficult to say I actually did put myself in the Thames.
I just get so bored.

Anyway I did that because I didn't know what else to do. I was
so lost.

I knew that no one could help me. Or can help me.

I LOVE CHICKEN TIKKA LASAGNE
FROM ICELAND

June 1st, 2011

02:33 pm

I attended two AA meetings after that business in the Thames. As usual it was the same mixture of reformed criminals and wife-beaters. The few women there all had the same story. Children being taken into care. Drinking straight vodka constantly.

I realised that these people had a lot emotionally wrong with them in the first place. They kept talking about making a list of all the people they've hurt. That's one of the twelve steps. I was thinking who've I hurt? I rang my Mum and Dad and they said I hadn't hurt them in any way. My sister said the same. Well, I think I'm a really good person. Everyone I meet reckons I'm really nice too. These AA people are really awful though. They beat people up all the time and steal things and say horrible things to people. I don't do any of that. I just get pissed. Not every day but the days I do get pissed sometimes I wake up and I think, well that was a bloody good session. And then the nice relaxing hangover comes and it's lovely when I can just sit there and watch telly and look up things on the internet.

My happiest moments are spent in the pubs in the morning, when I know I've got all bloody day. It all went wrong that day by the Thames cos I'd drank a bottle of wine when I woke up and I don't usually do that so early. It's usually just lager. A pint an hour from 9am. I felt really down after going to AA cos I thought if I do this then I will never be able to have a drink again. Holding onto that thought really depressed me. Alcohol makes me feel at peace but when I don't drink then I don't even think about it. Like that day in Basildon, I wasn't drunk and I wasn't hungover but there wasn't any point in that day when I thought ooh, I'll just pop into that Wetherspoon's pub. Drinking is either on my mind or it's not. Apart from when I'm at work but that's because it makes the shift go faster.

I didn't drink for the six hours I was at work last night though. I'm not after your approval. It sounds like I'm trying to justify my deciding to carry on drinking.

I feel okay about death now.

It's Michael's birthday today. I love him so much. I always go on about how much I love Michael but it's true. I love putting the microwave meals in the microwave for him and making him cups of tea. That sounds really anti-feminist doesn't it? He cleans a lot though and when I'm busy he puts the microwave meals in the microwave for me. I would never put a microwave meal in the microwave or make a cup of tea for any other man ever. Just Michael. Perhaps my Dad too if he needed to sober up a bit.

PISSING BEHIND TREES
IN EPPING FOREST

June 8th, 2011

03:20 pm

I took a trip to Woolwich Arsenal on Monday afternoon to visit my friend Porno Steve. He had no money so I thought I'd be benevolent for the first time in my life. We met at the Wetherspoon's and spent a good few hours in there drinking pints of Kronenbourg and a strange cocktail called a "Skittle". Steve talks a lot about cocks. He'd do well as a stand-up comic. I reminded him about that time he woke up on the grass outside a Novotel with his trousers round his ankles. And that time when he woke up on the grass of a roundabout in rush hour, again partly naked. He went to America a few weeks ago and woke up in a trailer park with a man cooking him pancakes and bacon. As they do out there. Oh, to be gay and so free and easy. I think he should start charging.

Resonance FM want to do a radio interview with me for their show Daily Subversions. Grayson Perry was interviewed last week so I'm in good company. I'm not very good at talking though. Whenever me and Michael have an argument I go back to Leytonstone and leave him two sheets of A4 with my thoughts on. We don't argue anymore though. I found it very difficult when we first started going out because I'd never had a boyfriend before. I never knew that when you meet your boyfriend outdoors you're supposed to kiss him on the lips. And when they get home from work you're supposed to kiss then. Is that right? Anyway, it still seems odd and quite contrived. I'd kiss Michael anytime though cos I love him.

Some well-dressed people came to my disco last night. A girl with a big beehive all dressed in black was the most stylish. She had no eyebrows. They were Americans. They stayed right till the end and sat with the old man that always comes in. He's a famous jazz drummer from the 50s and 60s. He's played with all the greats.

Then a group of MPs came down. I just saw one of them earlier on Prime Minister's Questions. They're lovely people, so great in fact that I'm tempted to vote Labour at the next election. I always vote for one of those strange parties that never get in. The Natural Law Party, that was it. I rang up their helpline after an election broadcast in 1994 and spoke to a very nice woman who seemed to be happy to talk to me forever even though she knew I couldn't vote. I rang the Coca Cola helpline after that but they weren't so helpful.

I went to Epping Forest yesterday. I sat outside The Alfred Hitchcock Hotel with a glass of lemonade. Lemonade because the old woman won't serve me in there, no matter how sober I am, just cos I went in pissed up a few times. It's annoying cos I used to really enjoy my afternoons in there. And it's not like anyone else uses the place. It's always me alone so I'm not going round bothering other customers. I just want to sit with my notebook and write stuff down while looking out into the forest. Bastards.

I get a six-pack of Holsten Pils and sit on the grass opposite but it's awful having to go behind a tree to piss. And that area is renowned for dogging. I don't want to be caught by some Godless pervert with my knickers down behind a tree. Mind you, I bet Steve would.

MY FATHER THE CHRONIC ALCOHOLIC

June 15th, 2011

11:37 am

I decided to come back to Oldham for my sister's birthday. It started off nicely. My Mum cooked me a nice roast dinner and made me a heart-shaped chocolate cake of E.T's face.

Yesterday I decided to visit my Dad. He had his prostitute there, Pamela. We sat and talked for a bit. Who he gives his money to is his business and I'm not bothered. She invited round a drug dealer to score some drugs. I told her I didn't think that was right, asking my Dad for money to fund her drug habit. It was then that she punched me on the cheekbone. It was quite a hard punch and she tried to launch for me again but I went into the kitchen and pulled the door tight shut. I thought she was going to kill me. I rang 999 from my mobile and she kept shouting, "If you call the police I'll fucking kill you". Anyway, she eventually left. I bolted the front door and sat in the armchair shaking. All this time my Dad was comatose, not knowing what was going on. He'd drank a litre bottle of Bell's whisky for the duration of my hour visit. After half an hour a policeman came. I told him I couldn't press charges due to the fact that it would put my parent's life in danger. Which it would. My Dad said that he didn't see anything. He kept calling Pamela a "good woman". I said, "Dad you saw what she did. Look at the bruise". But my Dad ignored it in his comatose state. I was wearing my glasses so my nose had a red indentation too.

After the policeman left, my Dad fell over so I had to call an ambulance. He looked as if he was having a stroke. They made me put him in the recovery position and check he was breathing. He was. Then he started slurring and I realised he wasn't having a stroke. He was just completely pissed. I cancelled the ambulance and tried to lift him but he was a dead weight. He was naked apart from a dressing gown and he had pissed himself and stank of shit. I got him some underpants to protect his dignity but what had he left? I rang my sister and she came in a taxi to help. We lifted him into the armchair and left him. I said it's pointless even talking to him. He doesn't know we're here or what's happened. She rang for a taxi and I kissed my Dad on the head and said, "Dad, this is the last time I will ever see you. I'm being truthful. This is it, this is the end". The taxi beeped and we left.

I told Mum. She was really upset, to say the least.

I always believed there was a tiny piece of hope. My Dad was lying dormant and he could become the person he used to be in 1985. But, no, alcoholism took its chronic hold and now he might as well be dead.

SINS OF DAD

June 17th, 2011

10:50 am

My right eye is still bruised. When I close it or lean on my pillow I feel as if Dad has done it to me. By denying it, he has. Well, he might as well have. I don't think of the prostitute, Pamela. When I close my eye with this pain I think of Dad.

I've been numb. I just got on with things last night. Tarted the bruise up with a smoky eye shadow and got back to work. I tried to smile but still found it difficult. I thought everything would be fine as soon as I got back to London. I saw people smiling and dancing again. Some told me how wonderful I was. You can't hold a living out of people's pissed up love though. I felt disconnected with the crowd so drank a bottle of wine. I then worried about becoming Dad. The wine made me feel better and soon I was chatting to the crowd whilst playing Wham! and Human League and the rest.

I decided not to tell Michael about the incident. He'd have been done for murder by now if I had. He doesn't read this. My sister banged a door into my face just in case. Accident.

I have an interview with Resonance FM this afternoon. I'm going to talk about drinking alone in the morning. In pubs like.

MUM AND DAD IN LOVE

July 3rd, 2011

01:35 am

My Mum has decided to divorce me Dad, after all these years. And it's all because of me.

I feel awful, responsible and shit.

I haven't spoken to either of them since the incident.

The dreams that I have, they always take place on Manchester Street in Oldham. Last night I dreamt I saw the prostitute, Pamela. She was picking up heroin needles in the undergrowth and putting them into lager bottles.

My other sister wants to go to Australia. This is not a dream. She texted me yesterday. I think Mum ought to go too. My sister said she needs a rest. From the chaos I cause?

My Mum divorcing my Dad is final. I can't get that scene out of my head though. The one where my Mum and Dad were hand in hand with me and I was in the middle and we were walking down Blackpool promenade. The sun was setting. I was about five. We were all watching the sun set. We'd just been to Mass. It was a Sunday evening. I was carrying my Alf doll and I'd left E.T. in the caravan cos he was too precious.

It's all my fault, and for being born it's all my fault.

Well they can go. They'd have a happy life out there. My father will do exactly what he needs to.

July 13th, 2011

09:41 am

I'm not sure whether anyone will have the attention span anymore. Everytime I click on this thing it asks whether I'd want up for some other fucking advert.up with that fucking moving advert.

No. I fucking won't!one l know Right, can't be arsed writing. If any one knows this is not placre ia am bored. want to write but this log is fucking shot shot shot shit.,,,,,.......

PEROXIDE GLAMOUR IN THE
HEIGHT OF SUMMER

July 19th, 2011

11:40 am

I hope you all listened to my radio interview on Resonance FM the other week.

My interview is number 9 on the right-hand side of the page. I'm interviewed in the second half of the programme. I repeat myself a bit. I'd been up all night drinking at the time of the interview. It took place in The Blue Posts on Berwick Street in Soho and the kind interviewer bought me a pint of Kronenbourg.

The Coach and Horses on Greek Street has gone right downhill. It's been bought by Fullers now so I hope they shut it for a week to sort out some carpet and those dreadful toilets. I'm not into posh pubs but when you're paying £4 a pint the least you can ask for is a toilet that's not brimming with shit. I think the manager took to concentrating on the twee tearooms upstairs. For fucksake why does no one want to drink properly anymore? I don't see many people pissed nowadays. They go out and have two poncey cocktails, talk about their boring jobs and then they go home. No wonder I stick to pubs that attract the more chronic alcoholic.

I went to a club called Hula Boogie at South London Pacific in Kennington on Sunday night. Everyone looked young and healthy. Too healthy. They looked happy too. And worst of all they looked nice. Like they'd be nice people. That's the worst thing you can be. Nice. Soon's me and Michael got home we were laughing at them all. Synchronised dancing. Lindyhop. Swing. Give me dirty rock 'n' roll anytime with those pornographic sleeves. I said next time we go we're gonna really show them how it's done. I'm gonna get really pissed and then we're gonna have a punch-up outside.

My band rehearsed on Sunday afternoon. It was a top rehearsal and we wrote three new songs. We've got a new guitarist from Leytonstone so we'll be able to do more gigs now. Ben, the bassist, replied to an ad on Gumtree where a guitarist was looking to join a band. I'd never seen him around Leytonstone before, so he mustn't be a big drinker. That's a good thing.

I'm gonna be thirty in October but I still don't feel a day over seventeen. I'm excited by things still. As I've always said, it's only other people that make me depressed. Soon's I'm on my own everything is absolutely wonderful. People have always said to me that I'll die lonely because sometimes I'm not very friendly. I don't reckon so though. If you feel comfortable with loneliness you'll never be lonely.

I don't think I'd be a very good DJ if I craved company. I jump sometimes when people come near the DJ booth.
But I think that's my nervous disposition. I shouldn't be frightened of anyone because I know I'm better than all of them.

THE GARDEN OF EDEN (HEATHCOTE ARMS)

July 20th, 2011

03:44 pm

Sitting in The Garden of Eden with a pint of Stella. Inside The Jeremy Kyle Show is on the telly. The imbeciles I left behind.

I blow an out of date dandelion, one o'clock, two o'clock, but the only thing that ever rocks is me and Michael. If this was 1956, I would have been taken away and put into an asylum.
Instead I'm here. My phone has gone again and I'm glad.

At last I am alone. Those that are comfortable with loneliness are never alone, after all.

I put on the jukebox earlier. Why must I always do that? It was all that crap R'n'B shit that they were playing. They just seem to have lyrics about sex.

Morrissey – Our Frank
Elvis – Kentucky Rain
Billy Fury – Once Upon a Dream
Blur – To The End
Gene Pitney – Twenty-Four Hours from Tulsa
Gene Pitney – Town without Pity

I went to the bathroom while the landlord was sorting out his sachets of sauces into pots. "Are you feeling saucy?" I said.
He laughed. That's the first time I've heard anyone laugh at one of my crap one-liners in quite a while.

The Elm Trust charity shop has closed down that's opposite the pub. I bought the Bet Lynch style dress I'm wearing from there. It was a quid. I used to go in there just for a chat. A person that actually speaks to me is such a rarity nowadays.

"Oooh. I see the rain is coming," as I used to say while flicking through the rails.

The nice black lady would be singing along to Premier Christian radio.

"Oooh, yes, but it's gonna recover for da weekend darlin!"

She was always so optimistic and she made me feel happy.

Anyway, it's all gone now.

It's strange this part of Leytonstone.

Last time I went to the toilet in The Heathcote the landlord said, "But you did that half hour ago!"

I said, "Now you're taking the piss!"

So back to The Garden of Eden. And loneliness. Wonderful loneliness. Amazing isolation.

Apart from being with Michael I can't think of a better way to spend an afternoon.

WHAT I DID ON MY HOLIDAY TO A HOT COUNTRY WITH THE SEA

August 12th, 2011

08:41 am

I went abroad last Friday, first time since 1997. Michael and I travelled to a remote village in Greece.

Taking off on the aeroplane was wonderful and romantic. We held hands. I forgot how much I love flying. There was turbulence and I was hoping it would crash. Half an hour into the flight they came round with the food. I had a cheeseburger.

Landing was good. I walked down the staircase like I'd seen Marilyn Monroe do on the telly. I waved at all the people in the terminal that were boarding the Ryanair flight after us. Ryanair has a quick turnover y'see! I felt really glamorous.

Michael's brother and sister-in-law met us at the airport. His sister-in-law is Greek y'see. We were here cos of the christening of their newborn child. They live in Newcastle normally.

Thessaloniki airport is an hour's drive from Stavros. I found the tiny chapels by the road fascinating and asked what they were for. There were so many.
"Those are for all the people killed out here on the road," Michael's sister-in-law said.
I realised that everyone was driving madly as they do on the continent. Michael's brother wasn't though, so I didn't feel so reckless as to hope for death again. I didn't want to die until the holiday was over anyway.

The hotel was the poshest hotel I've ever stayed in. Chandeliers, marble, pool, terrace. The breakfast was amazing.

When the fascinating Greek Orthodox christening was over we spent the whole time eating and eating and eating. In Greece they have these long drawn out meals. Well, they're not drawn out. I learnt on the first night you're not supposed to eat everything at once as you do in England. You're supposed to take your time in Greece and talk. It was difficult for me. I don't have much to talk about at the best of times and I'm a terrible talker. I was desperately trying to find some anecdotes in the back of my memory but they all involved arrests and drink, Pakistanis or when I was in the riots in Oldham (Michael's half Pakistani).

Michael's mother looks and talks like Helen Mirren. His brothers are posh too. I felt a world away from where I belong and awkward. A bit too awkward to speak. I tried to tell a few stories but as I say, I was limited. I was so nervous I kept losing trail of the anecdotes and then I'd let them interrupt me and I'd get back to my eating.

I realised quite quickly that you can't wear much make-up in hot weather so I couldn't even look pretty while sitting there. Both Michael's brothers are married. His other sister-in-law is about to have a child too. The child that we were there to see was cute. We were there for five days and I didn't hear or see her cry once. Greek Orthodox christenings go on for a while, an hour at least. They immerse the baby fully in the water naked, John the Baptist style. Then they cut her hair and dose her with incense. If all babies are like that then Michael and I would have one now and sell it for £500,000. I could buy my four bedroomed Victorian home in Wanstead then.

SOCIOPATHS ANONYMOUS, SAY WHAT YOU FEEL

August 19th, 2011

02:48 pm

When I see people with useless careers and those that have families I feel like I'm really successful and I get a dull satisfaction from what I've achieved. Like, it could have been worse.

Instead I'm in London, DJing in Soho and I'm happy but I'm not happy enough because I'm not doing enough. People ask me why I don't do more but I just can't be bothered.

I watch telly a lot and lie on the settee flicking through the channels throughout the day. I'm on the internet Googling my name and the name of my club to see what they've written about me. All the reviews are fantastic. But still.

My band doesn't seem to go anywhere and that's my doing. I don't go anywhere and that's mostly because I don't bother to leave the house if it's not for a drink.

I sometimes just wear my slippers, pyjamas and a long coat to go down to Ladbrokes at the end of the road and put on a bet. That seems to be the only time I ever leave the house nowadays.

The fun in life has been dragged from me. I see people I used to know and still do now on the TV. When 8pm comes I'll put all the make-up on and a dress and walk to the tube. I'll see people holding hands or coming back from the theatre. They look so dull. I wonder what time they get up in the morning and just thinking about them bores me.

I can't wait till I start work again at seven tonight. I don't like DJing much but sometimes it's just really wonderful. I like to be in control of all those people. Knowing that it's me they have to rely on for a good or bad night. I mean, I could just play The Fall and obscure Morrissey all night if I fancied. I am in control of them. Hitler would have written something similar to this. Most psychopaths would. But I'm a sociopath.

TOP TEN SUICIDE SPOTS

August 26th, 2011

10:43 am

I spent yesterday looking up ideal suicide methods and spots where I could do myself in.
I found a few but then I went to work.

I woke up this morning laughing from a dream and I didn't feel suicidal any more.

I wish I could have written yesterday. It might have been more articulate and perfect. Instead I stared at the walls and couldn't even bring myself off the settee to write.

A woman stood next to me last night after asking for Michael fucking Jackson. She wouldn't leave me. I felt so trapped. I didn't play him. Told her to go opposite to Little Italy.

I woke up the other morning in O'Neill's, Leytonstone. I can't remember anything.

That dreadful Coleen Nolan is presenting This Morning today. She's one of those women that would absolutely hate me. Daily Mail readers, they're all the same.

Last night I drank white wine as usual and I felt a lot better. I didn't feel suicidal any more.

BEING MARRIED TO MISERY
MAKES ME SMILE

September 20th, 2011

09:20 am

My Dad always used to take photographs at family funerals before the service outside the church. He'd tell everyone to smile. It became like a ritual. Every funeral he'd be there with his massive camera, like a proper photographer's camera round his neck. That memory just came back to me now and I had to write it down. You forget these things. When he's dead all his photos will probably be chucked out.

I always smile at inappropriate moments. It's nerves I think. I remember having to tell my best friends at school why I wasn't in the day after my brother had died. It was in form class. I just burst into laughter and said, "My brother's been killed!!" They thought I was joking and we soon had to quieten down for the register. Then Mr Bonner told the class that my brother had indeed been killed in a road traffic accident and we should say the Prayer for the Faithful Departed. My friends looked shocked and disturbed by my earlier laughter. We didn't speak about it for the rest of the day and I just carried on. I remember looking through my exercise books at each lesson, turning back the pages and touching the dates, thinking, Stephen was alive then.

I've never smiled when I should. At Stephen's funeral I walked behind the coffin down the aisle. Everyone turned round to stare in that understanding sympathetic way of theirs. I kept grinning at them all. It felt like I was getting married. Perhaps, in a sense I was. Marrying the misery that has made me who I am.

I DJ'd at a wedding on Saturday. I couldn't smile. I don't believe in vows and promises as you never know how you're gonna feel tomorrow. Sometimes you can just fall out of love with someone.

I can't fake a smile cos it hurts. But when someone makes me smile naturally then it's the easiest thing ever.

I was in an off-licence on Poland Street on Sunday evening buying ten Marlboro Lights and the man asked me how old I was. I told him thirty. Well, nearly. He just said, "No, you just look so happy. That must be making you look younger".
"I like the smell of this incense," I replied.

Wow! I'm so happy now and each time I'm miserable I feel happier.

COCKROACHES, SWORDS AND HAPPINESS

October 9th, 2011

10:23 pm

My life has changed in these last five weeks. I have too.

Something happened and I couldn't go back to Michael again. Something changed in me. Everything became clear and it was and still is an amazing feeling. I felt I could trust myself again and these last five weeks have been euphoric. I don't want to do Michael down here and I have nothing bad to say about him.

I'm back in my room in Leytonstone, living the life I've always wanted. It all feels like a film.

Nothing matters now.

The man downstairs carries round a samurai sword all the time. Years of drug taking have finally led to this. I went into the kitchen the other day to make a cup of tea and he was there with this sword and its three foot blade. He told me how there were people by the railway line trying to cut through our fence. I told him I couldn't see anyone. Then he went outside and came back in without his sword. "Where's my sword?" he said.
"You took it outside," I replied.
"Oh yeah," and then he comes back in with the sword.

I got back into my room and couldn't stop laughing. The whole situation seemed quite bizarre. Three hours later I left the house to go to Wetherspoon's. There he was at the front of the house waving his sword about. "They're in the trees. They're trying to get onto the roof. Look, can you see them?"
I looked up knowing full well that this was still a hallucination. "No, I can't see anyone."
He went on for a bit waving this massive sword about. "I've got to

342

meet a friend now," I lied. I walked off down the street laughing.
I came back a couple of hours later and he was still outside staring
up at the trees but minus the sword. An Asian man in his sixties was
talking to him. No doubt some relative.

The kitchen is crawling with cockroaches. If I go in there at night
and turn on the light I see them running everywhere. They've taken
up residence in the microwave mainly. Still, I don't care. I'm so
happy and have been like this for five weeks. It was always one day
off and one day on with me and happiness, but to constantly feel this
amazing has come as a shock. I do believe that this feeling is going to
last. Never felt so certain about anything.

I could have gone back to Michael's. He says I can stay there
whenever I want still, but each time I finish my shift I just want to
be back here in this room. I don't care about the hour-long bus ride
or the dangerous walk down this desolate street. I'm trusting in God
and the universe completely for the first time.

Tonight I went to St Paul's Cathedral for the evening service. Walking
into that place on my own felt so perfect. I forgot how beautiful
that cathedral is. The service was all about Sarah, Abraham's wife. A
chorister sang towards the end of the service and the congregation
was invited up to the front to light a candle. I lit one and it felt so
special, like the universe and God had worked everything out for
me, that I didn't have to worry about anything anymore and that at
last after all these years I had found true happiness.

NO, I'VE NOT BECOME A BORN AGAIN CHRISTIAN

October 11th, 2011

06:36 am

I'm here in my room again, not feeling lost any more, just totally secure.

I don't care what's going on around me. Just a complete happiness surrounds me. Am I still interesting? Is what I write not fascinating any more? I wonder.

I went to a place today. A cellar somewhere in Kings Cross. I read a few entries out from my old journal. It took a lot for me to get up on that stage and read shakily from that journal. But I did. I stand by every word I wrote. I meant it all. In that journal the bedbugs were bothering me. It's funny how the insects are always there. Cockroaches in the kitchen don't seem half as bad now. The shit in the bathroom is still coating the toilet seat. I really don't care. I have antiseptic wipes and I'll clean that shit.

The man with the samurai sword is still stuck, asking me through the door as I went into the kitchen tonight, "Have you got a spare fag?"
"Yes." Well, who's me to argue?

Tonight I drank a bottle of wine and a can of Grolsch to settle down my nerves from the state they were in. I don't feel nervous any more.

I feel happy still. I don't need to wait for the crash as I know it will never ever come again.

In this star-stricken room, God, I wish I could show you. I prayed so pathetically tonight. Got down on my knees and recited the prayers that once you're a devout Catholic you can never forget. It was so wonderful. Everything is so amazing. I love God and The Universe and everything that He has created. Even the people I don't like I now love.

Something has changed in me. You might think I've turned mental or something. I've not. I just have a peace about me. A peace I could never have imagined. I've never felt this great or felt a greater power for what I can do now.

I HAVEN'T CHANGED SINCE 1981

October 23rd, 2011

06:42 am

I'm back in my room. Bottle of Jacob's Creek Pinot Grigio on my bedside table. Stomach making strange noises. Haven't bothered to eat for thirty-six hours. Still not hungry. I don't care about alarm bells or warnings.

I went to my acting class this morning. Charles said my voice wasn't right. I blamed it on smoking and then realised that I didn't smoke enough. I was in the club tonight, shouting about The Stone Roses reforming when dealing with a Stone Roses request. Oh, that's it then. Yes, my voice is exhausted from shouting above the music and telling people to fuck off most of the time while ingratiating the rest.

I went to a music festival on Upper Street today run by Oxjam. A cropped haired Northern lesbian stopped me on Upper Street. I'd been playing on that £2 to win claw machine for a bit in The Queen's Head. Y'know when you've got to manoeuvre the metal claw to grab a soft toy. I couldn't be bothered in the end. I gave up and hoped some child would carry on my game.

Anyway, the nice lesbian got me into The Wenlock on the corner of Essex Road. I couldn't be arsed seeing the girl singer-songwriter though. What would she sing about? Love? For fucksake sing about something I'm interested in. I sat at the bar with the nice lesbian and we talked about leaving The North, her girlfriend and Michael, and why I left. Turns out she had lived opposite me and Michael for five years. London is not as big as I originally had thought.

The cropped haired lesbian disappeared after I went to the bog. Her girlfriend did too. I sat alone at the bar drinking a pint of German lager. £4.70. There was a handle on the glass and it was like one of these posh special glasses. It was very heavy. I finished it off and realised I still had the wristband on to see any of the other bands in any of the other pubs in the surrounding area. I wanted to go to The Hope and Anchor again. I hadn't been there in years and I just kept thinking about Joy Division and how thirty people turned up and paid 60p to get in in December 1978, how Ian Curtis hated that gig, how he expected London to be so much more than it was. And still is. I'm still writing where I sober up and my madness turns into perfect prose.

I turned up there and they told me I'd have to wait an hour to see a band and I should go to one of the other venues with my special wristband. I explained, "I only want to be here, I have to go soon". The main bar was packed and there were no seats. Just groups of friends. Fuckinghell. Friends. That loathsome word. Groups too. Sitting around like they're all in some fucking T-Mobile advert. I was wearing my navy blue and orange lined parka. My Sony cassette Walkman was weighing heavily in my inside pocket making the parka lopsided. I always pull at the other side of the coat, nervously, at regular intervals to make the parka seem more even. I've done this for years so there's a part where my parka has worn away. Michael always hated my parka. He always went on about buying me a new coat. I love my parka though. It is everything I am and I feel secure when I'm wearing it. I don't wanna be hanging around with posh people on Saga holidays. All I want is no friends, a room full of B.T.s, a

Well, I went upstairs and found an empty room. I sat there drinking my pint and looking out onto Upper Street and Canonbury Lane. I saw wedding parties walk past at frequent intervals from the nearby town hall. I kept thinking, their love won't last. They don't know what love means yet. They've just made the biggest mistake of their lives. I could see it. I just could. Everyone seems so afraid of loneliness. I'm the least alone. People just get married to try to combat the fear. With me, the fear never began. Being alone is me.

The sun set and the neon surrounded me. The barman came into the room. I'd taken the door stopper off the door so no one could interrupt my solitude. He said, "What are you doing up here sat in the dark?"
"Finishing my pint," I replied.
I downed the quarter and left.
After going into my room I soon had to leave for the club. It was a

busy night and I made no friends. It was lovely to sit on the Night Bus and listen to my Walkman once I had finished. Alone but with someone. A voice.

THE LANDLORD'S ARREST

November 3rd, 2011

06:29 pm

I'm thirty.

Sitting alone listening to my Roxy Music "Avalon" tape.

Last Monday was a difficult day. The man downstairs cracked. The landlord's wife claimed she had been raped by him and then changed her mind. I'm so glad I took a few swigs from my bedside Pinot Grigio that morning. It's my constant friend. I heard shouting and screaming, all in Urdu like. It was 11am and I was quite obsessed about getting to Wetherspoon's. I'd done my make-up 80s style. I was posing in front of the mirror when the screaming started. I locked my door and took a few more swigs. I even turned down the album I was listening to. The Good, the Bad & the Queen.

The police turned up. I knew it was safe when I heard their walkie-talkies. I went downstairs with an ambition to get out. I asked the young police officer what was going on. Vans were everywhere. I didn't feel nervous. I had an oversized lighter with a naked woman on the front. I lit a fag and had a bit of a laugh with the policemen and women. I asked what was going on but they said even they didn't know. I saw Shazia, the landlord's wife. She was crying by the lamppost up the street. A policewoman told me to go in and get her a coat and scarf to make her warm and cover up her head. I did, but her room was shut. I didn't know what to do and had to think fast. On returning to my room I took another swig of the Pinot Grigio and grabbed my fur coat and a skull-covered scarf.

I gave them to Shazia. It was terrible watching her cry, dressed in my tarty fur coat and skulls. Her husband (the landlord) turned up. He drove onto the roundabout to get to his wife fast. His British Gas van screeched. He got out. Really mad. The police held him. He wanted to go inside and kill his brother. It took six police officers to get him onto the floor and handcuff him. I just stood there in my Raybans and parka going, "Oooh, he's done nothing wrong. It's that drug dealer you should be arresting. He's got a sword!!!!"

Shazia was next to me while her husband was screaming and pleading for mercy. She knelt down and started praying to Allah, tearing her hair out. Then there was an African lady. I thought she was something to do with the police but after speaking to her, well it turned out that she's my next door neighbour. I said, "Well, I'm a Christian so I might start praying to Jesus in a bit". I asked her if she had been to the Methodist Church on The High Road. She said she had. We had a polite conversation about the local churches and which ones we liked. We tried to shout above the screaming and walkie-talkies. I talked for a couple of minutes about injustice. Then the landlord's brother rocked up, started calling Shazia a whore, how her Mum was also a whore. Shazia is lovely and has never been a whore. When she first became the landlord's wife she knew that I was always at a loose end and starving. She'd knock on my door and give me curry and those spicy parcel things with meat and potato inside. She's lovely.

I dread to think what the landlord's brother reckons of me.

Once they got the landlord under control and into the van, the police prepared to leave. I said, "Look, this woman needs help". The young police officer said, "This doesn't have anything to do with you. Don't get involved and go and find yourself a new place to live". "It's sixty quid a week all in here though."
Anyway, I thought for a bit. I wanted to look after Shazia but wasn't going to put my own life at risk. I'm crucial to this world and I don't think Shazia is as crucial as me.

I walked off in my Raybans and parka. Went straight to Wetherspoon's. I had been aiming for Wetherspoon's to start off with. I ordered a pint of Kronenbourg and sat in the corner. Alone. Writing down people's conversations. I prefer the banal ones. They make me feel relaxed.

PENS BUT STILL SWORDS. I JUST WANT SEA. AND DEATH.

November 6th, 2011
07:38 am

I've been crying at frequent intervals today. I'm so glad my Raybans are always by my side.

I couldn't get up to go to the bathroom and take my make-up off or clean my teeth. I got up to piss though. This deep depression has come. I never thought it would. I thought I had the world. It just encompasses me. One person understands but most think I'm just a drunkard.

I have to get on and do this gig tomorrow with my band. DJing and being in front of anyone or actually being in a room with anyone when I'm like this, it's hell. Never mind bloody having to speak to people. Sing in front of them? I just keep crying. I'll be okay. But I still keep looking around this room and working out how I can kill myself quite fast.

I won't. I can't bring myself to do it. I've been through these times before. Some external force has brought me through.

I made the mistake of writing my personal diary in a Pilot G-2 pen. The tears on my diary have smudged all the words. I don't know why I keep that diary. I can't write about most things on here. I carry that diary everywhere, constantly updating wherever I am.

My Pilot G-2 pen ran out every third day. I go straight in to WHSmith and buy another. It's a smooth pen but being waterproof is important.

I haven't even written about my holiday to The Isle of Wight. I'll write about that at a different time.
I'm so cold in this room. Yes, I came back to my room. The man with

the samurai sword is still living downstairs. I spent all my money on drink and gambling. How am I going to afford double for a room? I don't worry. If he kills me he will be doing me a big favour. Right now, I don't want to live any more and for someone to do me the favour of killing me, I'd be ever so grateful.

FREE TICKET FOR THE PERFECT LONDON SUNSET

November 11th, 2011

05:49 am

There were many things that I did last night, there were many places I went.

I woke up alone on a settee somewhere. Someone was trying to help me out again.

The sun was shining and making me scramble into my bag for my Raybans. I looked out of the window from wherever I was. I looked back at the empty room. Everyone had gone. I was glad to be alone. I walked out onto the street and found a bus stop. 59 Kings Cross. I saw The London Eye from the top deck. I realised the clocks had gone back. Sunset would be soon.

The sky was turning into Turner. That perfect Turner sky. I got off the bus at County Hall. I walked while listening to Avalon, that album by Roxy Music. I bought the tape for 50p a few months back. It makes me feel really great, like I'm in a film or something, It's become a soundtrack. THE soundtrack of late.

I waited in the line of screaming children and rich American tourists. I asked the man in front of me how much it was to get on. He said, "Well, we're going as a family but we have a spare ticket".
"Wow"! I didn't want to hang around in his capsule though but that was alright with the ticket vendor. She said I could go whenever I wanted to as long as it was before 8pm.
I gave the nice Indian family a tenner.

I watched the sky turn. I got in line then. It wasn't a big line. "Are you alone?" said the attendant.
"Yes, it's me, it's always just me." I stepped on. Inside that capsule.

It's like a drug.

Everyone was having their memories saved upon digital. Flashes were constant. I stood to one side and put my headphones on with my "Avalon" tape by Roxy Music.

I got to the top and looking down upon London. Well, I realised I'd arrived. The sky was scattered with cumulus. The red, pink and orange came from everywhere. I looked towards The North, East, South and West. I have them in the palm of my hand. I own London. In that sense, London owns me.

TAKE YOUR HANDS OFF ME
November 16th, 2011

11:44 am

I went to my own birthday party on Monday. It was rather wonderful. Subdued like, but that's how I like it. That's why I had it on a Monday. Being antisocial and not understanding people and their normal lives. Day jobs and evening meals. I still can't get my head round it.

It took place in The Phoenix Arts Club on Charing Cross Road. They don't mind me in there. I don't reckon they like me but they don't mind me and I'm grateful for that.

There weren't many women. I don't understand women. They're not like me. I can't talk to them about the joys of betting and drinking like I can do men. I do my make-up but I just tend to get on with things like make-up. I don't want to fucking talk about banalities.

I got up and sang a song after in The Alleycat Club on Denmark Street. My friend Lee was doing an acoustic cover set. I sang Sunday Girl, Hanging on the Telephone and These Boots were made for Walking. It was alright, I'd had about eight pints and was still sober. I felt slightly awkward but was wearing an Alfred Hitchcock type pale blue dress with a short jacket to match. Just like Tippy. I'd had my hair done too at Altered Images on Leytonstone High Road. I was looking really good.

I went to The Bar on Hanway Street after. Stayed there till after 5, drinking bottles of Stella and smoking all my fags. Just listening. I don't remember talking. I tend to let other people spout their useless bile. I just sit around looking really fucking wonderful. I know I'm fantastic. Everyone else feels like they have to prove something. People are forever saying to me, "Oh, you're not as thick as you make yourself out to be". Well, I made myself out to be a lot of things and have tried for quite some years now. It's just cos I can't hold my own in a discussion of any kind. I just sit watching and listening. They teach you stuff like that, like how to have a conversation or debate. That kind of stuff is for boarding school kids and people that have gone to university. I'd rather be a voyeur. I'm always watching. I'm an avid listener. I may seem away but I'm always listening.

Afterwards I went home and played Say Hello, Wave Goodbye by Soft Cell. Twelve-inch. I just kept playing it, dragging the needle back to the smooth part and playing it again. I cried for hours, just listening to that record. Over and over. I drank myself into wonderful unconsciousness after taking some old codeine. I didn't dream but when I awoke, I realised I was still alive. Well, I started crying again, face smashed into the itching carpet. I played Say Hello, Wave Goodbye again. I drifted in and out. I hoped I could just stay out. I came out of it and it was dark. It was time to go to work then. I took last night's make-up off and restarted. I drank another couple of bottles of white wine when I got there. Doctor Who's red-haired assistant was in. Johnny Vegas too. I played Say Hello, Wave Goodbye again. Final track like.

I AM AN INSECT AND I AM A POET. I MUST ADMIT I'M VERY PROUD OF IT...

December 4th, 2011

10:30 pm

I wonder sometimes what I've written about before and I wonder whether I'm running out of memories.

I was drifting on the bouncer's settee this morning. He had to rescue me last night because after my set I was wrecked. Memories of my Dad came back. How I'd sit in the back seat of the Polski Fiat with my E.T.s. I'd go on his calls. He was a TV and radio engineer. I'd sit outside the house, wherever it was. Oldham mostly. I'd never bother him. I was a silent child. I've realised that men always love the silent.

I spoke to my Dad this morning. He was there but almost not. As usual he hung up on me. He always does that, halfway through what I'm talking about. If I'd have stayed silent he would still have hung up.

I rang my sister after. She said that my Dad's house is now a crack den. Prostitutes and dealers, comings and goings.
"They've taken him for all he's worth," said Anne.

I wonder what he was worth. I wish he could have bought me an education. I'm just getting bitter now. But then again I can't stand all them educated lot. So contrived.

Michael's found another woman. Someone a bit steadier on her feet than me. Good luck to him. She's better-looking anyway. They can talk about clothes and stuff like that.

I sat on the tube crying but no news there.

The club's been packed. I hate most of them. They don't understand me. Not like you. They dance, laugh and smile and I just can't understand them. My most hated songs are the ones they dance to. They throw their hands up, look to the ceiling, move their feet. It's always a rubbish song like Stevie Wonder or Michael Jackson. I hate them two.

I ran out of fags on Wednesday morning. I couldn't be arsed going to the shop so I knocked on the door downstairs, the man with the samurai sword. He made me a roll-up out of old dimps from his ashtray. I was grateful because I was desperate. He insisted that I sit with him so I did. His swords hung by a string above the easy chair I sat on. He has BBC News 24 on all the time. I hear it when I walk past his door.

We talked about our pathetic love lives. I realised he was just as alone as me. He chucked me out in the end. He said I was disturbed. I was thankful for that.

HOW TO DO A NIGHT'S WORK
AND SAVE WOMEN

December 7th, 2011

08:59 am

I got over that last depression. It must have lasted forty-eight hours. I stayed in bed for that length of time. I had loads of bits and pieces over the bed. Fur coats mainly. I was so cold. Three jumpers on and just drifting in and out of sleep. I was so down and just wanted to sleep forever.

I turned on the internet for a bit at four-ish yesterday and heard an interview with Damon Albarn. He said he has a steady work ethic. A way of working that has always meant something to me. He works 9-5, five days a week. Rule of behaviour.
But unless I really have to go to work, I'm never bothered.

This job I've got now, DJing in Soho. Fuckinghell. I like that. It does my head in sometimes but I always show up. My sets are always the best. No one bothers me or talks to me so I just get on with what I'm doing. I think of new records to play, constantly try to surprise them. I hate the crap ones I always pick out of the case, like Madonna and Blondie.

Last night I played Little Roy's "Come as you are". I played it early on, well 11:40 and I'd been DJing since 8 and did till 3.

I make two trips to the toilet in a night. Women. I can never forgive women for being so honest with other women whilst I'm pissing. They go on about their boyfriends, sex lives and everything about men. Or women, sometimes that's the case.
When I come out of the toilet I always give them some sound advice. Stay clear from men, women, friends, people, but most of all: Sex lives. I reckon women get emotionally attached.
Once I've said that while washing my hands, I see them talking about me. They're on the dance floor then. They're going, "That DJ is a fucking nutter".

I have this gift for remote hearing y'see. I can hear what the crowd are saying about me. But those desperate women, I only want to help them.

I got my lonely macaroni cheese at the end of the night. Job done.

LET ME HAVE MY FINAL WORD
11:24 am

I just need to have that.

I remember my Dad saying to me, "Would you like a last look?"

Grandad was looking quite black in patches on his face. In a white shroud. His hands were porcelain like the statues he used to pray beneath, holding his rosary beads. I felt disturbed, looking upon him in his coffin. It wasn't like he could do that death rattle to me now. I visited him for ages but he was always there. We'd pray together. I said a few Hail Marys while holding his dead hands that day. My tears fell upon his decaying face. 2003.

"Do you want to look at him?" said my Mum in 1995.
"No." Simple answer. I'd never seen anyone dead before.

My sister and Mum told me how he looked. Hair slicked back in a style he never did himself. A scratch on his forehead. Almost still bleeding. Peaceful, slight smile.

Sometimes I think about death. Well almost always. I think about watching your baby starve to death, your husband killed, me being raped while they're massacring your whole family.

I think, these accidents and death, well in this Western world, it can't be too bad just having to put up with this.

I DRANK WHILE STARING AT THE MIRROR

December 8th, 2011

12:24 am

I'm not so cold any more. The landlord sorted me out with a fan heater.

I started off at The North Star, up the road. It was nice. I walked in, the landlord said, "Pint of Kronenbourg, Scarlet?"
"Yes." That's all I had to say.
Remembered my name and not barred. Good sign.
I drank that while staring at the mirror. Then the barmaid comes in. She's so clumsy and beautiful. I never know whether she's just attempting to be or if she actually means it. She doesn't seem too innocent with it. She's the perfect wife. I fell in love with her for a short while, last week, just sitting there. I had to go. She gave me the creeps. I didn't want to be a lesbian and I'm not.

I went to Wetherspoon's. My day seemed to be going into reverse. Children were running about the place but they kept getting caught by their mothers. I really worry about the fact that I'm always alone and I look the double of Myra Hindley. I would never kill someone. Myra's face must hang heavy. An icon almost.

I worried about the children and went to The Sheepwalk. I bought a half of Stella. Sat for a while with that woman that looks like she's got Down syndrome but doesn't. I got bored of talking to her so went to Coral.

I put on a bet for Man City to win 3-1 to Bayern Munich. I was talking to a record producer outside for a bit. He was the area manager of Coral. He used to be in that 1980s band called The Colours. He has his own recording studio and I was just listening before I mentioned that loud sentence, "I'M IN A BAND CALLED IRAQ!!!"
"Change that name for a starters." They always say that.

"No I like that." I always do the whole thing down. Perhaps Iraq is my downfall.

We've been writing top songs lately and it's only for me to know and the rest of you to find out.

I went to The Red Lion. It was alright apart from some woman that asked me if I was a Polish prostitute. I must look like one. I decided to go home, sit in my lonely room on my own. I wondered why people avoided me and I wasn't arsed. At least I'm warm. As for her, the cold fucking bitch. She can stay cold forever for all I'm concerned.

MY GRANDAD THE WARTIME CABARET SINGER

December 10th, 2011

07:12 am

When I went to view my Grandad his face was all black in patches and it was strange to see him dead.

I'd been waiting for him to die and then I was going to get on the bus to his funeral, which I did. My Grandad wanted to die for ages. He hated the care home. He was so cool though. When I lived up there I'd go round and just talk for a bit but then things ran out. What to say? He died when he was ninety-six. He never got dementia. But he was so cool. I remember how, whenever we'd go on a coach trip he'd go into the aisle of the coach. Not even ten minutes from leaving Oldham, he'd get up and do a song. More often than not it would turn into a two-hour set. We'd never go more than a hundred and thirty miles away. He would stand in the aisle of the coach the whole way, just singing in his operatic voice, all these ancient songs from 1886-1948.

It was genius looking back. At the time though most people were going, "Will he ever shut up?"

We all have our ways of never shutting up and we all believe we need to be listened to. I do it here but most people do it privately with their hers and his. Friends even.

I just wanted to say something about my Grandad Crosby. I thought he was so cool. And he was blind. Well, when he was eighty-odd he was registered as that. It's weird cos all his children have got perfect eyesight. Apart from me and my other sister. The optician told me I will go completely blind eventually.
I wouldn't like children but despite confidence and singing, the genes are alright.

CHRISTMAS PARTY!!!!!!!!!!!!!!!!!!!!!!!!!!!!!!

December 12th, 2011

03:34 am

Everyone was having a row at Waterloo. It was the club's annual Christmas party.

Earlier we had speed-boated down the Thames. Then we went for a meal at Chez Gerard. It was the toppest day out ever.

Anyway, this row was going on. Everyone wanted to go somewhere different after the owners left us. The owners are like our Mum and Dad and without them we get slightly lost. We walked for a while. The rain was heavy. Tim, my fellow DJ, held my pink leopard print umbrella above our heads. We followed Neil. He said he knew a pub. We got there. With it being a Sunday it was closed. Everyone berated him. Yukio kicked Matteo in the balls. I'm not sure why he did that. Yukio tends to go a bit mad when he's had two drinks. It looked well painful and when Yukio ran away, me and Tim stood by Matteo. We couldn't help him but we just kept saying, "Oh God! I can't believe he did that to you!"

Everyone wanted to go to Soho and get pissed. More pissed than they were. I didn't take advantage of the free drink with the meal or the free drink in the bar after. I couldn't be arsed. I'm either in the mood for drink or I'm not and once I'm eating then my taste for drink has gone. I have problems with drinking on Sundays too. I just find I get really down if I drink on a Sunday. I was just after going speed-boating down the Thames and having the best meal I might have in my life.

I had this amazing mushroom soup for starters. It was the best soup ever. It had proper mushrooms in and I found bits of potato at the bottom. I had bread with real butter and the bread was really nice. The butter was a bit too cold and I found it difficult to spread so I just put bits of it on the bread and dipped it into the soup.
For my main course I had turkey. It's Christmas. It looked a bit like

364

salmon. It didn't look like any turkey I've seen. It was all posh. It looked like a fillet of salmon but turkey. Bacon all wrapped round the outside. Then when you cut into it, stuffing on the inside. I ate it well fast. It was top. I liked the vegetables too. They were perfectly cooked. The carrots and potatoes were miniature but lovely.

Next up was dessert. We had to wait a while as everyone wanted to talk. I find talking difficult so I just listened and waited for my pudding. I got slightly restless after a while. I can never drink when I'm eating. Or when I've just eaten.
I didn't know what to say.
My pudding was a chocolate torte. It was a hot chocolate cake with coffee ice cream on the top. Again, it was well nice.

I love my bosses for organising everything and they just sat in our private dining room at Chez Gerard being as cool as they usually are and I looked at them and I thought, "Wow! I love them!"

They've been so good to me. I work really hard at the club but I like working for them because I like them. They're nice to us. The club is going really well, mainly because of me and Tim's DJing to be honest. And the bar staff and their faultless service. And the bouncers. Especially Trevor.

Back to when the owners left us and I was left with my beloved colleagues. I escaped them in the rain. Walked over Waterloo Bridge. Alone, I thought, well, I don't want to argue now, after all we have to do.

I put on my Roxy Music tape and walked up The Strand. I sat alone and had a Peroni in The Coal Hole. Punch and Judy next. I stood on the balcony staring out at the Christmas tree in Covent Garden. Ten minutes, then some German tourists disturbed my solitude. O'Neill's next. Alone again. Thank God. I walked up to The Salisbury next. Thought I was barred but it was different staff. London is so transient. Had another. Last stop was The 12 Bar. Saw a band, girl, American, so meaningful and so Patti Smith but none of her words meant anything to me. Some people seem bitter but I believe that life is opening. Despite my constant upsets I'm really happy. I just need to keep away from people.

£60 A WEEK ALL IN AND SO MUCH
BIN INCOME

05:55 am

I'm going to put on my heater again. I still haven't paid my rent in two weeks but I feel quite bad about that. I don't like drawing out money. Money isn't a big deal cos nowadays I always have enough.

My landlord and lady live in the room down the corridor. I talk to myself a lot and I'm sure they get pissed off about that. They can always tell when I'm in, bottles smashing and me crashing around the room. I keep music at a constant low. Y'know, the last thing I want to hear is loud music too. I can't help my footsteps and I'm sorry. The fact that I never bother to pay my rent, I dunno, I really can't take care of things like that. It's a menial task. Can I hire someone now?

I like it here though, with the strange man downstairs with that samurai sword. He's misunderstood, like me as I said.

I could get a better room, but this one suits me. If I talked to myself the way I constantly do in this one, in another room, they'd have me out in an instant. I reckon most people think I'm mad and should be hospitalised. I don't feel too crazy.

Michael always used to say, "Who are you talking to?"
My Mum said the same.

Myself though because I need to practice but my practice has never made it. Like when I was in Groucho's the other week, I still can't do it. I stay silent. Egotists love the silent and that's why I have so many friends in high places.
I don't know what a high place is because a lot of the time it doesn't seem that they are happier. They seem down and upset and I try to help them. Jude Law for instance. He poured his heart out to me and I couldn't help. Even getting him into my club. Well, I couldn't even get him in. I was DJing. It's not about who you are or even if

you know me down at mine.

The first tubes run across underneath, making the wall I lean upon shake. I should sleep and think. I am happy. Happier now.

CRISIS? WHAT CRISIS? I'M IN THE PUB

December 15th, 2011

05:42 am

I can't remember what I've done today or what I haven't.

I got my roots done with a bottle of Sauvignon Blanc on the go. I thought it may be less painful that way and I was right.

After that ordeal I sat in The Red Lion and ate a steak. It cost me £20. I wasn't bothered. I thought, the week everyone else seems to have been subjected to…Well…

I went to Coral after. I tried to put on a bet but got sidetracked talking to the bookies about my life, their lives too at some point. Well, my horse didn't come in cos I didn't bother to bother.

The morning was taken over by police cars and vans surrounding my house. (It's all coming back to my broken mind now.) I walked out and I said, "Is it me again?"
"Yes," replied the young police officer.
Samurai had gone mad again, stabbing the trees.
I said again, "I rent a room at the back. That's it".
I rolled my eyes. "I'm just off to the pub."
They let me go. They'd heard my story before so it didn't need repeating.

Always off to the pub. Crisis? I'm off to the fucking pub. When I was born, guess where my Dad was. You'll never guess.

I sat in The North Star for most of the day. That pub works well for me now it's midday opening. Free credits on the jukebox. Food too. I sit at the bar drawing up plans about how I can take over the world in one easy swipe. And I will.

A STAR-RIDDEN WALL AND A PISS-STAINED MATTRESS

December 16th, 2011

06:39 am

It was a new man working at the 24 hour shop next to where I live this morning. He wasn't going to serve me my usual Pinot Grigio. I wasn't pissed. It takes me two days to get pissed but then again my drinking is constant. Apart from when I'm unconscious or just so tired I can't lift a glass.

I've been feeling happy even through the drink and the hangovers. Not that I even get hangovers. The Pinot Grigio I'm drinking now is only 11.5% and tastes like water, it's so weak. This is the time when my fellow alcoholics move onto Special Brew and strong cider.

I ate a roast dinner this evening that I bought from 99p Stores. It was pretty vile. God, I'm cold. Just a minute, I'll put on my heater.

I'll be warm soon.

Last night my friend Alwynn Davies took me out for a drive in his Porsche. He took me to Muswell Hill and I talked for a bit. I rarely speak to people so it seemed strange. He talked too. He's still in love with a woman he met in the 1980s. He told me not to write this here but who'll read this anyway?

I felt lucky enough to have never fallen in love. Then everything including your career comes crashing down. Michael still loves me. He can find someone more stable. He says it's not like that, that he can get anyone, and he's gorgeous so he can. I just keep saying to him, look, I'm wasting your time. He doesn't want children so he has the rest of his life to find someone perfect, without all these flaws. He should go out with another model.

I don't want children either. It seemed like the perfect match. I hate thinking of him alone in the bed we once shared. I was an awful girlfriend. I'd lie and lie on the settee saying I'd been to places where I hadn't, making out that I'd not been sitting in the pub round the corner from 12 until 5. I'm being honest now but this diary is no alcoholics anonymous. You know who I am.

I never cooked. Michael didn't mind that. We just lived on ready meals. My skin is perfect considering. And even now, it's Wetherspoon's or USA Chicken.

I finished work at three and got home at five this morning. I drifted on the bus and wrapped my handbag handles round my hand loads. I'm so worried about that journey and dread coming back. Once I'm in my room it's fine. I worry about getting attacked. People have been saying to me lately, "How do you do that, on your own?"
"I always have and I've not thought anything of it until you just said that."

Why do people say that? It's made me so nervous of late. Of course it's dangerous but ten years and everyone seems alright. South London was the worst but where I am now, well, I never see a soul apart from the men in the 24 hour shop. They like me. I also know that the man with the samurai sword, he would kill anyone that touched me. Now that's a bonus.

THE DARKNESS OF SOHO

December 19th, 2011

12:47 am

Friday was strange. I was walking to work down Frith Street when I saw that my part of the street was in darkness. There's so much neon round there, the street lamps were off too so I knew there had been a power cut. I walked into the club, there were a few candles on the stairs. I was informed the power had been off since one. I thought, well this is cool, at least I don't have to work for a bit. The owner insisted that I stick around. The Friday before Christmas is the busiest night of the year. I'll give it to her, she still opened and lit the place with loads of candles and people came down. It soon got busy like it usually does and everyone was talking to everyone. People like a crisis. It gives strangers the opportunity to talk just because they have something in common at last.

I was hungry so went off to The Stockpot. I asked the owner to give me a call when the power came back. I sat with a cup of tea and ate some pâté on toast. I listened to the tourists and they all looked at me on my own with interest. I kept thinking, I bet they think I'm a model upstairs. I was wearing my leopardskin bomber jacket and had my new tacky diamond bag by my side.

I was halfway through my pâté on toast and hadn't touched my cup of tea when she rang me and said the power had returned. Oh dear. I spread the rest of the pâté quickly upon the toast and downed the cup of tea. I walked back to the club and the street was still in darkness. She called me again. Yes, it had gone again. Well, I was there now. I sat on a stool at the bar drinking white wine. It was nice and everyone was going on about how much they preferred the club like that. They could hear each other alright and they seemed to be having such a laugh about it. It was like the blitz they all said. I reckoned it was well okay. I didn't have to work but I felt awkward because I knew that these regulars knew who I was. They all have

371

friends and I don't. I guess sometimes you meet friends at work but I never do. Acquaintances I suppose but these people all know the ins and outs of their friends' lives. No one knows about the comings and goings in mine, even the people that read this. You will never know the true story.

The people all looked really posh. I never knew what the clientele looked like until now. I try not to look at them when I'm working otherwise they come over and ask me for requests. I could hear their accents. All posh. No cockney or Northerner in the whole place. I never knew it was like that.

At eight the lights came back on. It disturbed everything and everyone was going "Noooo!" And I was going "Oh noooooooooooooo!!!!!"

I had to go up to the DJ booth then. I played There is a Light that Never Goes Out by The Smiths as my first song. It was lost on them. Funny lot that crowd that go for cocktails in there of a Friday. They all work in Soho for those media companies.

I just played 40s stuff then and they seemed to like it.

I sat bored and alone trying to overhear conversations. I'm a good earwigger me. Nothing of interest cropped up. You'd be the first to know if it did.

BEING BULLIED AT ST DISGUSTINES IN OLDHAM

07:02 am

I used to eat slugs and worms upon the bin lid… Just to get some attention.
Really, I am serious. I worried my Mum. When they split up I said to her,
"If you ever get a new boyfriend I'm going to kill him".
She never did. She believed that marriage was for life as I do now.
I hope she never believed my threats over her youth and happiness.

I held a chainsaw over my sleeping sister's throat one quiet afternoon.
I said, "Tell me I'm beautiful".
No one had ever told me that before. Guess what? She did.
"Sarah you are beautiful."

Anne wished for a little sister in 1981 and she got me.

We've laughed about it since but that evil little sister pops up now and again. The evil daughter too. I worry about myself.

I don't want to be that way. I'd like to be nice. I'd like to love like the rest of the world. They find it easy. I could make excuses about my father but I'd prefer not to chase those. My father is a person who will never be caught.

He taught me how to drink and I'm thankful for that. He taught me how to be intelligent and I'm grateful for that too.

I chased the bullies with my chainsaw in the end. They drove me to it. I even stole the batteries from my sister's Walkman. Seeing their scared faces did a lot for me.

The chainsaw only required that. Then when I found that hand grenade with my fellow dog walker's metal detector, a nice old man, that was it.

Selena was her name. She'd stuck a sarsaparilla in my hair at Laser Quest in Whitworth Street in 1995. I said, "Right, you want a fight, then you're gonna have a fight!"

I didn't swear then. It was April 1995. My brother had just died in the March and I was tenuous.

She agreed to meet me in the A Floor toilets. So there I was. I was wearing my dead brother's two-tone parka, hand grenade in my right-hand pocket. There was quite a crowd. This girl, Selena had the whole school on her side. The Down syndrome kid I hung around with backed away. They can sense danger. A stupid teacher came past, knowing that something was about to take place. I piped up, "We're all doing a project for CDT on inside plumbing".
"Move on children, move on."

"Right," I said knowing full well I was about to murder her, "let's go behind the sixth form block".

The crowd was getting bigger and I just kept holding the grenade in my pocket, thinking, I might blow up all these kids in any second and I don't care.

The deputy headmaster came out and he said, "What are you all doing here? This is sixth form ground".
"We're studying the architecture of modern 90s sir," I said.
I really did say all this. I can't believe I said what I did but I really wanted to get to a quiet place where I could do her in. She and her friends had been bullying me since I arrived in the school. They took the piss out of me for liking E.T., then for having my sister's flyaway collars and then they kept going on about my Mum and Dad being poor and then when my brother died they just didn't stop.

I said R.E. block now. I kicked off then. Everyone clapped as I threw the first punch. Then she tried to scratch my face. My Deirdre Barlow glasses came off my face. I held onto her hair. She only had three fingers. Did I mention that earlier? She was winning by this point. I grabbed the grenade from my right-hand pocket. I was about to launch it down onto her head. A hand in slow motion came down and grabbed it. So strange and so clear even after all these years. It was a man's hand, Mr Crosby, the R.E. teacher. We fell silent. Oh dear. I was worried about the grenade going off and killing Mr Crosby. I always got on with teachers.

He took us both to the headmaster's office. It was weird then. We waited outside the door. Mr Kennedy, the headmaster, and Mrs McGonagle were there when we went in. Mrs McGonagle said it wasn't right for girls to be fighting.
I said, "I've put up with this for so long Miss, I'm sick of it. I'm sick of her and I'm sick of the rest off all them pulling my hair".
"Shake hands and let no more be said of this," said Mr Kennedy.
Alright. So I shook her three fingers and decided to not fight back any more.

I was nicknamed Psycho for the next three years. I wore my brother's old jumpers cos I thought Stephen might protect me. I even wore Stephen's old bloodstained rucksack on my back for a year, the one he was killed in. No one ever knew what those dark stains were. It just looked like red pen ink gone old.

I couldn't go into Oldham Town Centre after that. Eventually did.

At sixth form college I used to see them pushing their prams. I doubt I'd recognise the bullies now.

Going back there Wednesday and I look so fabulous, they'd never recognise me now.

IS IT CHRISTMAS?

December 26th, 2011

03:52 pm

Oldham is as bleak as it always was. More of the surrounding streets have been demolished. An old woman went back into her property today. The roof is just rafters and the windows are all smashed. Net curtains still blowing though. She got taken out by some men in fluorescent jackets. She looked so vulnerable. She refused to leave when the bulldozers were two doors up. My Mum kept seeing her peeping out of the net curtains. My Mum said she looked so scared, she called the community policeman. I didn't bother telling my Mum that the lady had returned. My niece is coming from Australia today and my Mum was busy tidying the house. I just watched the old lady from my bedroom window. It was a sad scene.

On Christmas Eve I went to visit my Dad. I bought him some cheese and cat food. My Dad was sitting there with his bottle of whisky watching E.T. It was strange him watching E.T. I wondered whether he remembered how much I was obsessed with E.T. Still am in fact. My Dad didn't know it was Christmas. I told him it was Christmas and mentioned it now and again. Each time he slurred, "Is it Christmas?"

The house smelt bad, he smelt worse. I fed the cat. My Dad can hardly walk nowadays so he just sits in his chair pissing himself. The bottle of whisky is always at his feet. He was using an empty biscuit tin as a makeshift table for it. He refuses all help and accepts no visitors apart from the crack addicts and prostitutes. Wonder why he let me in? They buy him the whisky and he gives them his pension. Not a good deal in my book but he gets his fix I suppose.

His sister had arranged for him to go over to her family for Christmas Day but when they arrived to pick him up he asked what day it was.

"Christmas Day" she said, "I'm not good company today". He made his excuses and they left him to it.

It's strange, I can understand how he feels. Just because it's Christmas Day does it really mean you have to be with people? The world says yes but I say no. I suppose my family like me but sometimes I'm such a pain with my drinking and silence. I think they'd be happier without me when I'm like that.

I didn't bother wrapping the presents I bought for my sister and my Mum. I said, "Do you mind if I don't bother wrapping them cos I can't be bothered now". This was at 1pm once they had returned from church. They rolled their eyes and said that they didn't mind.

My Mum wasn't keen on the arthritis medication I had bought her from Holland and Barrett. She gets all that free apparently. I'll take it back tomorrow and get myself something with the money. I bought my sister a vase and a David Bowie picture book. I think she liked that.

I bought myself (most important) a bottle of Chanel No 5 from Harvey Nichols. I used to wear it when I was eighteen. No one really likes the smell but I suppose it might mask the smell of piss and vomit if I get like my Dad anytime soon.

I watched Doctor Who, then went to bed at 8pm. I got up at five this morning and felt slightly better. I've got to go to the airport in a bit to meet my niece. My Mum has warned me that I'm not to get pissed while my niece is here as it will traumatise her for life. Being traumatised did me no harm. I'd have nothing to write about if it had never happened.

A DARK ALLEY WITH AN OLD MAN

December 31st, 2011

03:34 am

As soon as I see that Piccadilly platform moving away from me I smile. I grinned today. My Mum and my niece stood on the platform waving. I hate that. I told them not to come and say goodbye. It's a cliche. I'm alone and I hate feeling that there are people that do care. I had to smile and wave, pretending I was going back to London to live some kind of normal existence.

As soon as my mother and niece were out of sight, I put my headphones on and pressed play on my Walkman. "I am Hated for Loving" by Morrissey came on. It was rather perfect. My seat reservation was a backwards facing one. I looked out at Manchester's skyline, growing smaller and smaller. The raindrops streamed against me. I kept thinking, thank God. I am my own. I belong to me.

That Manchester to London Virgin train, it's the best. Once I sit in my window seat I am happy. On the way up I listened to Roxy Music, Avalon. My tapes are everything.

I found twelve notebooks last night. They were in my wardrobe. They were from a time when I described everything I did in vivid detail. I was intrigued about the men I fancied. The men my Dad left me with. I was fifteen and they were forty or so. I never had sex till I was eighteen. I never ever let the men that walked me home touch me. They always tried but they'd buy me a drink the next time I'd see them and apologise. I was drinking cider at this time.

I never had anything to go upon. It disturbs me to realise the kind of men he left me with. I trusted my Dad but the men would always try and snog me down an alley and I would throw them off me, sickened.

I believed these men were friends. Well, it never works out that way. I wrote my diaries and forgot about them until yesterday. Re-reading all this. I can't blame Dad. I just don't know what to say.

I

NOWT TO SAY AND I'M PISSED

January 10th, 2012

12:38 pm

The title was restored from my saved draft. I must have been attempting to write while pissed as usual and that's all I could come up with before falling unconscious.

It's nice to read everyone's "Year in Review" musings. I wanted to do one myself but I can't work out how to copy and paste so I'll write my own. This will be a bit like the process Morrissey goes through before he does an interview.

1. What did you like most about 2011?
   Wednesdays and drinking. Writing loads in pubs. DJing when I was really into it. When the crowd was decent. Finding new mixes to incorporate The Fall and Hawkwind into my set while keeping the floor dancing.

2. What did you dislike the most about 2011?
   I can never remember the tears but they came often as I'd wake up with mascara run. I don't remember being depressed or crying but I'm an emotional drunk, so I'm led to believe. My Mum and Dad are both bad on their feet and seeing them get old is sad.

3. Did anyone close to you die?
   I saw an old man being brought out on a stretcher in Leytonstone Wetherspoon's in December and I haven't seen him since. I used to talk to him a bit. He might have died. People I drink with are the closest people I have. On a sadder note, a man I knew quite well from the clubs I used to work in was stabbed to death on 21st December. He was a bouncer and it happened in Archway. Just some nutcase did it. He was trying to split up a fight. He wasn't even working and had just gone out for a Christmas drink.

4. Which countries did you visit?
    Greece. It was alright but I wouldn't want to go to a hot country again. I found out that you can't drink as much and they constantly ply you with food so you can never get pissed. Family is important to them but I was so impressed by the way they all smoked. I liked the style of the widows all wearing black as if they can never love again.

6. What would you like to have in 2012 that you lacked in 2011?
    I'd like some friends. I know it's dangerous but I would like people to not be too afraid of me. I know I never know what I might do next and they all hate me for giving them drunken phone calls at 6am. I can never arrange outings and I can't always promise that I'll be there for them but I'd like some people just to hang around with and not take friendship too seriously.

7. What was your biggest failure?
    Constantly being late for work. There's always some part of my make-up that's not quite right. I have over twenty coats in my wardrobe and I can never decide which one to wear. Stuff like that makes me late.

8. Did you suffer illness or injury?
    No. Same as last year, cold sweats and the shakes from drinking too much but nothing that my two-day rule doesn't solve. (That's not drinking for two days.) Good NHS guidelines them.

9. What was the best thing you bought?
    A HTC mobile phone that is a bit like an iPhone. I lost all the connection leads cos I was completely pissed when I bought it. I would never spend £200 on something, being the alcoholic that I am. However, I still have the phone! I Twitter constantly when I'm at work. This device has helped my boredom no end.

10. Whose behaviour made you appalled and depressed?
    People that asked me for Rihanna or Beyonce when I was DJing. That poster of Rihanna with her tongue out that I have to walk past on the tube. Women that let themselves be pimped out like

that. I feel sad to be a woman sometimes and seeing how the media portrays women, well I worry a lot about being raped on my way home.

11. Whose behaviour merited celebration?
Tom Watson. He's made me vote Labour. He should be prime minister.

12. Where did most of your money go?
Same as last year (almost). Drink, horses and surprisingly candles and church collections. Been generous this year and it has come back tenfold.

13. Compared to last year are you happier or sadder?
Happier. A million times more. Apart from when I'm drunk and suicidal. It's lucky I've done this quiz in a manic episode.

14. What do you wish you had done more of?
I should have gone more to Charles Verrall's acting classes.

15. What do you wish you had done less of?
Nothing. I mean I should have done less thinking. I thought too much before taking action.

16. Do you hate anyone that you didn't hate this time last year?
Alphabetical order? Everyone knows I'm a failed pop star but I absolutely loathe every female pop star. I'm so glad I'm out of the competition. I would never wear their ludicrous outfits or sing about "love". I'm older now and I'm a clever swine. Thank God.

17. What did you want and get?
A pay rise. They keep giving me pay rises. Oh, and I got a tax return £120. Alright. I spent the lot on fucking booze and horses, that's what I did! Huh huh...

18. What did you want and not get?
I wanted a pint several times and didn't get served (had enough

apparently). Ended up in Epping Forest with a few cans most of the time. Good job weather was warm.

19. How would you describe your personal fashion concept in 2011? Covered up Bet Lynch. Roots darker than my soul. Earrings bigger than Princess Diana's heart.

20. What kept you sane?
Nothing. But who's to say I'm insane? I lit candles in churches and knelt down in side chapels. I prayed loads. I prayed really hard. I was thinking of joining a convent and becoming a nun. I haven't heard God's voice calling me back though and when I pray nothing that spectacular seems to happen so I don't know whether it's working. I think I'll keep praying for the rest of my life though cos you never know.

21. Who was the best person you met?
There's a barmaid that works in The Red Lion in Leytonstone. She's called Laura. I like her cos she speaks to me and she's a nice person too.

22. Tell us a valuable life lesson you have learned in 2011?
Never make someone a priority who only ever makes you an option. Everyone has always made me a priority but I read that quote and it stuck with me. I tend to give women advice that are having trouble with men. Although I love men. Men have always been lovely to me. I speak as I find.

THE PIGEON FANCY

January 18th, 2012

02:13 pm

Alone. A woman shouting at me.

Fuckinghell, now a group of white builders.

So can I get on? Can I fucking get on?

What I hate is absolutely everyone. That's what I hate.

Can I get on? Can I fucking get on?

I know no one likes me and I'm happy with that. I long to speak to that dead woman again. The son is the pigeon fancier.

A PRACTICAL INTRODUCTION

January 25th, 2012

06:32 am

These people need to have a word.

I sit in a lonely room. All I hear is a weather forecast. At a quarter past six, I am now hearing the sport.

I hate everyone. No one ever liked me. Why does no one like me?

Directors of big films, well, I overheard how they were casting people from RADA. Fuck them I thought. Why not look and choose me? Naturally, they didn't. I just carried on and DJ'd. I felt alone again.

I played records for the rest of the night. I kept thinking, well, whoever you will cast, well, they will never be able to put this sadness across that is forever in my eyes.

DEATH, CODEINE AND WISHING SUICIDE

07:27 am

There was a man that died. I couldn't begin how to explain. He'd been coming to my disco. The fact that he'd been found dead, in his flat, alone.
The only person that he had rung was another DJ. A lonely voicemail: "Could you get that 96 Tears record played tomorrow?"
So sad.
I have it and shall never escape it now. He was found dead. And the last person he rang was a DJ. He didn't hang himself. Cos I keep going on about killing myself upon a belt, I'm troubled, I'm deeply troubled. This man just had diabetes.

I often saw him in my club. I haven't been worse for wear lately. I don't know what to say. So many of my friends have died. I tear my hair out. It's bleached and it's easy. I hate it, I absolutely hate it.

From Saturday till Tuesday (until I had to go to work on fucking Tuesday), well, I lay in bed. I didn't even know he was dead but I wished I was dead. I don't have anything in common with anyone. Even Michael. I just feel dead. Dead is how I wanted to be. I took some codeine and I felt nothing.

I woke up. This is Wednesday.

MY NIGHT IN THE HOUSES OF LORDS AND COMMONS

February 1st, 2012

06:32 am

Yesterday I went on one of those walks. I'm trying to do so many things like that when I'm sober. Sometimes I'm sober for two days. I feel so happy.

I did The Old Westminster by Gaslight walk. It was the coldest day of the year. I asked my friend Alda and Michael if they'd fancy it. I hate leaving people out. I knew they wouldn't be into walking around cold. I did it alone in the end. The Americans were there, naturally.

The cold held nothing to me. I was fascinated by everything about the posh, down-on-her-luck, theatrical, Julie Christie (as she must have been). She was interesting. I ended the tour wanting to know more about her than the bloody buildings that she has to go through, talk about, day after day.

I wish I could just have a lecture and hear about people's lives when they're not pissed. Not in pubs like. Just when people are sober. I'm fascinated about lives.

I ended up sitting in The House of Lords gallery. She (that wonderful tour guide) left me there. I looked down and listened for ages. It was all really boring. I saw John Prescott hang around for a bit. He was restless. There were some women that all sat together on the backbench towards the left. Three of them all on their iPhones. They all seemed to be having a joke. A Lord was talking about asbestos, trying to get somewhere, no doubt.

I got a bit bored so I moved to The House of Commons. I've forgotten what they were talking about but I think it may have been that small claims bill thing. Then they all said "aye" for quite a while. It was then adjourned as it was 9:30pm.

A backbencher then started to go on about the holocaust and how it was of complete importance that children in Stoke-on-Trent needed to know about it as it was a big BNP town. I felt like shouting, "hear, hear!"

The adjourned speech was the best one. I hate racism. Being from Oldham, y'know me? I'm always in the minority.

I walked across the bridge, caught the tube, listened to Billy Bragg and went to sleep, safe that some MPs have the correct idea.

DANGEROUS DREAMS = DANGEROUS PLACE

08:14 am

Light strikes above the second panel here.

I'm trying to write but I know nothing will ever come. I'm attempting to write but I don't care if I go into an offal.

Struggle as I do. But I mean as I meant. What did I mean? To be heard?

Forever was a troubled story. I won't go into that. My father, well, he is in his own place now. Ha ha!! I hate that, I laughed at that tonight, I hate it when people in rehab or have just come out of something like that, I hate it,
"I'm in a good place now".

So what leaves me with anything? I feel so happy. Until here it felt that there was someone here writing this with me. In the provisional eye. Is that madness? I haven't drank too much tonight.

The nightmares strike each night when I am sleeping. If I sleep in Leytonstone everything is fine. I slept in the other place and dreamt of car pile-ups and being executed at Auschwitz. I can't escape these nightmares. Michael has to often hold me back because I wake up in such a panic. I then switch on the news. 501 and 503. I'm in such a state by this time. It seems so real. I can't tell you. I get so upset.

If I'm in Leytonstone I don't have the dreams. Just nice dreams.

February 15th, 2012

06:23 am

My unsteady hand lingers around this keyboard. I don't know what to do. The lights flicker and, well, I've nowt to do.

The bouncer snores and maybe I should talk about Trevor. He'll take me out tomorrow if I don't get up before him. We like to watch the obscure channels. See Hear, etc, etc, etc. Repeats, repeats and bloody more bloody repeats.

I hear him now, unsteady with his breathing. It's Valentine's Day. Stupid that, my Grandad's birthday. Ex-boyfriend too. He was alright but I don't reckon he was too into me. I was never good at Valentine's Day, getting cards and stuff. It seems so boring. Like paint. Like getting DIY.

I feel upset. The fact that I have gone and gone and gone and gone back to my house. I bought a massive lined piece of paper thing, with a margin. Hardback book. An elastic thing holding the bloody thing down. Just so no one can ever see it. Maybe I shall start.

Michael always says, "Have you got anywhere?"

"No."

It's the only tr

I WOULDN'T LOOK ME IN THE EYES

February 20th, 2012

05:10 pm

I'm writing this for the first time sober in months. I'm in Leytonstone library. I always used to write it here. I feel at peace here.

I went to The Walnut Tree for a roast dinner this afternoon. Next time I shall have the courage to ask for more gravy.

I DJ'd on Friday. Not before I'd covered most of the pubs in the Waterloo area. It's really shit round there. I felt quite uncomfortable. I ended up taking the tube back to Leytonstone and going back to what I know and like. I ended up in my favourite pub, The North Star. Someone had left a Valentine's Day card in there for me. Well, at least they knew where to find me. It was anonymous of course.

I went home and there were another two cards pushed under my door. One claimed their undying love for me, the other was just the usual blank "?"

I got really pissed at work and fell asleep at the end. Michael was round the corner at St Moritz so he came to collect me. I managed to DJ alright though. I shouldn't have drunk before work but I'd been on it since Tuesday and that was the end for me. I was only sober on Monday last week. The rest of the time I was just topping up.

I rehearsed yesterday. The band is sounding good and I'm really enjoying doing the new songs. I love the lyrics I write. I have great confidence in the band now, more than I ever have before. I'm getting on. I'm thirty but I remember thinking I was getting on when I was twenty-three so nothing changes. I think about the great musicians of the 40s and 50s and most of them were in their forties and fifties. I'm not too worried about my age anymore.

I deleted all that bollocks I wrote about being suicidal. It does my head in that I do that, but I'm glad I do it here because I can just delete parts of my life I'm not happy with. That's what I do in my mind too. If I've done something particularly disgraceful, I just don't think about it and then it goes away. I hope nothing comes back to haunt me. It did the other day though. I was sitting watching telly and then I remembered those two lesbians. The one that slashed her wrists and the other one that jumped in front of a car because of me. I thought it was quite funny at the time. Women and their emotions and all that. They survived but the scars on her wrists are still to be seen. I thought, I wonder if when she looks at her wrists, she thinks of me. Then I began to feel bad for five or ten minutes. Then Dickinson's Real Deal came on and he took my mind off the whole morbid episode.

YOU AND THOSE OTHERS ARE MORRISSEY

April 4th, 2012

07:33 am

I've taken my snake bracelet off, my dove and skull ring too.

I have something to say. Because I've been bored. I've been sitting in Hollow Ponds attempting to write. I only read the newspaper yesterday. It seemed you had no troubles.

The club I work in, Soho, is that different?

I feel wonderful every single night.
Nothing matters to me.

I hear doors crashing downstairs, and what goes on beyond them fascinates me the most.

So without reading stupid newspapers and without listening to radio stations.
Without watching Television…

CAN YOU LISTEN TO ME?

IGNORE ME

08:06 am

This time last week I was in Brighton. I had no reason to be there. I'd woken up in a bad state. I'd even lost my Walkman. It was quite ridiculous.

I found another Walkman and marched to London Bridge. Whilst I'm typing I'm hearing Brian Ferry's voice. Just greatest hits now.

My favourite time was when I was hearing Roxy Music's Avalon. It's ok. I'm ok now. I'm really ok.

My friend's son committed suicide, hung himself. In the same way I was going to do. I'd planned it with a belt too. I keep having to watch this bloody sun rise.

I saw his mother yesterday. And she couldn't stop crying.. No more... I can't put anyone through that... Ever...
So that is selfish, so what on earth do I do?

THEY TOLD ME TO GET A JOB AT THE BODY BAG FACTORY

09:25 am

Just got off the phone from my Mum.

Smoke and all sorts coming down her chimney. God, I wish I was there. I could really sort that John Prescott's ideas out. How the fuck can they do this?

My street is the only one with my bedroom and my Smiths, Bowie and Fall records, my E.T.s and stars on my wall, mantelpiece with every Virgin Mary, St Anthony, St Teresa too...

They want to kill everything in Werneth just to make it a bomb site that they can never afford to build up.

I'll call up my Father and I'll tell you what he has got to say on the matter. He's boarded himself up in his home. Number 5 Bath St. Kill him if you dare. You never will. He'd prefer a Setons body bag.

BHAKTIVEDANTA AS ALL...

10:54 am

I feel awkward. Oh, don't feel sorry for me now.

I chose to turn the television off and conquer this. And still my head slides uneasily towards the television.

I spoke to my Dad just now. He was okay, not knowing where he was going. I don't know whether he was saturated in piss. I don't think about that now. All I remember are the good times. It's strange, he was always the best father. Never did anything bad. It's terrible how many women have been sexually abused. I have not. Me and my Dad had more of a drinking relationship. We just hung around and drank.

My friend still said, "The reason you are drinking is because your brother died!!!!"

I don't reckon though. I like drinking.

I AWOKE A LOWLY CREATURE

April 11th, 2012

02:06 pm

I awoke sober on a Wednesday for the first time in ages, perhaps even over a year. There's only so long I can sit around watching telly or just staring at the walls thinking about I don't know what.

I came to this internet cafe on Kennington Park Road to do something rather than drink. Well, I am drinking Cherry Tango. I love experimenting with soft drinks. I don't tend to do that with alcoholic drinks. Last time I tried cocktails I ended up taking a piss in a gated community garden in Notting Hill. Next thing I know I'm in The Royal Albert Hall at The Proms.

I was thinking about epiphanies this morning. I was thinking about the epiphany I had in September. Hardly anything is in the now. It's an old cliche to go on about living in the present but it really works. It's impossible to do most of the time. I'm still attempting to not watch television or read newspapers. But listening to music is even taking your mind off now. I've got Jazz FM in here. Fuckinhell. Jazz? Anyway, when I'm writing music or writing then I find that is now. And sitting over in Hollow Ponds with my cans of Kronenbourg doing my writings, that's probably my peak moment of the week. I sit in front of some bushes by the lake watching the swans and ducks for the first few hours. I watch the cloud formations and the sun change its light. I sit in the long grass in the middle of the field for the final hour. It's a right bother when I need to piss. Too many dog walkers and perverts about. I've started to pop into The Alfred Hitchcock Hotel if Vinegar Tits isn't in.

I don't mind DJing. Most of the time it doesn't feel like work. It just feels like a night out. Of recent times I haven't been able to DJ without drinking, just because I'm so bored of it. The music that John Peel used to play, that interests me but they wouldn't employ me if I started playing Mogwai or something. Of course, I get away with playing The Fall and a bit of Hawkwind but I've lost interest in all the songs I play. I've been to a few clubs but they just play hip hop as that seems to be the fashion nowadays. I'm getting too old for all this. I'll keep doing it though until I find what it is I want to do with my life.

Michael's been very affectionate of late. He even bought me a bunch of flowers on Saturday, of the Narcissi variety. He told me he didn't realise. I like the fact he doesn't do this drinking game. All that "one of us has got to be sober and it's not gonna be me" stuff. That makes sense. Thanks Jeff.

My band has a gig at Proud Gallery in Camden on Wednesday 25th April. Do come along. I think we're on at 8:30.

I really enjoyed that day in Brighton. I touched upon it in my last entry. I feel so free when I go out to the seaside and spend the whole day on a pub crawl with myself. I went in most of the pubs in that road to the promenade. I took my notebook and did some of my writings. It was nice because all the pubs were empty and I had got to Brighton at 11am. I just had half in each pub and moved on. I got through so many pubs that day. I ended up at some pub on the seafront watching that big upside down ride turning. I had another epiphany. "I'll go down that pier and go on that ride," I thought. I think I was about four pints in and I was still drunk from the previous night. Anyway, I walked down the pier and went on the ride. It was alright. I like rollercoasters and rides that go upside down. It was a bit of an anticlimax really and didn't give me much of a thrill. Perhaps my senses had been numbed by the alcohol. When I got off the ride I saw the ghost train and remembered that famous scene from Brighton Rock. No one was around so I bought some more tokens and went on that. That gave me more of a thrill. It had a strange resonance as death has always been so close to me. I like the bit when the old dead woman pops out. After that I went to Horatio's Bar. That's the bar at the end of the pier. I liked it in there. I saw couples and families and thanked Our Lord I was alone. I was having such a top time.

I went to see the fortune-teller after that. He was in his caravan on the pier. He read my Tarot cards. I know a fair bit about Tarot as I worked on a Tarot line for six months in 2000. He didn't give me much specific information. Usual stuff. Said everything was gonna be fantastic for me but I bet he says that to everyone. He didn't mention children or marriage though so I was well relieved when I got out.

I made my way back up some other street and carried on my drinking. Soon it was 8:30 and it was all dark so I made my way home. I still had a can of Holsten Pils in my bag from the previous night so I drank that on the train back and listened to the soundtrack of Merry Christmas Mr Lawrence. I was satisfied.

IT'S NOT JUST ME

June 20th, 2012

06:32 am

Yesterday I hung around West Norwood Cemetery. Sunny day and all that. I felt nothing at first. I craved to feel death. I spoke to the gravediggers and they chatted to me for a while.

I moved on. I ran to a lonely place. Lonely ivy-covered graves. Oak trees covered me. The graves too. I found babies' graves.

I sorted out the teddy bears and put them in order.

There were some graves that said "No Regrets".

I looked at the dates and a lot of them were 1995. I thought well, the family were going through their tragedy as I went through mine. So who's to say my tragedy is mine only? There were others. 1988. 1983. 1997. 2003. Young deaths. In my family.

I began to see that everyone had been through losing people young. It isn't just me.

But on that Monday 13th March 1995, my brother was taken from me by a cement mixer. The driver failed to look.

AVOIDING SUICIDE

07:42 am

I've been trying to do a different thing each day. Avoiding television, newspapers, boring stuff.

I read books. Listen to my Walkman. A-Ha. Though, the job that I have is amazing. It's the only job that inspires me but that sounds shit. My last job made me contemplate ending my life. I used to sit in Old Street Cemetery. For an hour I would crave death. Sometimes I would never go back. I've worked at my place for eight years and I've only called in sick once. I am never ill. I am so happy now.

A few weeks ago I saw my Dad. He could not talk. He was stuck with a bottle of whisky by his side. He smelt of piss. The chair next to him was saturated with piss too and stank just as bad. I am writing this because it needs to be said. My sister and my Mum have really tried to help him but it is an impossible task.

There is nothing that can be done. There are crack addicts and terrible people that surround him. They use his house as a crack den. The police know about this.

It just pains me to think of the Dad he once was. I'll never get my Dad back.

ALONE AMONGST THE DANDELIONS. ONE O'CLOCK...

June 26th, 2012

10:51 am

This morning I sat beside the lake. I watched a swan drowning a small bird. I let cruel nature take its way.

Last night I read my diaries. They were rubbish.

I've had nothing to say in ages. I'm in Leytonstone Library.

People surround me typing meaningful words.

There's dirt beneath my nails where I've been grabbing onto soil. I rang Mum. I rang Michael. I even rang Dad.

I sank into that familiar place. Do tragedies overtake us all? We surely cannot live through these. I don't like people that have never lost. I prefer a person that can second-guess.

A hero is always alone. I didn't cry today.

I'VE HAD A FEW... I WORRY WHEN I'VE HAD A FEW

July 4th, 2012

11:16 am

I worry about this when I've had a few... I've had a few.

I'm at Trevor the bouncer's flat. I don't have a computer because I can't be arsed getting my laptop sorted. The dongle just doesn't fit in any more.

I must have been watching something on ITV this morning cos I've just been woken up by that vile Jeremy Kyle show that my Dad loves so much. Oldham accents shouting. They're usually from round my way. I only narrowly escaped being an in-bred. If my Dad wasn't having a night out in London my Mum might have got away. She wishes she had. She says she wouldn't change things but if I'd had her life, to change fate would be the first thing I'd do.

Last night I took her to The Cambridge, that's that main pub on Charing Cross Road (Cambridge Circus). My Mum and Dad used to meet in there, mid swinging sixties for courting, That was when he was a slim, suited, handsome man with a rolled up umbrella. He was a mod. Looked just like Gene Pitney apparently. He wasn't a drinker for all those years but in 1981 he suddenly became an alcoholic.

Losing my Dad through drink is the biggest bereavement I've gone through. It's never been my brother. I know he's fine. He died as a Hare Krishna and who could get more close than that, to this God they speak of?

As for me? Well, I'm having trouble writing. I just DJ day to day. Four nights a week and I'm lucky. It is the best job in the world. My

Mum said that. She said, "Do you know you've got the best job in the world?" She was a cleaner and housewife so I suppose anything beats that. My band have just recorded some tracks with Criminal Records. We rehearse every Sunday at Enterprise Studios in Tin Pan Alley. We've got a gig at a place called Retro in Westbourne Park Sunday 22nd July at 8pm.

I feel I'm too old to be interesting to the teenagers. But if you continue to be an artist, someone eventually takes notice. I feel everything I do and write is an integral part of this world that YOU live in. I think the one thing that has saved me is my non-desire to have children. The time on my hands may be spent drinking but on the other hand I'm doing other stuff. Sitting in pubs and pissing in forests. There's always a pen on me and I've never got to change a nappy. Women that have had children give me the creeps. I feel bad for saying that but I can't understand them.

Women said I would get this urge to have a child one day. They always say one day don't they? I'm thirty. Can't think of anything worse. Nor can Michael and he's forty-nine. Never lets me tell people his age. Oh dear.

He doesn't read this. Him indoors. I always call him that. If I'm sitting at a bar and having a chat, I always refer to Michael as "him indoors" or "the Mr".

I reckon I've done more for feminism than most of them political women do in their life. What women should really do is go to pubs alone, sit at the bar and buy men drinks. Since I'm alright financially I buy myself one then go to whoever's talking to me, "I'll get you that!" Before the man knows it I've got my money out and paid, cos I see when the drink is coming down. Clever. But let no one take you for a fool girl! Don't be buying everyone drinks. You'll have nowt left!

YOU ARE SUCH A WELL-SPOKEN PERSON, SCARLET

July 10th, 2012

11:12 am

"You're such a nice refined person," says Alwynn Davies.

"I'll kill people!"

I get pissed off too easily. If they annoy me anywhere, I will. Michael spoke above a programme I was trying to watch on Sunday night. I was so pissed off. I was absolutely sober. I aimed two glasses at the wall. They did the inevitable and smashed. I'm not standing for anything. My temper is short. Then I went to Leytonstone, just to show him like. I'll remove myself and go.

How women put up with men. Well I won't put up with that. Michael was alright after that. Apology after apology, but it was too late.

I was sitting in the pub in Leytonstone. I've calmed down. I think I'm okay now.

BEATING DEPRESSION THROUGH ALCOHOL

August 28th, 2012

03:20 pm

I've been finding it extremely difficult to leave the house again. I'm in an internet cafe as I've failed to get my laptop fixed. It's difficult to concentrate. There is a radio on in here and I've never been able to write with music or radios on in the background. The space bar is broken and as usual with these internet cafes, they've tried to cram in the maximum amount of computers into a room that should only be used as a store cupboard.

So now I've done the Steinbeck introduction I'll go into my life a bit. I'm still drinking excessive amounts. I still tend only to drink in Leytonstone nowadays. I just prefer it there for people and pubs. I'm well-known in the area amongst other drinkers and they seem alright to me now they know I'm not a prostitute. Only after three years of drinking there have they finally realised I'm harmless and I'm not Russian. They would never trust me if I was Russian.

I don't feel so creative anymore. I thought it would be easy to just get on with my book. My filled notebooks have now risen to two foot in height. I feel excited by nothing.

I've never found art exciting. Despite my years of visiting galleries I now prefer to sit staring through daytime television. Half the time I just watch the Sky menu or The Landscape Channel, not enjoying it, just waiting. Sometimes I just wait for work to start. The rest of the time I wait for sleep to take me away. I don't feel the hope or joy that I once did.

The only thing I like is the drink. My favourite part of the week is Wednesday mornings drinking in Leytonstone. 9am in a dark corner or in the window of Wetherspoon's. In the window I'll watch the boring people going to work and in the dark corner I'll write while the air-conditioning units rattle and soothe me. I don't know why I call those people boring when I spend most of my time sitting in front of a television, just waiting for the moment I can watch them go about their daily business. They look sad, so their sadness makes me feel better. And I'm safe behind that glass and invincible with my pint of Kronenbourg.

I don't want to be a proper adult and now at the age of thirty I probably am. Michael talks about financial things like savings accounts but I still don't understand why I'd want to do all that. I'm still suicidal, suppose the only thing it would pay for is my funeral. People in the past have said I should go on tablets. I always resisted because I thought it would stop my creativity but what's stopping me now? I'd never take any tablets. Not even now. The drink on a Wednesday makes me happy but by Thursday I'm back to how I am the rest of the week.

The other week I fell over and cut my knee really badly. Blood was everywhere. I think I was somewhere in Wanstead. It's healed now.

I AM LIKE WATER MISSING
BET LYNCH IN A BATHING SUIT

August 29th, 2012

10:55 am

I've got that feeling, when I feel very warm and very relaxed and I don't know what's coming after this. Like this could be the end. It's okay. I don't fear the end. And I can type?

I rang my Dad the other day. I always tell here when I've called my Dad. My Mum and my sister tell me I shouldn't call him as it will only upset me more. He said that he has an infestation of fleas. I asked him if the crack addicts were still coming too. He told me they were. He said there's nothing he can do now. I said, "Dad, you need help".

"I know now." So went that conversation. He hung up then. I left him to his crack whores. My Mum and my sister have not been the same to him since he let his prostitute punch me. He did nothing to defend me and he was unable. Incapable. My Dad is the only person that has ever broken my heart and if I call him today he will continue to do so. My Mum and sister told me to put him out of my mind and treat him as if he's already dead. I'm crying now. Is this the grieving process?

On Sunday I was in a social situation with Michael's friends. I was out of my depth again. This whole conversation thing that is expected of me by the age of thirty. I am supposed to be able to throw back anecdotes and be fascinating. I can't. I just can't. Shall not too. I have nothing to prove. For me, being able to show up in a conversation is slightly like writing this and not knowing how to spell. My commas and quotes still need a seeing-to though. At least I admit my faults.
I hear a child shouting, "Mummy". Well Mum was forever the saint.

Six years in between myself and Anne so as a housewife, all the time was spent on me. God, I needed it. Monday's play group, Tuesday art gallery, Wednesday museum, Thursday music (pots and pans and things) and Friday, LIBRARY! That was my favourite day. I'd get my books. And then Helen, Anne and Stephen would come in and tape my fingers to the washing line and turn it upside down. Then they used to put me in the massive laburnum tree in the garden, leave me in the highest branches and run away. On Saturdays they would put me in a sleeping bag and tie it up, then carry it to the pantry. I would stay there for hours. All this was deemed as fun. And it was. Stood me in good stead for what was later to come.

06:32 pm

Women surround me. My head is in me hands.

A PRAYER FOR A HOPELESS CAUSE

October 11th, 2012

01:21 am

Now this is difficult to tell you. I'd like to talk about my Dad.
I came back on Sunday. It's Thursday morning now.
My sister came over from Australia in September and popped in to
find him sitting in an armchair. He was naked apart from a blanket
covered in piss and he was unable to speak. He'd grown a beard and
his shit was everywhere.

They've done so much since that day. The evidence of it being a crack
house was clear. I tried so much after his prostitute gave me the black
eye. I mean, it's not like he's on it. They just take vulnerable people
and ruin them. My Dad was an intelligent man until addiction took
hold. They kept him in that piss-soaked chair and they drugged the
whisky with sedatives. They had disabled his chair lift with a piece
of wood and cut the wires. The smack and crackheads then used the
upstairs for dealing and using. £10,000 has been taken out of his
bank account. I'm not joking. I'm not writing this for effect. This
has really happened to my Dad. It feels as if I'm watching a movie.
It feels as if this is not actually happening to my Dad. He had black
eyes and bruises on his wrists. He seemed so scared and told us he
had fallen out of bed. He hasn't been to bed since May. Where was
I when all this was taking place? In London, giddy London. I feel
guilty. I always call my Dad up once a week and sometimes he would
seem all there. Sometimes he would never answer the phone but
after all these years, he never did like answering the phone.

So my sister that's come over from Australia felt we had to do
something. She got the crackheads and smackheads out. She's tried
every avenue to help him but he doesn't want to stop drinking. We've
tried social services, we've tried the police, but no one wants to help
because he just will never stop drinking. He's destroying us all.

DREAD, SLEEP AND ALL OF A SUDDEN

December 7th, 2012

09:12 am

I've not been back. Why should I? He didn't get better all of a sudden.

My Mum is made to care for him, much to my distaste. Well, my Mum had done everything to get him out of our lives. Well, perhaps, keep him in a bit too. But Dad is such a bastard. I'm dreading going back.

Most of you can smell Christmas. I know the smell of urine and faeces. It's been a year and last year went and I met Dad. Urine and poo is the smell of my Dad at Christmas, not cos no one was looking after him when I was visiting. It was just cos he pissed and shit himself and I visited him at perhaps the wrong time.

Every day my sister in Australia says he's getting a bit better. Then some days she says he's getting worse. Am I to run forever up to Oldham to help him out? I need to put myself to sleep with alcohol.

Helen is making me feel guilty for not helping my Dad through his alcoholism.. My black outs are getting worse. U

I was cleaning in my room. I can't remember.

December 21st, 2012

07:35 am

So to go to Oldham on Sunday.

It's okay. I don't know what to say to him.

I'll play dominoes, Cluedo and Scrabble with my Mum. Monopoly.
I'm so lost.

I don't want to see my Dad. I'm crying so much now. I really don't
want to see him. Everyone said he'd be dead by now.
He's still alive sitting in the chair. It's not piss-soaked anymore. He
still hangs up his phone when I'm speaking to him. That hurts me.

Have I really got to keep strong? My hands are shaking and I'm not
sure what I can do.

Got some cans from heaven knows where. A fridge I found. So Dad
hanging up and Mother talking to me forever.

This Christmas makes me feel odd. Just odd.

Family. I feel like smashing the screen with the sight of that word.
Family.

And all those stupid family food supermarket adverts.

How the mother cooks.

I'm a woman. I never ever will.

CHRISTMAS TIME 2012,
OLDHAM, DAD, PISS

December 30th, 2012

06:21 am

I'm in Oldham and I'm not sure what to say.

I can't wait to go back in a few hours. I shall be relaxed then. My sister sleeps and my Mum sleeps in the next room.

My Dad. Well, I hope he's sleeping too. A ten minute walk up the street. I won't say goodbye.

I spent all day with my Dad. Boxing Day it was. I didn't quite catch his piss when he got his penis out and pissed on the carpet. I tried to get his piss bucket. The piss came quick though.

Before that incident we were talking about this and that. Watching the BBC News 24 channel if I remember rightly. Current affairs, politics and stuff.

People look the same here and wear the same jackets. They're small and all walk flat-footed. My Dad was lucky enough to marry a Londoner so I'm lucky. My brother was six foot tall.

I look upon these houses and I feel bad for thinking the thoughts that I do. I could never live in a town, just do a job and have a family and be content. Why try for everyone else? Why try for your child? I'm thirty-one now and I want to do something. People say I've wasted my life.

It doesn't seem long ago since I was young.

My thirty-one-year-old friends came to me with their children. The children made me nervous. I remembered how I was interested in bright bulbs and fires. I kept saying, "Make sure they don't burn themselves!" It was really nerve-racking.

Children and parents that were once friends went.
So I went to the pub with Anne, my sister with no children. We drank and talked about our childhoods. She's six years older than me and it's lovely how that age gap disappears, especially when no children are involved. I believe you only grow old when you have children. You grow stupid when you fall in love with a pathetic man.

Me and Michael though. I do love him and he loves me and neither of us want children. Job done.

We talked about Mum and Dad and our sister in Australia. I feel nervous now because Anne has woken up. I can't write.

Anne's gone back to sleep.

I was just listening to "Late Night Maudlin Street" on this computer. I don't have one of these computers in my house anymore, in London. My Mum loves these things. I'm still struggling.

So everything around me is pulled down. John Prescott's idea. Everything I grew up with. My block is one of the only ones left. Such a stupid idea. They ran out of money, whoever that was. So they couldn't afford to tear the final gorgeous blocks down. If they even try to knock down this final block I will be here till the end of time. I will give up my DJing and everything for this house. This house stays.

THIS HOUSE STAYS.

The man that built this street and designed the fireplaces. Well this was his house. It shall never go.

I HATE PRINCE AND THAT
PROSTITUTE RIHANNA

January 9th, 2013

04:26 am

If I'm left alone with a computer this is what I shall do. I'll try and type about my goings-on.

I don't have a computer but I'm at the bouncer's flat and he's gone to bed. Trevor doesn't mind me writing my journal. I'm glad David Bowie is alive. I heard rumours of a heart condition and Danny Boyle flew out to Manhattan or wherever but Bowie wasn't able to do the performance at that whole Olympic thing as much as he would have liked to. His new song puts me in mind of Thursday's Child from the Reality album. Good to hear David back up and running.

I've been DJing in my usual place. Sometimes I get upset cos people don't like the decent stuff and they just want to hear Prince and I absolutely hate Prince. Rihanna. I really don't like her. She's the worst kind of woman. I don't mind Lady Gaga with her bikinis but Rihanna is encouraging women to be complacent with domestic violence. I disagree with seeing Rihanna's tongue when I'm taking the tube to either my work or seeing her anywhere when I'm walking to my bingo halls. I disagree with women being placed on posters like that. It disturbs me.

I like Greta Garbo, Marilyn Monroe, Grace Kelly, Clara Bow, Ava Gardner, Rita Hayworth, Julie Goodyear, Pat Phoenix, Ena Sharples… The list could go on.

People like The Arts Club cos they know they're not going to get crap music. I'm happy because I try to give them the best music. And they absolutely know they are not going to get any Rihanna.

Song I finished on last night was "Drive-In Saturday" Bowie. I did my best.

THE SECOND MISTAKE IS YOUR LESSON

05:24 am

I feel like giving a second verse.

It's strange whenever I'm working, people all over Britain are watching telly. I despise people for not going out. If they are out they're looking at their stupid phones. Or taking photos of themselves having a "GOOD TIME".

They are so concerned about becoming appealing. It does my head in. I watch their little lives unfold. Week after week. I said to someone, "Don't bother, it will end". In the toilets that was.

Most things do but it ended drastically for her. I met her the next week and she was onto a worse man. Some people will repeat the same mistakes, as far as friends go too. But this was a man in her case.

I feel like someone else here and in my DJ booth (confessional booth) as it sometimes is. I love you all. You will repeat the same mistakes until you realise the lesson.

A FATHER'S PERSPECTIVE

January 23rd, 2013

06:55 am

So my Dad's mood wasn't very good. My sister's and my Mum's wasn't too.

I was okay.

Women's moods change with the moon. My Dad always pisses in his carpet. Middle of floor.

I try and change him but some things can't be changed. My Mum is fantastic. I'm tired tonight.

I wish he wouldn't hang up. I wish he could always be there for me. I feel so alone. I wish he was more like Trevor. Trevor is always there for his daughter no matter what. Sometimes you just need a Dad.

Sometimes you can't speak to your Mum about things. And you just need to have a pint with a man, see the men's perspective about stuff. My Dad is too far gone to do all that but Trevor is always ideal. Trevor is perfect. A father that I never had.

PRETTY KITTENS AND PISS

08:05 am

I can't compete with pretty kittens.

I'll let them be.

My Dad's pissed-up carpet. I'll let it lie. That awful carpet that I have to smell. I'm sick and tired of smelling.

Went to an acoustic thing tonight where the woman was going on and on and on about how much she missed her boyfriend when she was on some kind of tour. Well, well done. I'm bitter. My lyrics are all about my Dad's piss. No love. All strange hate.

I don't write about boyfriends and how much I miss them cos I don't. My lyrics are all to do with my Mum's area, Werneth… It's a suicide hot spot.

Loads of my sister's friends have topped themselves cos they can't work it out for themselves to just read books and get away from Oldham.

My Dad told me to live in Oldham and get a job in a factory. Thank the Lord I never took his advice.

The rest of my "friends" that avoided me at school have moved to the hills. You had to be really brave to talk to me in those days. You would have been beaten up if you were seen talking to me. I had a paper round that went round the houses. Some tart with her skirt up to there used to take my papers and throw them into the road.

I hope she's dead now. I shouldn't say that. I hope she's okay but I guess she's not doing this well.

FROM £60 TO £85 A WEEK! IT'S A BIT STEEP, THAT RISE!

March 20th, 2013

03:25 am

I'd rather come to you with no upsets but we all have our upsets do we not?

I'm smoking a fag. I only ever smoke when I'm bored. What have you been doing?

Those two last "paragraphs" were from something else I was about to write. Funny how it just says, "Would you like to restore?" OK. That was that. I must have been in the middle of a rant about something or other.

Saw my Dad today. He'd already got a bottle of whisky before I went up to his house. I was worried and still am worried about the sobriety of my Dad. He sought it out and I'm nervous, but I think my Mum knows that I did not get my Dad that bottle of whisky.

Everyone walks around like peasants round here. I suppose that is a bad thing to say but the posture in Oldham is something else. They all have some gripe. They all seem quite upset. I won't and I never will have any upsets. I reckon if you are upset you won't get too far.

My landlord put my rent up from £60 to £85. If he had done it over the seven years I had been living there, £10 here and there, I wouldn't have minded. But all of a sudden like that. I looked on Gumtree and found most rooms are now £85-£100. I don't understand that things go up in price. It's a bit like when people started asking for that vile Rihanna.

Horrible day on Saturday evening. He'd got some Polish men in and they started cooking. I used to share a kitchen with a witch doctor in 2005. I know bad cooking smells. Skulls involved and worse. But these Polish people are cooking vile smelling food. I hid my face underneath my duvet.

People ask me why I don't move in with Michael. Well… I think we need our own wardrobes, glamour and space.

PEACE WITH MY MUSIC [NOT THAT WHORE RIHANNA]

May 8th, 2013

06:24 am

It was easy. I don't have a care in the world.

But I do. My landlord seems to be getting thinner and thinner. I worry about him. It's ridiculous, he's put the rent up from £60 to £85 all bills inclusive. I don't mind. I still have a bit of quids to gamble and drink away and the rest I can give to Michael.

I must be the only person excited about going to work.
Last night I was really happy to be going to work, just to DJ and put on a few records. I felt ok once I did that.

I felt at peace then.

MICHAEL SAVES ME FROM
THE PEE-PING TOM

May 29th, 2013

06:25 am

When there is a child I really do feel writing is done. People have told me that.

The baby downstairs is screaming and each day screaming louder, disturbing me from some unforgotten sleep that I will never remember or get back. I'll never be the woman that you will leave your child or baby with.

I don't feel motherly towards it. It's just bothering me, its crying, its sadness, just reminds me of me in a sense.

A man was standing on the toilet and watched me take a piss on Sunday. I didn't know till I'd finished taking a piss and looked up. You can always tell when someone's looking at you. I'm just glad I didn't have the shits.

I was well depressed. And shaken up too. If I was drunk I would have punched his lights in and everything else but the men's and ladies' toilets were through many dark corners. I thought perhaps he's got a knife. Perhaps he's gonna rape me. So I ran up and got Michael.

Michael ran and got him. More or less.

A RIPPLING REFLECTION OF WHAT A WOMAN SHOULD BE

July 22nd, 2013

10:15 am

Most people think there is nothing more to me than my drink problem. I do not believe this to be the case. I think I've got a lot going for me. Well, that's what my Mum says. I embrace the drink. It's like the world is in Technicolor when I'm on it. Everything seems so clear through that blurred and bright vision.

Today I'm not on it. I've had my breakfast of the Traditional Wetherspoon's kind, a cup of tea and a glass of Pepsi. I've been manic for a fortnight now. God knows when the crash and suicide thoughts will come. Taking antipsychotic drugs has never crossed my mind. Michael said that I should be on some kind of medication for all this manic behaviour. I don't know what it is or why I'm like this. I find it's wonderful because right now I can't see the blackness. Everything is now. I've been sleeping for about two hours a night for this whole fortnight but I don't feel tired. Everything is now because if I miss these moments of happiness they will be gone and I'll be back in my slow suicide.

I went to Leytonstone Festival yesterday in The Henry Reynolds Gardens. I sat on my own with a couple of cans of 1664. I didn't feel sad. I watched the people with their friends and families and I don't think I've ever felt less alone. I can cope with being alone now as I know this will always be the case and I've come to realise I'll never get on with anyone. People will forever fail me.

I went to The North Star after drinking my two cans. I bought a pint of 1664 and felt uneasy and awkward. Still happy but people talk too much in The North Star and they've got to know me. It's them that's uneasy though. They're uneasy about me always being alone.

I hate the way people laugh louder and try to act like they're having a really good time once they clock I'm alone. I don't let it bother me though. I hate it but I don't let anything bother me now. I feel I'm beyond everything and everyone. I feel so wonderful, like I can change the weather, create sunsets and time.

I like changing time through drink. Sometimes I want to lose three days. Especially if I'm bored. I haven't been bored for a fortnight but I'll still linger and cling to the drink for a short while longer.

THIS IS STARTING TO SOUND RIDICULOUS

September 8th, 2013

06:05 am

These men and women about. They disturb me.

They did that weird dancing where they bumped and grinded in front of my DJ box. It disturbed me. I never dance.

I've had far too much to drink. I don't like them as they disagree with me. They have livelihoods whilst I have fuck all to lose.

Me with all my rubbish. There's a woman that keeps cooking me curry. She keeps asking me what I drink. I keep explaining how I've not paid the rent. No reason. I've got the money. Kind of.

I've heard about writers being alcoholics in love. I wanted to play her my song Nhilism. Can never spell, me.

My Dad was in love with my mother. They love me so therefore I can't commit suicide.

I want to kill myself so much. I don't self-harm and I won't but this depression hits me. Especially after my work. Everyone's been applauding me tonight. It's just like that song Backstage by Gene Pitney.

There's no reason I should feel this way. It's the drink. I always say it's the drink. Yet the only way to make myself feel okay is through the drink again. There is absolutely nothing and no person that will ever make me feel okay. I've tried marrying myself. I've married E.T. twice now. This is sounding ridiculous.

The terrible people with their awful lives. I love the way they hate Monday mornings. However I love mine.

WHILST RIDING A BICYCLE NEVER UNDERTAKE A LORRY AT A JUNCTION

07:08 am

I met a man. Well it was Wednesday afternoon. Must have been coming on for four-ish. It was strange cos he looked exactly like Stephen. You know, my dead brother. He was a painter and decorator too. I talked about him as if he was still alive. Stephen was the best-looking out of the lot of us. There were four. We always thought it was weird that he died. Perfect skin, eyesight and bone structure.

And then us three girls left. I always felt alone after Stephen did that, knocked over by a cement mixer turning left at a junction. I never got over that. I keep going on and on about it.

I wish he was here. My sister said he would not be happy and hate me cos he hated my Dad being a drunkard.

Perhaps I've said this before. He ended up a Hare Krishna devotee. He wrote a diary about how much he wanted to go back to God.

I was born dead. All the time with this useless time. I just keep thinking it should have been me that died. Boy, could he play guitar!

NOT TO WORRY

September 16th, 2013

03:48 pm

They have to be kind to me in this library. They'd get done if they weren't.

She laughed politely as I said, "Yeah seventeen, happiest year of my life that was". Numbers on these computers y'see.

I'd say thirty-one now. I've never been so happy. I cry myself to sleep within dreams of my happiness ending. I can't ever escape from the dreadful ending.

I went to The George in Wanstead this morning. That's a Wetherspoon's. I just sat alone on the top floor. There was no wake this time. The staff were putting up Christmas decorations. I watched them and attempted to make jokes about it being too soon. They smiled politely and continued.

I got on the bus after that. I always call those little single decker buses "the nanna bus". They're always filled with Nannas with trollies. The whole of the UK over. I get talking to them. I was talking to one today about her bits and pieces from the 99p Store. We had a lot in common.

I got off at O'Neill's. Green Man Roundabout they call that. The lack of Kronenbourg in there is rubbish. I sat in a corner booth and had to put up with their shit music whilst I drank half a Peroni. I stared out of the window and watched people going about their daily boring business. Prams and mobile phones seemed to be the main thing. A pram in the hall. I'll never forget that.

Next stop was The Crown (the pub formerly known as The Sheepwalk). There were two men sitting at the bar. Seemed odd as I'm always alone in there of a Monday early afternoon. They told me that Eddie had died. I had no time for him. I used to buy him a few pints now and again. He was homeless and would collect glasses in The Sheepwalk and The Wetherspoon's just for drinks. I had a friend that moved into his room above The Sheepwalk. It was full of pornographic magazine cut-outs of women. Oh well, each to their own. He died of a stroke.

THREE FRIENDS DEAD WITHIN A WEEK

September 27th, 2013

12:52 pm

Well.

I'm at Trevor's.

I was told that I'm selfish, awful and terrible by Michael. Last Friday I got out of my head at work and fell off my stool, DJing paralytic. I was drunk out of my mind. I still have the bruises. I was given a taxi to Michael's.

Back at Michael's he helped me out of the taxi as Trevor kept him on the phone.

I sat down on the settee and told Michael how I'd been seeing Gary, how we were going to Blackpool for a holiday on Monday. Michael wasn't bothered and all my worries had gone.

I slept soundly. I knew that when I woke up everything would be fine.

And despite all my bruises everything was okay. Michael was happy about Gary.

Then I woke up. Trevor and Costas (the owners of the club), always calling. Naturally I couldn't remember a thing. I didn't want to answer. I didn't answer.

Michael had to answer Trevor and Costas' calls as I refused to answer my phone. I felt like I was living in a nightmare and I really wanted to kill myself. Michael said, "Why you drink that Kia-Ora? Water! You need to drink water! Why are are you such a child?"

IT'S DREADFUL. AND I THOUGHT YOU WERE DEAD!

October 14th, 2013

05:49 pm

My friend said how it's weird when you have the kids and get married, you lose your name. You lose your whole identity, she said. It's a strange thing for the record.

I'm in Leytonstone Library yet again. My shakes are bad. Yesterday I went to two churches and one art gallery. I woke up drunk. I woke up today drunk. I've woken up six mornings this week drunk. It fails to disturb me. I wish I could bloody sleep without putting myself out the way in which I attempt.

The woman insinuated herself into my room this morning asking for £4. I'm glad I was fully clothed.

So back to that bloody Godless art gallery. Back to that bloody Godless Hillsong Church at The Dominion Theatre next door to Tottenham Court Road tube station. They prayed. I prayed because I'd been contemplating suicide as is of the normal nowadays.

I gave up on them.

I decided I'd go to St Patrick's in Soho Square. They were having Communion. I held out the palms of my hands and the priest placed the wafer in there. I felt at peace.

THE ROMANCE OF THE MILL WORKERS

October 29th, 2013

02:23 am

I could do with a fag. I always like to have a fag on the go when I'm writing but I'm back in Oldham at my Mum's so I'll have to write without. The return button isn't working on this keyboard and I do like my paragraphs, unlike our friend Steven. My Dad is looking better. Still pisses in a pint pot that he leaves in the kitchen sink but the house no longer smells of piss and he's looking younger and fatter. He doesn't look like he's in the last stages of cancer anymore. My Dad looks as if he will outlive us all. Good news. Not at all what we were expecting but wonderful how life takes kindly to some of us that choose to live with an addiction. He can't move very fast and he still reminds me of a tortoise. He wrote me a cheque for £50 today. That's the largest amount of money I've ever received from him in my thirty-two years here. I'm thirty-two today. It's my birthday. I took a bus up to Oldham town centre to put the cheque in and pay my rent at NatWest. All my direct debits had gone out so I just ended up paying £100 instead of the £140 which I owe. My landlord has defaulted on his mortgage so no doubt I'll be turfed out by the end of the year. I thought I'd use my last fiver to go to Oldham Wetherspoon's. It's called The Up Steps. I bought a pint of the cheapest lager which was Carlsberg for £1.95. I sat in a corner and listened to the low tone hum of older people's Oldham accents. It was relaxing and I pondered upon hardship whilst glancing at the people's friendly but troubled features. I thought about my life and how easy it is compared to them and those that have gone before me. Coming from this stock, you can never lose that sense of belonging. Despite my attempted escape, I will always be dragged back on a short but worthwhile visit. Above the low drone and sporadic coughing fits I homed in to a conversation on the adjacent table. A monologue rather. An old man, he must have been ninety-five, and an old eccentric dear was sitting opposite him. He was talking about how the mill workers used to wake him up with their clogs walking to the mill along the cobbled streets every morning. He'd put his trousers on and rush out to join them. No such thing as alarm clocks back in that time. Usually if you lived close enough as most people did, then the sound of engines starting in the mill would wake you up and you'd just get out. He was saying how one morning in the winter an engineer had gone in as the engine had malfunctioned and he had to start the engine up, but it was three o'clock in the morning. All the workers turned up to the mill not having a clue of the time. This man then broke into song, he did a rendition of Ground Control To Major Tom by Bowie. "Put your engines on," and all that... He sang it in the strongest Oldham accent I had heard since my Grandad. Must have got into Bowie in his sixties or seventies. He then told the old dear that using Durex was a bit like having a shower with a raincoat on. He misheard her. She was telling him what she's bought from Poundland next door. Must have sounded like Durex. After that they walked off hand in hand and it was one of the most romantic scenes I've witnessed in my life.

THIS TOOK ME MONTHS

May 28th, 2014

01:44 pm

I'm in Leytonstone Library.

Just taken my bracelets off. Makes it easier to type y'see?

My Mum paid me a visit from Thursday to Tuesday. It is now Wednesday. My Mum, as you know, is a wonderful woman. I always think because she's done such good I can get away with the bad life I live. I dunno whether it works so easy. What if you're the mother or father of that teenager that went on a gun rampage?

I've been feeling slightly hungry today and my dreams have been fast, just lasting three minutes a time when I feel two days have passed in the dream.

I've just been out for a fag. The man on the computer next door saved this computer for me.

I had so much I wanted to put down earlier but I can't think of anything now. I'm drunk. People are coughing and shouting, I don't know what about.

The police paid a visit to my house this morning. As soon as I hear an English voice I know it's the police. They usually have their radios on but this time at 8am they didn't. There was a domestic incident with the couple downstairs a couple of weeks ago. I told them to calm down and they did but the police need to follow these things up. They asked me if I knew anything about it but I said no. It's cheap rent. I'm not gonna tell anyone there was an incident and I didn't see anything anyway.

I tried to write some lyrics after that about the whole incident of there being an incident. What I wrote was okay but a bit rubbish.

I'm glad my Mum wasn't there. She would have been worried. The cockroaches came back after that. One by one they climbed my bedroom wall. It was like a procession, all coming from the crack beneath my CD/tape player combo. I think they came from the bathroom.

I sprayed them with a cockroach spray I bought from Robert Dyas. Rentokil stuff. Good brand that. It seems to kill them. I feel slightly bad about killing things though. My Dad once gave me a cockroach in a Ferrero Rocher box as a gift. I fed it at his house on lettuce leaves and dead ladybirds. I kept the ladybirds in an airtight container until they suffocated. They turn yellow and then white.

My cockroach lasted eighteen months. I was upset when it died. My Dad and me gave it a proper burial. The grave was close to Blackie's. He was a cat. I saw a few of his decaying bones as I dug the grave. I ended up digging a maggot-ridden mouse called Morten out. My sister forgot to give Morten water and didn't tell my Mum she was keeping a mouse.

My Dad and I got The Bible out and then we lit candles on the grave for this cockroach. I seem to remember his name was Ernest. We read him the last rites even though he was already dead.

We then went to The Hertford Social Club and I do remember having a glass of cider to celebrate the life of Ernest.

BENEATH ME

August 14th, 2014

12:36 pm

I'm sitting with the smelling people yet again. The mentally insane too. Some Romanian beggars that do know how to speak English when I have a little chat with them. Jesus. I try to act like I'm a born-again Christian or a Jehovah's Witness around them.

There's a man in here with a gas canister. You know? Like oxygen. I just keep looking at him across the room. Breathing in and out. Reminds me to remain calm.

I got a man chucked out just now for speaking on his mobile phone. I'm trying to achieve something here.
I've spoken to the security guard. I think I've caused more chaos than what was originally created by the mobile phone.

I hate that advert, saying her son has told her he loves her due to mobile phone technology. No!

Now that man that I tried to get chucked out of the library is back and giggling about me and taking pictures. There's nothing that can be done.

SURROUNDING MYSELF WITH SOMETHING WHILST WINNING AN EMPIRE

August 22nd, 2014

06:26 am

Taken off my bracelets and rings yet I struggle to write.

I'm in The Empire Casino where my Mum and Dad met. He walked down the spiral staircase with his rolled up umbrella and my Mum took one look and they fell in that stupid love thing. I wish they hadn't. Being in here she could have had an accountant. Instead, Dirk Bogarde lookalike. I chose a Morrissey lookalike.

I'm trying my best here to explain my hurt about inherited addiction which is never fully explained. It's always my fault. I feel devastated.

I keep feeling that everyone would be better off without the burden of me.

I haven't been feeling too well recently and I'm not sure what to do. Half the time I'm after suicide and the other time when I'm awake I'm after sectioning myself. I just can't see anything. I went back to my Mum's and refused to get out of my bed. I took all my E.T.s out of a box and surrounded myself with them. I didn't feel happy but they calmed me.

I don't think I can carry on much longer.

PRISONERS, SMACKHEADS AND A STRAW CAMEL

September 5th, 2014

03:18 pm

I've moved permanently back to Leytonstone and I feel most at home here. My depression passed when I woke up this morning in my little room and I felt happy for the first time in about two months. It didn't feel like it was ever going to pass and I was thinking of ways to top myself constantly. I was still going to work but every waking hour I just had that old mantra in my head… With knife, with drugs or with rope?

I'm finding this difficult because I'm sober and I can't write as well when I'm sober. My hangover's help me to write but I'm not even hungover.

I've just been to that pub called The Crown on The High Road. I said to the girl, "Bloodyhell, I've never been in here sober".
"Neither have most people," she replied. I'd gone in for a meal cos every time I'm in there the staff go on about how good the food is. It's always quiet too. I used to go to Wetherspoon's for a meal but I know too many of the alcoholics in there now and as I'm an unsociable creature I didn't want anyone sitting with me. One thing I can never do is drink alcohol with a meal. It stops my appetite. I don't associate alcohol with eating. I guess that's what's different on the continent.

I saw that man earlier. He's a tall man in his twenties and he walks around Leytonstone centre with a bloody bandage around his head. I heard from my friends in Wetherspoon's that he's been injecting heroin into his head. You see, I'm not that bad. There's always someone worse off than you as my Mum always says.

I've been spending a lot of my mornings in The Walnut Tree (that's Leytonstone Wetherspoon's). I really enjoy it in there. I like sitting with the other alcoholics. One in particular that I've become good friends with is a man named Harry. He's in his seventies and has been in every prison in London over the years. I was really impressed by this. He has bad D.T.s in the morning and as soon as he comes through the door I run to the bar to get him a pint so he can settle them. He likes to bet on the horses but has been barred from Coral opposite so often I'll go and hand the betting slips in for him. One of the staff recognised his handwriting though so I've started to re-write his bets out for him and I just pretend they're my bets. I take tips from him for my own bets though. Sometimes I win, sometimes I don't. It's about 50/50. Anyway, I have a really nice time with old Harry on our morning drinking sessions. I asked him the other day why he didn't mind me hanging around with him and he said, "You make me feel good". That's one of the nicest things anyone has ever said to me.

I saw the Co-op funeral director yesterday. Last time I saw him I was asking how much a funeral plan would be as I didn't think I had long left. I think he was a bit worried about me. I always see him having a fag outside when I've had a big session in The Walnut so I can understand that he wonders why I'm pissed out of my brain at 1pm. He said I was looking better yesterday.

I went to that little second-hand market up the top next to O'Neill's this afternoon. I sometimes go in there when I'm pissed too. I buy all sorts of crap from all these second-hand places in Leytonstone and when I come round I wonder why I've bought something like a straw camel or an ashtray shaped like a dinosaur. These things amuse me when I'm drunk but my room is tiny and it's full up with this type of stuff now. Just like Soft Cell's Memorabilia song. The nice big black Christian lady in the market said today I was looking well. I didn't buy anything so at least she makes a bit of money out of me when I'm pissed.

What's weird about being sober today is that I don't need to piss or have a fag every fifteen minutes. It's quite nice that, I can just get on with things.

I TERRIFY MYSELF…

September 25th, 2014

10:44 am

Suicidal tendencies. Lovely way to put things.

I tried to kill myself with Tramadol, ibuprofen and codeine on Friday. I woke up to the sound of thunder and those strikes of lightning. I'm not sure what hour it all kicked off but I lay in my bed and I had a feeling: as I'm dead everyone else must be dead too. It was a calming thought whilst the storm did her job. And so I drifted off again, believing that the world was to end.

I've failed to mention how I failed to turn up for work. I've been suspended now. I'll probably lose my job over my suicidal tendencies.

I woke up with the sun shining through my nicotine net curtains. I didn't feel too bad. For once I'd had a good sleep. I hadn't slept since Tuesday. Not sleeping for three days is a reoccurrence. I'll then sleep for twenty-four hours. I get manic about this book I'm attempting to get published.

On Saturday morning I went to the community garden. It's a bit of wasteland near my house that they've made the best of. They gave me an apple.

I knew I'd ruined everything due to my attempted overdose. I then went to Wetherspoon's. I sat in a corner bench. It's the seats that they put the Christmas tree and bookings forms on. I sat behind that Christmas tree and I cried. I knew I'd ruined everything.

I decided to text my boss and tell her all would be well but it was too late. She'd replaced me with another DJ and I was suspended. My heart, well it does go into your mouth sometimes. Even now writing this I'm in tears.

They summoned me to a meeting on Monday. I attended. Oh I dunno the outcome. I think they'd prefer it if they never saw me again.

So I need to provide proof that I will never drink again. Just to regain my job would mean sanity and I wouldn't drink cos they've put me on diazepam.

I CAN'T STOP FEELING CALM

October 10th, 2014

12:26 pm

Silence at bloody last.

So we're all aware by now that I lost my fucking job. I do believe I
have sacked myself. It was all getting too boring.
I shan't say anything bad. But I've never been happier so what does
that tell you?

I feel calm, a total peace and it's the absolute best. I've always loved
Leytonstone and now I love it more than ever. I can't stop feeling calm.
There are certain places that put you on edge but Leytonstone... It
just does something that calms me completely.

I love the Autumn light, the trees.... Y'know the go...

So the doctor put me onto Turning Point which is a rehab daycentre.
I'm gonna fuckin murder that screaming child that has stopped my
train of thought.

Yeah, so with the screaming child gone.

So you hang around in this centre thing. There's crackheads and
smackheads but it's mainly alcoholics. They're not too fascinating.
I talk to them and play table tennis. Then there's this keyworker
person who talks to you about how you're gonna get off whatever
drug you're on. You have to sit around in this square room and rant
on about your affliction. The crackheads and smackheads succeed
in this field. Us alcoholics just stare into the white walls or at
photographs that ex-addicts have taken. They run many courses.

So I'll let you know how I'm getting on. But I'll tell you something...
I'm happy for the first time in thirty-two years.

CHANGE HERE FOR THE LIVING

December 24th, 2014

07:54 am

I'm back in Oldham as is per usual at this time of year. I mostly wake up at six each morning nowadays. I feel most alert at this hour.

After I lost my job in September Michael made me move all my belongings out of his flat. He had a new girlfriend and didn't want any remnants of me ruining things. Who can blame him? Gary booked an Addison Lee cab and I got busy on those little cans of pre-mixed spirits which I'd taken a recent liking too. Discreet for my handbag.

Upon arriving at Michael's there were twenty-two bin bags of my belongings. I felt very sad but the nervous breakdown had numbed me enough to zombie walk through the episode. I just kept drinking these little cans. I can't even remember what they were. Gary got all the bags out and we went back to Covent Garden where I left them and him. I felt bad about Gary helping me because I knew that as I had lost my job I'd lost my identity as disco queen or whatever it was he thought he was going out with. I knew that was over. It was as if all my redeeming features had been hollowed out of me. Everything I was had gone. Scarlet West was dead.

I went for a pint in The Hercules Pillars next door. The Kronenbourg helped me so I decided to walk to Holborn and get the tube back to Leytonstone. Apparently I was drinking a little can of Malibu and Coke when I struck up the conversation at Leyton. A man was reading an Evening Standard article about Stewart Lee next to me. I said, "Is he any good him?" I'd obviously waited until Leytonstone to speak as I knew I was three sheets to the wind and there's always a danger of getting chucked off a tube train by a concerned passenger and then getting locked up for hours until you sober up. I told him how I wasn't a nutcase and I was getting off at the next stop anyway.

He told me he was getting off at Leytonstone too so I asked him if he fancied going for a drink with me. He realised I'd had too much so we went for a coffee instead in that cafe at the end of my street.

It was strange being honest with someone for the first time. I told him everything I had gone through over the previous week and that day but then the subject changed to sunnier things. We were both Ken Dodd and Gene Pitney fans. There was all this obscure stuff that we were both into. He'd got on at Holborn as well. I hadn't realised we'd been sitting together the whole way. After we parted company I couldn't stop thinking about him. I bought more cans of 1664 as I had been constantly drinking in every waking hour for about a fortnight, and to stop now would have meant a really bad withdrawal. Before this meeting there was nothing to stop for.

I knew he wouldn't want to go out with a chronic alcoholic which was what I had become by the time I'd met him. I checked myself into an alcohol rehabilitation daycentre on the Monday in Walthamstow called Turning Point. They didn't make me stop all at once but everything seemed to fall into place and I started to feel less inclined to drink over the coming weeks through group and counselling sessions. It wasn't like all the AA meetings I'd been to over the years. I always found them too depressing and departed like I didn't have a problem.

I think falling in love for the first time has saved me. I'd written on here that I'd been in love before but nothing has ever felt like this and I think I was just confused with the rest. Tomorrow it will be three months since the day we met. I'd written an entry on here on the morning of that day. Thursday September 25th. Forever engraved.

DAD'S DEATH

February 6th, 2015

04:26 am

I was full of ideas as I was walking up the Leytonstone High Road to get fags. I knew I had to do this and I woke up at two-ish and I knew I had to write. I was out of cigarettes just when I needed them the most.

Dad died.

It was something I'd always expected. The grief! Bloodyhell, even he wouldn't believe! Relatives. It was like something else! He's been dead since Wednesday January 14th and I still haven't cried. I did my grieving for the loss of a Dad years ago. When his alcoholism took hold, by God I cried. When he put the phone down after a hello, when I fed him grapefruit and carried him up the stairs, aged eight. Well, I cried then.

I haven't cried since. I've only remembered the top times we spent together.

I did a small eulogy on Tuesday at his funeral. I thought that the grief would hit me as soon as I saw the coffin but it didn't and I was surprised. I talked about our pub crawls and how we got on as friends rather than Father and daughter. I suppose with me being the youngest, he'd given up on discipline or telling each how to live their lives. He didn't give any advice on how to live mine.

I've written so much about my Dad in this journal. I was so much like him. I meant to write before he died.

We sat on Boxing Day in his house. I'd had enough of my Mum. She's lovely but I always used to go to my Dad when I got bored. She's not boring but she doesn't drink and I was off on one. My sister doesn't drink either. I said, "Well I'm going to Dad's". I caught a taxi after my niece did my roots. I just wanted to get away from the women.

I called him up and gave him some warning I'd be over in five minutes. I walked into his house and sat down on the armchair next to him. My Dad had a bottle of whisky on the go. I didn't feel bad. He was watching some old war film and we talked about the film for a bit. He then gave me a tenner to get a few cans and some fags. I then went to Sunny Video at the end of the street. They knew who I was. I'd bought all my childhood alcohol from there, no questions asked.

Back at Dad's we had a right good chat. We laughed and talked about the war and rationing. We talked about the pubs and characters we knew. We talked about the family. We talked about Jeremy Kyle and daytime television.

I started to go on about Blackpool and we both admitted we were happy there. It was such a lovely four hours that Boxing Day. I even got his wedding album out and made him recollect the day. We smoked cigars that my sister, Anne, had bought. My Dad always used to like a cigar at Christmas.

At some point after getting drunk I can't remember much, but I just remember saying, "I love you Dad," and calling a taxi to Mum's. I remember giving him a hug and kissing him on the forehead.

I called him up on the Saturday morning before he died. We had a little chat and he seemed well. I talked about my gig the previous night.

Next time I called him on Thursday morning. I always called him whilst Jeremy Kyle was on. There was no answer but I thought I'd leave it as sometimes he wanted his peace. In the back of my mind though, I thought, he's dead. He's sitting in that armchair and he's dead. I kept it in the back of my mind though.

There was nothing anyone could do. My sister broke in and yes, he was dead, in his armchair. He died from a heart attack on Wednesday January 14th. Evening as the light was on.

The brass on his coffin read, "Peter Crosby died January 16th".

I didn't view him. I believe in remembering people. That memory of my Dad was perfect.

£10. NEEDS STEAM CLEANING

February 16th, 2015

10:23 pm

They asked if I wanted his house. I sat in his armchair, the one where he died. I positioned myself in the same place, asked my sister Anne for the pose of how she found him. No photos. Am I morbid?

I didn't think of much. I still haven't cried.

Why haven't I cried? It's not that I feel cold. I mean I loved the man and he did me no harm. I worry about delayed grief. Some of these things may hit you later, I'm warned. I don't feel that though and I don't feel any sadness. I've felt him sitting on my bed though and sometimes holding my hand. In a dream like. I did love him. I just think he wants me to know that he's okay.

I miss our two-minute phone calls;

"Dad, how are you?"
"Alright."
"What are you watching?"
"Jeremy Kyle."
"What's the predicament?"
"No teeth."
"I'll leave you to it."
"Bye."

He hated phone calls.

My sister has tried to sell the chair he died in on "Oldham Swap & Sell". She put it in for a tenner with the tagline, "Needs steam cleaning". Huh huh.

PETER CROSBY: 12TH DECEMBER 1944 – 14TH JANUARY 2015

April 30th, 2015

04:53 am

I'm in my room. I've put on "Rank". I love the way Morrissey never fails.

I've had many gigs in the meantime. David has given me much encouragement. I often feel the God's... or a really hard-working angel, a team of them perhaps... When he met me... Made me sit near him. I love him so much and was about to commit suicide.

I didn't see any light. My Dad was still alive then but I couldn't even see him. I called him at my worst, three times a day. I didn't miss my Mum but thought a lot about moving back up, quitting the band and living with my Dad. He meant a lot to me and I had a feeling he would go fast.

My feeling was right. I wonder about Anne's grief being recognised, finding him as she did. It was a heart attack after all and he'd lain dead for a day. That morning when I tried to call him, he'd died the night before. I had a feeling he was lying dead for something within me had gone.

I had David though and had fallen in love for the first time. Nothing as trivial as my Dad dying mattered and being in love for the first time... Nothing else matters.

The wonder of David helped me and I'm still indebted to him.

If I had have gone through my Dad's death alone, I would have topped myself. My Dad was one third of my world, if I can put it that way.

My eldest sister came over from Australia and tried to help my Mum. It was a busy day at the morgue when Dad died. Funeral directors too. They confided that they'd been swapping the bodies from their other outfit in Middleton. It took three weeks for the funeral. I wasn't in work but couldn't stand it up there. People were breaking down and doing crying and I just couldn't cry and still haven't. I patted a lot of shoulders during my time up there. I couldn't wait to get back. I didn't start on the drink as the majority expected I would. I had David and he kept me occupied. I'd never loved anyone before and I love him now and I'll love him forever.

The day of the funeral was soon arriving. I told Helen that I didn't wish to see the corpse. Helen said that I should. They said Dad looked peaceful and that it might give Anne some "closure" if she sees him laid out with his suit on. I'm not sure what that would have done to her mind after three weeks. She decided against the idea and so did I. I still can't get the memory of my Grandad (my Dad's Dad) out of my mind, lying there, rosary beads in hand, bruised through normal decay and just looking strange through the fluids they pump into them plus the make-up they shovel onto them. It's not them. I thought I'd test out a viewing with him but after that I knew never to be curious again.

SO FOR THE LIGHT FAILS US NOW

July 15th, 2015

11:39 pm

What did it matter or what could I say after that?

My Dad had died but that didn't give me any kind of right. I spoke to my Mother, my sister too today. They've healed and I have too.

My sister, Anne, and I went to the grave. Father's Day. Anne was born on Father's Day. And to have discovered him, death struck a strong cold hold. I still put on her situation, well I don't know how I'd feel, finding him dead like that.

He was struck off. Like me perhaps, he was a lot like me. I wish I had found him, undiscovered. The next door neighbours gathered round. Fascinated. The paupers.

Why should I say?

SILENT ARE THE ROOMS

July 16th, 2015

08:07 am

I'm going to stop writing about my Dad. He'd hate this. He was never one for publicity.

I wanted to go back to David's today. We'd had a slight disagreement on matters of volume. I won't speak about David today as he doesn't want or need the publicity.

I'm working as a cleaner now, just so me and David can be together. I'd do anything for David. Kill a person, anything! I don't mind cleaning though. I have The Ken Bruce Show, Woman's Hour and 6 bloody Music to keep me entertained. Domesticity.

I just regret turning down DJ work. I work all week now for what I could make in two hours. It distresses me. I'm glad of the job and I try to do it as best I can. Naturally, I get nothing from my Dad as he gave it all away to his crack whores. Yes, I can say that. We all know.

I've got to leave shortly to start work. It's a shame my publishing deal crashed. I thought this would be a book one day. David is not keen on that due to my lies and the menace.